THE ENCYCLOPEDIA OF
Stock Car Racing

THE ENCYCLOPEDIA OF
Stock Car Racing

FRANK MORIARTY
Winner of the STP Award for Journalistic Excellence

MetroBooks

An Imprint of Friedman/Fairfax Publishers

©1998 by Michael Friedman Publishing Group, Inc.

Library of Congress Cataloging-in-Publication Data available upon request.

ISBN 1-56799-459-8

Editor: Nathaniel Marunas
Art Director/Designer: Kevin Ullrich
Photography Editor: Sarah Storey
Production Manager: Camille Lee

Color separations by Radstock Repro
Printed in England by Butler & Tanner Limited

10 9 8 7 6 5 4 3 2

For bulk purchases and special sales, please contact:
Friedman–Fairfax Publishers
Attention: Sales Department
15 West 26th Street
New York, NY 10010
212-685-6610
FAX 212-685-1307

Visit our website:
http://www.metrobooks.com

DEDICATION

This book is dedicated to the late Alan Kulwicki, who not only was one of the first NASCAR drivers to help me when I began writing about racing but who also taught me a lot about working hard to make dreams come true as he raced to the 1992 Winston Cup Series championship.

And with love to my wife, Portia, who has supported me through all the craziness and long hours that go along with making dreams come true.

Contents

FOREWORD

The NASCAR Winston Cup Series has become one of the biggest success stories in all of sports. In large part, the fact that millions of people watch racing on television while millions more pack the grandstands of racetracks across the country is because of the R.J. Reynolds Tobacco Company and its sponsorship of NASCAR racing through its Winston cigarette brand.

When Winston made the commitment to become involved with stock car racing, NASCAR was in a vulnerable position. It was 1970, and the sport had just seen the end of a bizarre period of time when the automobile manufacturers had thrown money at expensive stock car racing programs in an all-out effort to win. Suddenly, the companies pulled out of racing. The racing teams that had come to depend on the vast financial contributions of the manufacturers found themselves to be independent racers again, just like in the early days of NASCAR racing two decades earlier.

But when famed car owner Junior Johnson went to Reynolds to pitch the marketing value of sponsoring his race team, Reynolds' Ralph Seagraves saw the potential of the entire sport. So the Winston Cup Series was born in 1971, and NASCAR entered what is called "The Modern Era," as the drivers raced for their share of the initial $40,000 point fund.

That point fund has grown to $1,500,000 in 1997—and the sport of stock car racing has grown to match those big numbers.

But on June 20, 1997, an agreement struck among forty states and the tobacco industry threatened to bring an end to Reynolds' involvement with NASCAR's top division. Tobacco companies would no longer be able to sponsor sporting events if the agreement is approved.

"If, in fact, we have to get out of the sport, we will do everything we can to make sure that we keep connected as well as we can," surmised T. Wayne Robertson, president of the firm that handles the sports marketing operations for R.J. Reynolds, on the day after the agreement was announced. "We have had a great deal of support from this sport, so we are not going to just turn around and walk away."

Speculation regarding which corporate giant might take over sponsorship of NASCAR's top series if Reynolds were ever forced to withdraw has long surrounded the sport of stock car racing. That speculation reached new intensity when word of the agreement spread through the garage area as the Winston Cup contenders prepared to race for the first time at the palatial California Speedway (a venue that exists because of the popularity NASCAR enjoys—popularity due in large part to Winston's support).

Regardless of the pros and cons of the tobacco industry itself, it should be noted that the reason any other corporation would leap at the chance to sponsor a stock car racing series is the loyalty Reynolds and Winston showed to NASCAR. And while the 1997 Winston Cup point fund is large, Winston has put more than $7 million more into racing for the less-famous motorsports divisions—including series where the NASCAR stars of tomorrow cut their teeth in short-track competition. Will other companies be willing to make that commitment to the racers of the decades to come? Only time will tell.

If this does mark the end of the Winston Cup Series as millions have come to know it, then this book will serve to help document an incredible period of more than twenty-five years of growth under Winston—a time in which NASCAR truly became a household word.

Frank Moriarty
October 1997

8

A Brief History of Stock Car Racing

Why, when there are racing series with high-tech motorsports machines using the latest computer-based technology, do millions of stock car racing fans sell out NASCAR races months in advance for a chance to watch coupes that are using carburetors on their engines do battle?

Perhaps the reason is right there. The NASCAR fans can identify with the cars that the stars of stock car racing are driving on the racetrack because many of those fans will be climbing into the same model car for the drive home after the race. And just maybe that use of carburetors harks back to a simpler time—a time when you could open the hood of your car and easily recognize exactly what every component under that hood did to keep your car running.

Or perhaps NASCAR's appeal is just the fact that thrilling, side-by-side competition is the norm in stock car racing. Where Indy-type open-wheel racers encounter disaster when their vehicles encounter each other, "tradin' paint" in NASCAR racing is an every-race occurrence. The bangs, dents, and tire marks that adorn almost every stock car after a race are testament to the rough-and-tumble action on the speedway—and the best drivers aren't shy about using a little on-track contact when it's needed.

Then again, maybe what draws the fans to NASCAR are those very drivers. Baseball players are spitting on umpires, football players are flunking drug tests, and rich basketball players are throwing petulant tantrums in front of the national media, but NASCAR drivers are signing autographs, posing for pictures with children, making telephone calls to hospitalized fans, and generally keeping in mind the NASCAR prime directive: without the fans, we're nothing. That's a rule most professional sports businesses in the United States forgot a long time ago.

But it wasn't such a long time ago that there was no NASCAR, or for that matter any truly organized stock car racing series. The history of NASCAR is one that dates back only about fifty years, and it can all be traced back to one man.

Bill France was called "Big Bill" because he was a big man. Standing at a towering six feet five inches (196cm), France moved to Daytona

Beach, Florida, with his wife, Anne, and son, Bill Jr., in 1934, leaving behind garage work in the Washington, D.C., area. The France family were uncertain as to exactly where in Florida they were going to settle, but they were charmed during a stop in Daytona and made the decision to put down roots right where they were.

Eventually France was able to open an Amoco station after a number of jobs working for other people. Meanwhile, he continued to race recreationally in Florida as he had done back in Washington.

But it was for his promotional genius that France would become legendary, and he got his first opportunity to try out those razor-sharp promotion skills by overseeing the running of a 1938 race on the Daytona beach/road course.

Daytona was already known as a center of mechanized speed, as land speed records for automobiles had been regularly chased on the wide, flat, and firm beach during the first decades of the twentieth century by a number of famous drivers. After Sir Malcolm Campbell set a land speed record of more than 275 mph (442.4kph) in 1935 on Daytona Beach, however, the speed record crowd turned to the even more wide open spaces of Utah's Bonneville Salt Flats. Meanwhile, motorsports action continued in Daytona on a racing course that used a stretch of highway for one straightway and the beach for the other.

France's first promotion was a success, and he continued his racing management activities through 1941. But by then the United States was fully involved in World War II, and racing was virtually forgotten as conflict raged around the globe.

After the war, in the hills of the Deep South, the first stirring of what would become major league stock car racing was felt.

It was indeed motorized competition, but it wasn't taking place on any racetrack. Instead, it took place on unlit roads that wound down mountains in the dark of night. The competitors: moonshiners and federal agents.

Moonshining had begun in the Prohibition era, and the sale and distribution of illegal whiskey was a sizable industry in the late 1940s and into the 1950s. It was the distribution aspect of the moonshining operation that set the stage for stock car racing.

Simply put, the moonshiners had to figure out ways to outrun the federal authorities while driving cars made heavy by their bottled burden. The methods they used to accomplish this goal formed the foundation of stock car racing.

Engines were finely tuned, springs and suspensions were beefed up, and high-speed reaction times were cultivated during high-speed pursuits. Eventually the moonshiners—who had become so highly skilled at mechanized evasions—began to compete with each other on an informal basis to answer the question that is at the root of today's modern NASCAR racing: who's the best driver?

The first races were held in settings that were a far cry from the luxury box–equipped speedways so common today. As often as not, a circular "racetrack" carved into a field set the stage for the race that followed.

But eventually actual speedways began to appear, with bleachers that held a growing number of people who liked to watch the moonshine gang do battle with each other instead of against the federal agents.

It was in this atmosphere that Bill France assessed the state of the sport of stock car racing. As often as not, promoters would cheat the drivers—France himself had discovered that during his own brief career behind the wheel. And there was no national organization to bring order or rules to the chaotic competition taking place throughout the country. France decided to do something about it and called together the most influential promoters, car owners, and drivers of the young sport.

The foundation that was laid in meetings held beginning on December 14, 1947, at the Streamline Hotel in Daytona Beach may have been fragile, but it was the bedrock on which a multibillion-dollar sports entertainment business was built.

Over the course of three days of meetings, the thirty-five participants France called together debated the future of stock car racing. France himself outlined his vision for a national series sanctioned by an organization that would ensure fair treatment of drivers while striving to further develop the sport itself.

The NASCAR tradition began here on the course at Daytona Beach, Florida. In February 1957, Cotton Owens was victorious in the Daytona event, beating more than fifty fellow competitors with an average speed of slightly more than 101 mph (162.5kph). When this photo was taken, NASCAR had been in existence for nearly a decade. Soon the stock cars would leave the beach course and move to the first modern super-speedway, Daytona International Speedway.

Atlanta's Red Vogt was a well-known racer and car builder in the early days of stock car competition. Bill France knew Vogt's input would be valuable if France were to establish a successful national stock car competition organization. Indeed, Vogt is the man who suggested the name now recognized by millions of race fans–NASCAR.

The group bought into France's vision and elected him president on the first day. Joining France in steering the new organization was a board of governors that included some of the best-known names in early stock car racing, including Buddy Shuman, Marshall Teague, Red Byron, and Red Vogt, a car builder from Atlanta who got his start building swift and sturdy vehicles for moonshining.

It was Vogt who conceived the name of the new motorsports sanctioning body. Although the popular vote was to christen the organization the National Stock Car Racing Association, Vogt pointed out that a group of promoters operating in his home state of Georgia were already doing business under the NSCRA banner. Vogt's alternative: the National Association for Stock Car Auto Racing, NASCAR.

It's important to note that the word "national" in the approved name was paid more than just lip service by Bill France. He had invited people involved in racing from all over the country to attend his pivotal meetings, not just racing folk from the South.

Newly christened with a catchy name, the sanctioning body was legally incorporated on February 21, 1948, just days after the first official NASCAR race. The winner of that event was one of France's thirty-five, Red Byron. The February 15 race, titled the Winter 160, was held on the Daytona beach/road course, and Byron's winning entry was a Ford.

But these first forays into sponsoring competition were in the Modified division, with rules that required only a 1937 or later coupe body with windshields and full fenders. France, though, wanted the racing on the track to reflect more closely the cars that rode the highways of the postwar era. His instincts told him that if he could get the fans to identify with the cars on the speedway, they would feel a closer bond to the sport.

With that in mind, NASCAR sanctioned a new division in 1949: the Strictly Stock division. And Strictly Stock was a good description of the race cars, for all parts on the vehicles were required to be available through the manufacturers' catalogs for each model. The vehicles themselves were required to be full-size passenger cars, with hoods, fenders, bumpers, and grilles attached to their complete bodies.

The first Strictly Stock division race took place on June 19, 1949, in a city that would become synonymous with the sport of stock car racing: Charlotte, North Carolina. The field of thirty-three cars was scheduled to run 150 miles (241.3km) on the three-quarter-mile (1.22km) dirt track at Charlotte Speedway. Among the competitors were names that would soon become legends of NASCAR: Lee Petty, Buck Baker, Jim Paschal, Herb Thomas, the Flock brothers, and more. Also competing that day—and credited with a fourteenth-place finish—was Sara Christian, who grabbed a claim to fame at the very first race by being the first female driver in the division.

Less clear than Christian's finishing position was that of the race winner. Over the years, stock car racing—being a sport based on technology and mechanics—has many times had to deal with the problem of race cars equipped with alterations that fall outside of the rules. That difficulty cropped up in this very first Strictly Stock race.

It was discovered that winner Glenn Dunnaway's Ford had completed the two hundred laps stabilized through the turns by illegal rear springs. The spoils of victory—$2,000 and the cheers of the thirteen thousand fans on hand—were transferred to Jim Roper. Although Roper completed only 197 of the scheduled two hundred laps as he trailed Dunnaway, he and his Lincoln were declared winners of this first race in the division that would one day become the NASCAR Winston Cup Series.

But there were many years of growth to come between that dusty Charlotte track and the huge speed palaces of modern stock car racing. Through much of that period of time, Bill France himself carefully guided the sport toward its destiny.

The first fine-tuning came prior to the 1950 season. Yes, the name Strictly Stock served as a good description of the type of car that was racing, but France felt that something with a bit more panache was called for. Borrowing from England's premier horse racing event, the NASCAR series—with its carousing drivers and dirty racetracks—was bestowed with the title Grand National.

Not that the Grand National name could calm the behavior of the men driving the race cars. The lifestyles of many of the NASCAR competitors rivaled the rough driving on the tracks, and racing lore is full of tales of brawls and all-night drinking binges. Driver Darel Dieringer once said, "If you went to bed for three days before a race, you weren't considered a real race driver."

In spite of that—or maybe because of it—NASCAR and its brand of mechanized competition began to build a base of support for itself among fans, especially in the South. But France's vision focused on much more than mere regional success, and in 1950 his cars raced in Ohio, New York, and Indiana.

The year 1950 was also noteworthy for the arrival of the first new NASCAR speedway. South Carolina's Harold Brasington, a successful peanut farmer, had attended the 1948 Indianapolis 500 and begun to ponder the idea of a 500-mile (804.5km) stock car race closer to home. After selling himself on the idea, Brasington purchased 100 acres (40ha) of land near Darlington, South Carolina, and set about the task of making his dream a reality. When he had finished building the 1.25-mile (2km) Darlington Raceway, Brasington aligned his completed speedway project with France's NASCAR—even though France was a bit leery of a 500-mile (804.5km) race's effects on Grand National cars.

Big Bill France found reassurance with the running of the first Southern 500 at Darlington Raceway, held on September 4, 1950—and Harold Brasington found his grandstands filled with twenty-five thousand fans out to gape at the spectacle of a seventy-five-car starting field.

It's hard to imagine a starting lineup nearly twice as large as today's racing fields, but on that day in September 1950 the cars lined up three across in twenty-five rows and set about the task of completing four hundred laps. Johnny Mantz was able to do it first, even if it did take him well over six hours behind the wheel of his Plymouth to wrap up this historic first 500-mile (804.5km) stock car race.

In 1951, France's vision of NASCAR expanded to new ground, as Johnny Mantz was assigned to supervise the organization's new West Coast division. As a result, NASCAR moved into new territories like California and Arizona.

Big Bill's keen business and promotional skills were in full display in 1951, when Detroit was planning a celebration to commemorate its 250th anniversary. France knew there was a 1-mile (1.6km) dirt track at the Michigan State Fairgrounds. What better way for the Motor City to celebrate its heritage than with a stock car race of 250 miles (402.2km), one lap for every year.

France proceeded to lobby the auto manufacturers to ensure they had vehicles representing their makes in the field of the August 12 race, witnessed by a full house of sixteen thousand. France's effort paid off, as the starting lineup featured autos made by everyone from Nash and Hudson to Mercury and Studebaker.

Tommy Thompson won the Motor City 250, but perhaps the biggest winner was Bill France himself, who had opened the eyes of the auto manufacturers to the promotional value of stock car racing. It was a sight they did not soon forget. In fact, the groundwork had been laid for the days of full factory-backed racing efforts.

As auto manufacturers began to brag about the success of their models in NASCAR competition—the first signs of the "win on Sunday, sell on Monday" philosophy—everything seemed rosy in the NASCAR realm. The manufacturers even began making "severe usage" packages available to the race teams, consisting of parts that fit within the NASCAR rules yet made the cars more competitive and durable. And the first large multicar, professional NASCAR team appeared in the form of the

NASCAR's legitimacy as a sport was dependent on the ascension of stock car superstars. One of the first and greatest was Glenn "Fireball" Roberts, who won the biggest races on the NASCAR circuit as the sport rose in prominence. Roberts' performances helped attract the attention of television programs like ABC's **Wide World of Sports.**

Multiple-car racing teams are common in today's Winston Cup Series but were the exception in the early days. Carl Kiekhaefer (left) fielded three entries during the 1956 season. Kiekhaefer's drivers were tremendously successful, sweeping the championship battle. Herb Thomas (second from left) was runner-up to Buck Baker (second from right) for the title, while Speedy Thompson (right) finished third. Kiekhaefer cars won thirty races in 1956.

Carl Kiekhaefer/Mercury Outboards Chrysler team that fielded up to five cars at a time for drivers like Tim and Fonty Flock and Buck Baker.

By the mid-1950s, specialized racing tires and flameproof suits for the drivers began to appear at the racetracks of NASCAR, along with other safety advances. But it was the safety of the spectators that concerned those outside the sport.

In June 1955, a disastrous crash took place during the famed 24 Hours of LeMans race in France. One of the cars lost control and plowed into the spectator area as it disintegrated in flames. The carnage it left behind was nearly incomprehensible: more than one hundred spectators were killed in the horrific tragedy.

A worldwide outcry against the sport of auto racing was raised. In the United States Senate, Oregon's Richard Neuberger called for the end of auto racing. "We allow children to visit race tracks where men and women are constantly in peril of being maimed or killed," Neuberger exclaimed. "If automobile racing is necessary to perfect motor vehicles—as proponents of racing ridiculously claim—then I sup-

pose next we will hear that we must run stallions off cliffs to improve horse flesh."

It was a dark time for motorsports, and the danger hit home for Bill France and NASCAR in 1957. On May 19 at Martinsville Speedway, Billy Myers' Mercury made contact with Tom Pistone's Chevrolet. Myers was sent hurtling off the racetrack surface. His car landed in an area clearly marked off-limits to spectators, but fans who had ignored the warnings were in the path of Myers' racer. Several were severely injured, including an eight-year-old boy who suffered grave head injuries.

Fully aware of the negative publicity surrounding the incident, the media-conscious auto manufacturers made a big show of distancing themselves from France's NASCAR. The factory-backed drivers suddenly found themselves independent racers once again.

In lesser hands, this situation could have turned into a collapsing house of cards. But the guiding hand of Big Bill took charge, encouraging promoters to sweeten race pots while France himself provided travel money to his racers to help weather the storm and keep stock car racing growing.

And grow it did. NASCAR badly needed a hero, and in 1958 it got one: Fireball Roberts. A string of incredible performances throughout the season opened the eyes of the sports world to Roberts and NASCAR as Fireball led nearly half the laps he drove that year.

Edging back toward respect, stock car racing needed a true showplace for its competitors. It was Bill France who provided one.

France had long dreamed of building his own superspeedway, one that would outshine Harold Brasington's Darlington track and allow the NASCAR drivers to compete at breathtaking speeds—and he wanted to build it in Daytona Beach.

France originally envisioned Daytona International Speedway opening in 1955, but a series of unavoidable delays prevented the grand opening of the track until 1959. But what a track it was.

Grand National drivers who entered the speedway through the tunnel under the huge track's fourth turn were dumbstruck upon seeing the vast infield stretched out before them. And around the infield expanse was a ribbon of asphalt wide enough for plenty of side-by-side racing, with turns banked at more than 30 degrees, and measuring in at an astonishing 2.5 miles (4km) in length. At a time when the drivers were still competing on racetracks as small as the .25-mile (402.4m) bullring at North Carolina's Bowman Gray Stadium, Daytona International Speedway was truly mind-boggling.

In preparation for the very first Daytona 500, the Grand National drivers found themselves running at speeds that were once unimaginable. They also found themselves having to develop a unique set of skills for superspeedway racing, including the new strategy of drafting. Drafting involved pulling up right behind another car, allowing the two cars running close together to race along faster than they would be able to do trying to cut through the air by themselves.

Bill France wanted close competition to be what everyone remembered about the first Daytona 500. He got far more than he had bargained for.

The February 22, 1959, event drew a crowd of more than forty thousand to watch a fifty-nine-car field compete for a winner's share of $19,000. But it was determining just who was the winner that day that became the big problem for NASCAR.

After three and a half hours of competition at speeds of 140 mph (225.2kph), the two strongest cars were the Oldsmobile of Lee Petty and the Thunderbird of Johnny Beauchamp. As the cars roared out of the fourth turn on the final lap, Beauchamp and Petty were side by side. They flashed across the start/finish line in a dead heat.

NASCAR declared Beauchamp the victor, but Petty and his team vigorously protested the decision. Bill France declared the race unofficial, pending a review of all available photographic evidence. Three days later, it was Lee Petty

The aftermath of racing's darkest day. In June 1955 more than one hundred people were killed when a car lost control in France's famed 24 Hours of LeMans event and crashed into the crowd of spectators. Only Bill France's firm hand at the helm of NASCAR prevented the backlash from the tragedy from damaging stock car racing.

who was declared the first winner of the Daytona 500.

Despite the controversy, the race had been a tremendous success, and Big Bill's amazing speedway set the tone for a decade of growth. While the sport needed new fans to prosper, it needed a growing infrastructure on which to build the foundation that would support the future of stock car racing. New superspeedways in Atlanta and Charlotte helped meet that demand.

Many new fans were introduced to the sport thanks to the debut of stock car racing on national television. ABC's *Wide World of Sports* began covering NASCAR in the early 1960s, and CBS and NBC dabbled in racing coverage as well. The partnership of television and NASCAR was one that would flourish in the years to come.

Part of the reason for that was a growing stable of colorful stars who wheeled the Grand National cars on the nation's racetracks. The first generation of NASCAR stars who had raced throughout the 1950s were yielding to a new crop of drivers like Junior Johnson, David Pearson, Buddy Baker, and Richard Petty.

And the Grand National cars these drivers raced in were undergoing their own metamorphosis. In the early days of NASCAR racing, the cars were almost entirely stock; tying the drivers into their seats with rope was considered a safety feature. As the 1960s progressed,

though, the automobile manufacturers made a full-scale return to NASCAR racing.

While the cars looked like passenger coupes on the outside, under the skin things had changed. Specialized chassis designs were developed and mammoth powerplants were stuffed under the hoods. The manufacturers studied ways to meet the requirements of NASCAR's rulebook while achieving their desired results. Ford managed to fit a 429-cubic-inch (7030cc) motor into five hundred examples of the compact Mustang, thus satisfying a NASCAR rule covering the number of production models that must be made available to the public—and thereby making the behemoth powerplant legal to go under the hoods of their Grand National cars.

The manufacturer melee reached its peak in the 1969 and 1970 seasons, as Chrysler and Ford pitted their engineering and aerodynamic teams against each other in an all-out battle for NASCAR supremacy. Ford developed the sleek Torino and the Mercury Cyclone, but Chrysler went a step further. Its weapons of choice, the Dodge Charger Daytona and Plymouth Super Bird, had pointed snouts up front and huge wings at the rear and almost overnight became legends of the NASCAR circuit.

Driver Bobby Isaac and brilliant crew chief Harry Hyde won the 1970 championship with their Daytona, while Pete Hamilton drove a Petty Enterprises Super Bird to win the

Opposite: *Although NASCAR was becoming known as the elite motorsports sanctioning body in the United States, smaller racing organizations still flourished by promoting events locally. A non-NASCAR race at the treacherous Langhorne Speedway in Pennsylvania in October 1951 was brought to a halt by this crash on lap 86 of a scheduled 100.* Above: *Jim McCuirk spins backward in his 1959 Pontiac while competing in the very first Daytona 500, held at Daytona International Speedway on February 22, 1959. The spectators who filled the grandstands and crammed into the track's infield were drawn to the new track by the promise of unprecedented speeds. The Daytona 500 has since become a February tradition.*

extent where every week they came down with a new gimmick or a new car or a new something, and NASCAR couldn't keep up with it. They said, 'Hey—it's our ball game! We want you to play with our bat and ball, and we're going to tell you what that bat and ball is going to look like instead of you telling us what it's going to look like.'"

The manufacturers reacted by once again scaling back their racing involvement, feeling that they had proved their point on the race-tracks of America. But in 1971, a new force arrived on the NASCAR scene to fill the void.

Junior Johnson had approached the R.J. Reynolds company about sponsoring his racing efforts in 1970, but by the time all was said and done, Johnson's negotiations led to Reynolds' Winston brand becoming sponsor of the entire NASCAR Grand National division. Thus was born the Winston Cup Series and NASCAR's modern era.

The first noticeable effect of the modern era was a trimming of the race schedule. For years, the Grand National series had criss-crossed the country, racing several nights a week. Not all drivers raced in every event. Even though the schedule had been pared somewhat by the late 1960s, France and Reynolds wanted to create a more compact schedule, one that encouraged every driver to show up for every event. The itinerary of NASCAR's premier division dropped from fifty events a year to a more manageable thirty races per season.

Having guided the sport to unprecedented success, Big Bill France decided to surrender the day-to-day reigns of control over NASCAR in 1972. But the organization that he had so carefully built was well taken care of, as Big Bill's son, Bill France, Jr., became the new head of NASCAR. And the younger France eagerly set about the task of moving the sport of stock car racing toward even greater achievements.

Among the changes that characterized NASCAR racing in the 1970s was an influx of new sponsors. Traditionally, racing sponsorship had been supplied by manufacturers and distributors of automotive supplies. But in the 1970s, marketers of consumer-oriented products began to see the value of placing their logos on the quarterpanels of the cars competing in the Winston Cup Series. Joining soft drink giants Pepsi and Coca-Cola in the sponsorship trend were companies like Shoney's Restaurants, Coppertone, and Citicorp. With the days of full factory support becoming just a memory, the arrival of these new sponsors helped offset the expense of maintaining a racing team.

Modern Winston Cup racing is built on team efforts. Although it is usually the driver who claims headlines in the wake of a victory, it is the work of his crew that builds the foundation for success in the Winston Cup Series. Motor specialists, like those of the Robert Yates team pictured here, work within the rules of NASCAR to maximize horsepower and performance.

Daytona 500 and both races at Bill France's new 2.66-mile (4.2km) superspeedway in Talladega, Alabama.

Big Bill was alarmed at the direction of the sport. His brand of stock car racing was based on cars that fans could identify with. What he saw racing on his tracks in 1970 was a hybrid of automotive and aircraft technology. In fact, much of the Chrysler engineering talent had moved to the manufacturer's auto racing program from Chrysler's missile division. The aerodynamic Chrysler vehicles—with their wings guiding the cars through the turns of superspeedways—were pushing stock car racing away from the common fan.

Bill France had the power to change things and he used it, instituting engine limitations so restrictive that Ford's and Chrysler's aerodynamic cars almost immediately disappeared.

"What happened where it was getting out of control was that Detroit was controlling NASCAR," said Richard Petty. "I mean to the

The sponsors doubtless noticed that stock car racing was slowly but surely growing in terms of visiblity and importance in the world of professional sports. Part of that was happening as a result of the increasing television coverage of NASCAR events.

In 1976, ABC Sports broadcast the finish of the Daytona 500 live. Millions of viewers tuned in to see five-time Daytona 500 winner Richard Petty in a heated battle for the win with David Pearson, racing hard in a quest for his first Daytona victory. The two cars were charging toward the start/finish line on the last lap when they crashed exiting turn four. Pearson managed to keep his battered Wood Brothers Mercury running, slipped the car back into gear, and limped on to the checkered flag as Petty sat stalled behind him. The bizarre finish to NASCAR's biggest race attracted national attention.

But an even bigger attention-getter came in 1979, when CBS became the first network to broadcast the entire Daytona 500 live. It's doubtful that the television network executives could ever have imagined the amazing programming they got on that Sunday in February, as race leaders Cale Yarborough and Donnie Allison crashed on the last lap and Richard Petty secured the win, his sixth Daytona 500 victory. That was exciting enough, but when Yarborough, Allison, and Donnie's brother Bobby all got into a fight at the site of the final-lap accident, CBS was assured it had carried programming that would have the entire nation talking.

As the 1980s dawned, the drivers of the Winston Cup Series were forced to react to the trend in the automobile world toward smaller cars. The Winston Cup cars up to this time had been lumbering beasts with huge powerplants to propel their bulk along at 200 mph (321.8kph). (One of the longest cars, the Dodge Charger Daytona, was 19 feet [5.7m] in length.) But in 1981, the wheelbases of stock cars used in Winston Cup competition were limited to 110 inches (279.4cm).

But the competition on the racetrack was what really mattered, and it was as exciting as ever. Late in the 1981 season, the ESPN cable sports network televised its first live race, and the partnership of live sports coverage on television and NASCAR's premier series helped elevate stock car racing further in the public consciousness.

A new group of driving stars flexed their muscles in the 1980s, as many of the drivers who had established the sport throughout the 1960s and 1970s retired from competition.

Names like David Pearson and Cale Yarborough faded from the top of the points standings, to be replaced by drivers like Bill Elliott, Darrell Waltrip, and Dale Earnhardt. The sons of earlier NASCAR Grand National champions created a second generation of Winston Cup drivers, as Richard Petty's son Kyle, Ned Jarrett's son Dale, and Bobby Allison's son Davey all began racing on the speedways and superspeedways.

The decade of the 1990s has been characterized by the full acceptance of stock car racing and the Winston Cup Series by the sports and business worlds. The range of sponsors is greater than ever and the sum they must spend to back a top team is also greater than ever—up to $6 million for the 1997 season alone.

Such a huge expense is considered to be worthwhile because of the number of people they will reach by sponsoring a car. In 1995, the total attendance at the thirty-one races of the NASCAR Winston Cup Series was approaching 6 million people—people covering all demographic territories. *Forbes* magazine estimated that total annual NASCAR and race team merchandise sales tops $500 million (Dale Earnhardt alone accounted for $50 million), and that the entire sport's annual take—that of NASCAR itself, the track operators, and race team income—is $2 billion.

Those astronomical numbers are reflected in the speedways themselves. New tracks like the regal California Speedway near Los Angeles and the Texas Motor Speedway near Dallas are truly state-of-the-art in every aspect, from the garage areas where the teams prepare the cars

Like Fireball Roberts did before him, Jeff Gordon has become a NASCAR superstar. Personable, well spoken, and a hard-charging driver, Gordon meets the specifications for success on and off the track in an era when the ability to interact with the media and the public is almost as important as the ability to race.

Right: *Since NASCAR was founded, safety has been an overriding concern for the sanctioning body. As a result, fatalities in competition are rare. Today competitors often walk away from the most violent of crashes with only minor injuries, even from those as spectacular as this one, involving Bobby Labonte.*
Opposite: *Proof of the appeal of NASCAR's Winston Cup Series is seen in the logos of the major corporations of all types that sponsor race teams. These companies feel that the millions of dollars required to sponsor a top team is a sound investment.*

to the luxury boxes where wealthy fans dine as they watch the race unfold far below them. The older tracks that NASCAR built its foundation on are struggling to upgrade themselves lest they see NASCAR take away a precious Winston Cup date and give it to another track in another market—as happened to North Carolina's historic North Wilkesboro Speedway.

While the longtime drivers retain the southern heritage of the dirt tracks that NASCAR racing cut its teeth on, many of the new drivers are well aware that they represent a new breed of stock car contenders. They hail from all over the United States, and while they may carry a helmet in one hand, many also tote a briefcase in the other. They are well spoken because they have to be—sponsor commitments and appearances are a given, as are live television interviews.

Perhaps the driver who best personifies the modern Winston Cup star is young Jeff Gordon, who won what may prove to be the first of many championships in 1995. But in spite of his media-perfect good looks and his ability to almost always say the right thing, Jeff Gordon is still a racer. As such, he is fully aware of what it means to walk in the footsteps of such legendary drivers as Allison, Petty, and Pearson. "Oh, I know how special it is to be Winston Cup champion," Gordon said in a conversation shortly after winning the championship. "It's something that I'll be able to remember and enjoy for the rest of my life because every time they introduce me it's going to be as the 1995 Winston Cup champion. That's a great feeling. It's a great accomplishment and I'm very proud to be a part of it. I'm glad that my team could be a part of it. I'm just looking forward to all of the great things that

are going to happen in the future from this championship."

Like the legends who came before him, Gordon knows that you can never be satisfied with what you have already accomplished. To keep your edge, you must keep aiming higher. "Great champions in Winston Cup...are the ones who have won more than one championship," Gordon said in 1996. "That's something that is very, very hard to do. I'm very proud to be able to say that I've won one and it's quite an accomplishment, but to be able to say I've won more than one is something even greater." Gordon won his second title in 1997 and can now count himself among the greats.

As long as NASCAR is able to feature drivers with that level of determination, the fans will continue to fill the grandstands and stock car racing will grow.

As for the future of NASCAR itself, Bill France, Jr., still remains solidly in control of the empire that his father started in 1947. But many observers speculate that Bill Jr.'s son, Brian, will one day take the reins of stock car racing's most important sanctioning body. Brian France already oversees the marketing efforts of NASCAR, and his flair for business makes him a likely candidate to take over when his father decides the time to step down is at hand.

It seems that after a whirlwind five-decade existence, NASCAR and its top division are poised for ascension to a level of popularity and status that Big Bill France might have found unimaginable. Then again, watching the steady growth of the organization that he envisioned in the meetings at the Streamline Hotel back in 1947, perhaps the elder France would have expected nothing less than to see the public fall in love with the sport—just as he did.

ALLISON FAMILY

Rivaling the Petty family in significance, Alabama's Allison family has played a crucial role in NASCAR's history. Sadly, though, the family's contributions to racing—which just a few years ago seemed poised to stretch long into the future—will now live on only as part of the past.

Bobby Allison (retired, born 12/3/37) was the first of the Allisons to enter NASCAR Grand National and Winston Cup racing. After growing up racing at short tracks in Florida during his high school years, Bobby and his brother Donnie (retired, born 9/7/39) moved to Alabama to challenge the competition in one of the national centers of stock car racing. From there, having found great success in his new home, Bobby moved to NASCAR.

After a dozen races between 1961 and 1965, Allison went at the NASCAR schedule full-time in 1966. He came away with his first three wins and a tenth-place ranking in the season points tally. In 1971, he collected eleven victories, and followed that up with ten more the next year. With the DiGard racing team and crew chief Gary Nelson—one day to become NASCAR's chief rules enforcer—Allison won the Winston Cup championship in 1983. Fans voted Allison most popular driver in 1971, 1972, 1973, 1981, 1982, and 1983, a testimony to the soft-spoken driver's easygoing nature off the track. Bobby's record also includes three victories in the Daytona 500.

Bobby Allison's career was cut short after a devastating crash at Pocono in 1988. The accident left Bobby with neurological problems, and his return to the sport came as a team owner. In recent years he has helped the careers of younger drivers like Jimmy Spencer and Hut Stricklin.

Donnie Allison followed his brother into NASCAR racing, starting his first races in the top division in 1966. In the two decades that followed, Donnie drove to ten victories in more than two hundred starts before he, too, left competition in 1988.

But the Allison family still had one member competing in the Winston Cup Series, and he seemed to have the potential to outshine the accomplishments of those who had raced before him. Davey (born 2/25/61, died 7/13/93) was Bobby's son and grew up watching his father and his uncle race in the Winston Cup Series. After getting his own start racing on short tracks and in the ARCA Series, Davey Allison entered Winston Cup racing in 1985 and 1986 on a sporadic basis. Showing great promise, the young driver managed a top-ten finish in each season.

Dale Earnhardt after winning a Winston Cup race just days after the death of Davey Allison:

"You're happy about winning a race but to win it and have the death of Davey hanging in your mind, and his family down there, to have those folks in mind—they're part of our family and they've been through so much. David Smith had a word of prayer with all of the crew members and prayed for the families and then we took a victory lap in memory of Davey and Alan [Kulwicki], too.

"Davey was a heck of a good friend and a racer. I had a lot of great memories of racing with Davey. He'd get under your skin and outrun you—but I'd have been glad to be second to him today to have him back."

Left: *Bobby Allison (right) and his son, Davey, celebrate their first- and second-place sweep in the 1988 Daytona 500.*
Opposite, top: *Victory lane was a place where the Allison family could often be found. Here Donnie Allison celebrates after winning at Charlotte Motor Speedway in 1969.*
Opposite, bottom: *Donnie Allison held a commanding lead in the 1974 Daytona 500 with just eleven laps to go. Then disaster struck: track debris blew out both front tires, forcing Allison into the pit. Though the DiGard crew quickly replaced the tires, the delay enabled Richard Petty to win the race.*

Davey Allison
on setting up passes in
Winston Cup Series competition:

"You have to go on instincts for one thing—and hope that your instincts are right. I think that after you make enough mistakes you learn when they're right and when they're wrong. You have to be careful about when you pass and where you pass. And if you make a move, and it doesn't look like you're going to be able to be successful making it, then rather than trying to make a hole to get back in line you just have to accept it and fall back in where you can. The way I tell is I look over my shoulder before I move back in line. I don't just pass somebody and move over, I look and make sure I'm in the clear. That way it takes all of the guessing game out of it—you either know that you are or you aren't.

"The hardest part of being patient is knowing that you want to move up, but you don't have an opportunity to—and accepting it."

In 1987, he began Winston Cup racing for real and won twice that year. The first win came at Alabama's Talladega Superspeedway, a race in which his father's car became airborne and crashed. Bobby was not seriously injured, so the day had a happy ending. Even happier for Davey was the 1988 Daytona 500, where he watched his father win while Davey himself finished second. After his father was forced to retire from driving as a result of the Pocono crash, Davey won the Daytona 500 in 1992.

In 191 Winston Cup starts, Davey Allison won nineteen times and almost won the 1992 championship, which was captured by Alan Kulwicki. But in July 1993—just weeks after his younger brother Clifford died in a crash at Michigan in a Busch Grand National car—Davey was killed when his helicopter crashed at Talladega Superspeedway. Davey and long-time Allison family friend Red Farmer were flying to the track to watch a test session that Neil Bonnett and his son, David, were taking part in. Davey lost control and the aircraft

Two Ford Thunderbirds in flight, as Davey Allison runs on the inside of Alan Kulwicki in 1989. Allison and Kulwicki, along with Bill Elliott, staged a thrilling battle for the Winston Cup championship in 1992. Kulwicki claimed the title by just ten points. Sadly, less than a year later both Allison and Kulwicki were killed in separate aircraft accidents.

Left: *It was a dark day for NASCAR when Bobby Allison's career was brought to a close by a crash at Pocono International Raceway on June 19, 1988. Head injuries sustained in the crash left Allison with partial amnesia, unable to remember the day he won the Daytona 500 and his son Davey finished second.* Below: *The ASA and ARCA racing organizations provide many drivers with a chance to gain speedway experience. But that learning process can include accidents as vicious as any in NASCAR, as shown in this photograph of Jack Shanklin's 1967 crash at Daytona International Speedway during ARCA competition.*

crashed in the infield. Farmer survived, but Davey never recovered from his injuries.

Davey's death brought to a close the legacy of the racing Allison family, which suffered through tragedies but enriched the sport of stock car racing with their laid-back demeanor and superior racing skills.

AMERICAN MOTORS CORPORATION (AMC)

The tiniest of the major U.S. automobile manufacturers predictably faced overwhelming odds when it competed in the Winston Cup Series. Nevertheless, the small company did achieve some success in the NASCAR wars, winning three times alone in 1975.

AMC began competing seriously in NASCAR in 1969 with its Javelin model, entering into the division now known as the Busch Grand National division. But it was with the Matador that AMC had its best results.

Roger Penske and AMC teamed up to bring the Matador to the Winston Cup Series in 1972. With lead driver Mark Donohue, the team had a disappointing year with aerodynamic problems plaguing the boxy Matador. But on January 21, 1973, Donohue drove the Matador to victory in the road race at Riverside. A redesigned Matador, driven by Bobby Allison, won at the old Ontario, California, track at the end of the 1974 season.

But 1975 was the big year for AMC's NASCAR efforts. Allison won at Riverside and placed second in the Daytona 500, then won both races that season at Darlington.

After the 1975 season, Penske and AMC parted ways, and American Motors' brief NASCAR effort came to a conclusion.

AMERICAN SPEED ASSOCIATION (ASA)

Racing on short tracks throughout the Midwest, the American Speed Association provides a fertile breeding ground for future stars of NASCAR Winston Cup stock car racing. Although ASA cars are lighter and slightly less powerful than their Winston Cup brethren, the fundamental approaches to racing learned in ASA competition can help drivers who make the move to NASCAR's Busch Grand National

John Andretti on how the personal aspects of Winston Cup racing differ from other racing series:

"When our first child, Jarett, was born, it was December, the off-season, and we really didn't hear any more from people than you would expect from family and close friends. I was in IndyCar at that time.

"Now, I'm in Winston Cup, and after Olivia was born, the first thing that happens is I show up at the track and I see 'It's a Girl!' on the spoiler of the race car. And then all of a sudden every autograph session I went to, even that first weekend, everyone was congratulating me on having that baby. We keep getting cards, gifts, and letters from fans.

"When I went home after Bristol the house was filled with flowers. It made us feel great. We feel like we're part of the NASCAR family. Nobody calls me an IndyCar driver anymore; they ask if I'm going to run the Indy 500 but now it's like a NASCAR guy might go over to run the Indy 500.

"This is what you work to become. I've shed one skin to get a new one in NASCAR, and I like the new one."

and Winston Cup divisions. Well-known Winston Cup drivers who have passed through the ASA Series include Alan Kulwicki, Mark Martin, and Rusty Wallace.

While NASCAR has benefited from the presence of drivers with ASA heritages, the ASA has been aided by the explosion of interest in Winston Cup racing. Directly as a result of the stock car racing fever brought on by widespread NASCAR coverage, many ASA events are now broadcast live on national television and provide a high-profile classroom for tomorrow's Winston Cup drivers.

ANDRETTI FAMILY

IndyCar legend Mario Andretti (retired, born 2/28/40) showed that he had talent for any kind of motorsports competition—and he proved his point in his infrequent NASCAR Winston Cup starts. Although Mario competed in only fourteen events in NASCAR's premier division during his entire racing career, he came away with two top-ten finishes and one win. And what a win it was.

Despite his background of success driving in all kinds of race cars, Andretti was considered an underdog in the 1967 Daytona 500 despite the fact that he was driving a Holman-

John Andretti and family celebrate Andretti's first Winston Cup win, in July 1997. Andretti raced in a variety of motorsports series before entering into Winston Cup competition, and some doubted if he had the determination to weather the process of building a reputation while learning how to race in NASCAR. But Andretti persevered, and made his mark with this first win for car owner Cale Yarborough at Daytona International Speedway.

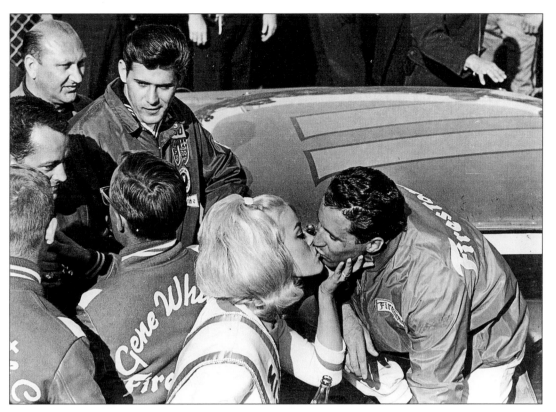

Left: Thirty years before John Andretti won his first NASCAR event, uncle Mario Andretti captured his own win at Daytona International Speedway when he emerged from his car victorious in the 1967 Daytona 500. Below: *One of the drivers Mario had to beat was Richard Petty, modern-day owner of the number 43 Winston Cup entry, a car seen here leading Terry Labonte's Chevrolet. In late 1997, John Andretti was announced as Petty's driver for the 1998 Winston Cup season.*

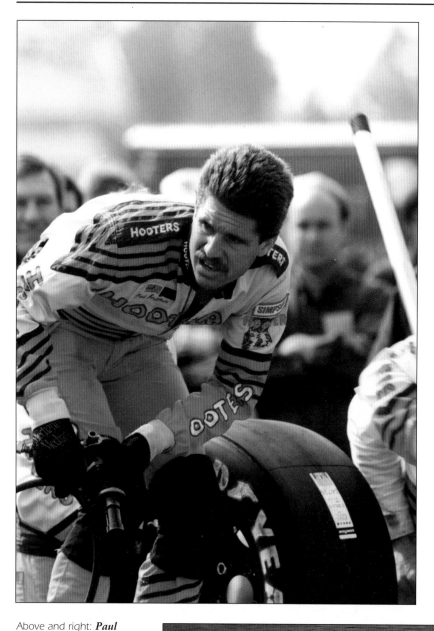

Moody Ford. After all, he was competing against NASCAR's best drivers, some of whom had hundreds of starts compared to Andretti's paltry few.

Even though Mario started the race back in the twelfth position, by the twenty-third lap he had taken the lead. Andretti stayed at the head of the field for much of the race, leading the most laps in the event. Although he was running low on gasoline, Andretti charged on. Then a late race caution flag came out when Richard Petty's engine failed, allowing Andretti to conserve enough fuel to hang on for the win as he took the checkered flag under caution. The only other car on the lead lap was Mario's Holman-Moody teammate, Fred Lorenzen.

Even though Mario Andretti never won another NASCAR race, he had won NASCAR's biggest race.

Mario's twin brother, Aldo, has a son who carries on the Andretti tradition in modern NASCAR Winston Cup Series competition. John Andretti (born 3/12/63), after trying his hand at motorsports competition ranging from the Indianapolis 500 to the 24-hour race of LeMans to NHRA Top Fuel drag racing, settled on a NASCAR career and made his first start for Billy Hagan in 1993.

Andretti learned quickly in the Winston Cup Series and, after driving for the Michael Kranefuss operation in 1995 and most of 1996, helped revitalize the Cale Yarborough team in 1997 with strong race performances and his first pole position.

Above and right: *Paul Andrews was crew chief of the number 7 stock car team when Alan Kulwicki captured the 1992 championship in a Ford Thunderbird. At Atlanta Motor Speedway that year, the two men carefully calculated the number of laps they needed to lead by in that race to win the season.*

Opposite: *Don Bitner survived this crash in 1960, at Lakewood Park in Atlanta, Georgia. That same year, the Atlanta suburb of Hampton became the site of a brand new superspeedway, Atlanta International Raceway.*

In May 1994, John Andretti gained tremendous media attention when he competed in both the Indianapolis 500 and the Coca-Cola 600 on the same day. Immediately after the 500, Andretti flew from Indiana to North Carolina. Although he missed the mandatory NASCAR pre-race drivers' meeting, Andretti did arrive at Charlotte Motor Speedway just in time to start his car in the 600-mile (965.4km) event, becoming the first racer to ever drive both races on the same day.

John Andretti's first Winston Cup win occurred behind the wheel of a Ford Thunderbird for owner and NASCAR legend Cale Yarborough at Daytona International Speedway on July 5, 1997. In 1998, Andretti drove for NASCAR legend Richard Petty.

ANDREWS, PAUL

One of modern Winston Cup racing's most respected crew chiefs, Paul Andrews (born 5/25/57) demonstrated his outstanding abilities when he guided the understaffed and underfunded Alan Kulwicki racing team to the 1992 Winston Cup championship.

At the age of nineteen, Andrews began working with Rusty Wallace, and over the next ten years he began to acquire the knowledge that can make or break a crew chief. Kulwicki hired Andrews in 1988, laying the groundwork for the championship.

After Kulwicki was killed in a plane crash in April 1993, Andrews stuck with the team, helping to hold the group together until Geoff Bodine bought the operation later that year. With Bodine at the wheel of the team's Ford Thunderbirds, Andrews won four victories by the end of the 1996 season, bringing his accumulated total to nine.

After directing the Bodine team to its final win in 1996, Andrews left to work with young driver Jeremy Mayfield.

ATLANTA MOTOR SPEEDWAY (AMS)

Unlike most Winston Cup racetracks, Atlanta Motor Speedway has never developed a colorful nickname, other than ones inspired by the track's legendary postrace traffic jams—nicknames that can't be printed here.

But what the Hampton, Georgia, facility lacks in nicknames it more than makes up for in excitement. The racing action became especially challenging during the era of restrictor

plate racing, when Atlanta—where teams did not have to use plates—was the fastest track. This led to lap speeds in excess of 185 mph (297.6kph) around the 1.522-mile (2.4km) oval.

The track's unique configuration—half-mile (804.6m) turns with 24-degree banking at each end of the oval—created a history of outstanding competition from the track's 1960 debut onward. AMS traditionally hosts the final race of the Winston Cup season, and as a result it has been the site of many memorable events, like the finale of the 1992 season, when Alan Kulwicki placed second but won the championship by just ten points over race-winner Bill Elliott. That race was also Richard Petty's final entry in NASCAR competition.

The history books reflect the fact that Virginia's Wood Brothers racing team has had the best luck at AMS, with its drivers claiming a dozen victories over the years.

Unfortunately, in 1997 track owner Bruton Smith succumbed to his lust for tri-ovals, and AMS's famed configuration was altered to clone Smith's Charlotte Motor Speedway and Texas Motor Speedway. As a result, the track's current length is 1.54 miles (2.4km). At that configuration—and newly paved—Geoff Bodine qualified on the pole for the first race on the "new" AMS with a speed of 197.5mph (317.7kph), more than 10 mph (16kph) faster than the old track record.

This is the original configuration of Atlanta Motor Speedway (which was called Atlanta International Raceway until its purchase by Bruton Smith), with its vast turns. In 1997 the track underwent a face-lift. The start/finish line was moved to what had been the back straight-away, but more important to the drivers was the track's change from an oval to a tri-oval shape. Expectations were that speeds might decrease, but Geoff Bodine qualified on the pole for the November 1997 race with a speed of more than 194 mph (312.1kph), the fastest qualifying speed at any track in 1997.

AUTOMOBILE RACING CLUB OF AMERICA (ARCA)

Although ARCA sponsors several divisions of motorsports competition, its stock car class functions much like NASCAR's Busch Grand National division as a pipeline to the Winston Cup Series.

ARCA's stock cars are virtually identical to Winston Cup cars. In fact, since ARCA allows older body styles to compete, many Winston Cup cars that have outlived their NASCAR usefulness are reborn in ARCA competition. ARCA is also beneficial to young drivers hungry for experience, as the series often competes on the same tracks as the Winston Cup Series, including Pocono International Raceway, Charlotte Motor Speedway, Talladega Superspeedway, and Daytona International Speedway. Many ARCA events are now televised.

Among the Winston Cup drivers who have raced in ARCA competition as they gained stock car experience are Benny Parsons, Davey Allison, Sterling Marlin, and Kyle Petty.

BAHARI RACING

Bahari Racing—formed in 1987 by owners Chuck Rider, Lowrance Harry, and Dick Bahre—has become a consistent presence on the NASCAR Winston Cup Series circuit for the past decade. With a name formed by combining the first part of each of the three men's last names, Bahari Racing became a two-owner team just months after its inception when Rider and Harry bought out Bahre. Although Bahre left the team—eventually opening New Hampshire International Speedway—the Bahari name remains.

Michael Waltrip drove for the team from 1987 until the end of the 1995 season on a seemingly futile quest for both his and the race team's first Winston Cup win. Waltrip came close—with one second-place finish and four third-place finishes during the years—but luck never seemed to shine on Bahari Racing.

Frustrated by years of falling short of the goal of victory, the parties mutually agreed to split before the 1996 season, with Waltrip moving to the Wood Brothers Ford team. Bahari Racing turned to a talented young driver, Johnny Benson.

Benson won the 1993 ASA stock car championship (ASA is the division where drivers like Mark Martin, Rusty Wallace, and Alan Kulwicki got their starts). After moving to the NASCAR Busch Grand National Series and winning the Rookie of the Year title in 1994, Benson won the series championship in 1995.

Poised for Winston Cup stardom, Benson nearly won the 1996 Brickyard 400 for Bahari Racing and helped the team become even more competitive. Then in 1997 Benson announced plans to drive for Jack Roush in 1998. Bahari Racing welcomed former Daytona 500 winner Derrike Cope as the team's 1998 driver.

BAKER FAMILY

North Carolina's Buck Baker (retired, born 3/4/19) and his son, Buddy (retired, born 1/25/41), accounted for a total of sixty-five victories in the combined four decades that the two men drove in NASCAR's top division.

Buck Baker was among the first drivers to compete in NASCAR Grand National competition, finishing in eleventh place driving a 1948 Kaiser in NASCAR's first true stock car race, on June 19, 1949, at the Charlotte Speedway dirt track. In 1952, Baker won his first NASCAR race, driving his Hudson Hornet to victory in Columbia, South Carolina, on April 12.

Driver Michael Waltrip's career-best finish to date (second place) in official Winston Cup competition came in 1988, when he was driving cars prepped by the distinguished Bahari Racing Team

Buck quickly got the hang of winning in NASCAR, as he went to the victory lane forty-five more times in the twenty years of competition that followed. His last two wins came in 1964, although Buck did compete in the Winston Cup Series sporadically until 1976. During his career, Baker was NASCAR's champion in 1956 and 1957, and his achievements include wins at the 1953, 1960, and 1964 Southern 500s at Darlington.

In recent years, Buck Baker has started a popular stock car driving school based at North Carolina Motor Speedway.

Son Buddy's first Grand National start came just ten years after Buck's own NASCAR career got under way. Buddy's first win came at a high-profile event, the 1967 National 500 at Charlotte Motor Speedway. Baker drove his Dodge to complete the 500-mile (804.5km) distance ahead of NASCAR's biggest stars and became one of the few Grand National drivers to beat Richard Petty (during a season that saw perennial champ Petty win an amazing twenty-seven races.)

Buddy Baker's aggressive driving style served him well during the rough-and-tumble years of the Winston Cup Series. He won the 1968, 1972, and 1973 World 600s at Charlotte;

the 1970 Southern 500 at Darlington; the 1975, 1976, and 1980 Winston 500s at Talladega; and the 1980 Daytona 500.

Buddy Baker also became the first driver to run a lap at more than 200 mph (321.8kph), in March 1970 at Talladega. Supposedly conducting transmission tests on a winged Dodge Charger Daytona, Chrysler's Larry Rathgeb was determined to set the mark and chose Baker as the driver who could achieve the feat.

Above: *Buck Baker sits in the Carl Kiekhaefer entry on the sands of Daytona Beach prior to competition in 1956. Baker was one of the first to open a racing school using the tracks of the Winston Cup Series as a classroom.* Left: *After retiring from his own legendary NASCAR career, Buck's son, Buddy, now teaches at the school his father started.*

Buddy Baker on being the first driver to turn a lap at more than 200 mph (320kph):

"You know, I've had records—I still hold the fastest 500 that's ever been run in Daytona and all—but someday that's a record that will go down. But nobody will ever beat me at 200 mph. It'll never happen, and that's one of the few things in racing that they can't take away from you.

"With the Daytona 500, I've held the record there for thirteen years now, the fastest ever run in Daytona, but that will someday go down. I mean that's why they call it a record—you can break a record. But a milestone in the history of the sport, they can't take that away from you. It's like the guy who made the first 100 mph [160kph] run on a major speedway, and then there's 200 [320kph], and the next one's 300 [480kph]—and I want to meet this guy because he's going to have a pointed head, I believe!

"It didn't mean that much at the time—it was a good race car and a good group of people, but it didn't really mean that much at the time. But now, as I get older in my sport, and things are beginning to take shape as far as your future and what you do and I'm doing television and I'm doing this and that, all of a sudden it means as much as anything I've ever done in racing. It's just as important as winning four times at Talladega like I have or four times at Charlotte or whatever you might have done in the sport. The Daytona 500 is very important, but it's not any more important than the 200-mph run simply because of the unique car and the situation where the next barrier is 300."

Buddy Baker retired from active competition in 1994 with nineteen Winston Cup victories. He has become one of the most popular and knowledgeable television commentators for stock car races, and also instructs students at his father's stock car racing school.

BEATY, DICK

Dick Beaty (retired, born 1923) was NASCAR's Winston Cup director from 1981 until his retirement in 1992. The years leading up to Beaty's tenure saw competitors coming up with any number of outlandish methods to circumvent the rules in search of a competitive advantage. But Beaty is generally credited with tightening the reins in the garage area. By increasing the scrutiny of the race car inspection process, cheating had become an unusual rarity by the end of Beaty's reign over the NASCAR Winston Cup Series inspection line.

BECHTEL, GARY

Gary Bechtel (born 1951) is one of the newer team owners in NASCAR's Winston Cup Series, but he has become influential quickly. Having made his fortune in large-scale construction, Bechtel first entered Winston Cup racing in 1990.

But it wasn't until 1994, with Busch Grand National champion Steve Grissom signing to drive for Bechtel's new Diamond Ridge Motorsports team, that the team raced a full Winston Cup schedule. Grissom left the team during the 1996 season and was replaced by

Right: *Buddy Baker at the wheel of a Dodge Charger Daytona, en route to shattering the 200 mph (320kph) mark.*

BENSON, JOHNNY

After winning the 1993 ASA stock car championship, Michigan's Johnny Benson (born 6/27/63) set his sights on a career in NASCAR racing. His rapid rise to the Winston Cup Series is a testament to Benson's talent behind the wheel.

In 1994—his first season in NASCAR's Busch Grand National Series—Benson won at the challenging Dover Downs International Speedway on his way to Rookie of the Year honors. In 1995, Benson swept to two wins and twelve top-five finishes as he captured the series championship in just his second season of NASCAR competition.

For 1996, Benson made the move to Winston Cup, replacing Michael Waltrip in the driver's seat of the Bahari Racing Pontiacs. Benson quickly made a mark on NASCAR's top division, winning the pole position as fastest qualifier at Atlanta Motor Speedway in just his

Left: While overseeing Winston Cup competition for NASCAR, Dick Beaty is credited by many competitors as being the man who reined in cheating— or "creative interpretations of the rules," as it might sometimes be called. Below: Clean competition within the rules makes sponsors like the Cartoon Network feel comfortable sponsoring entries (owned in this case by Gary Bechtel) in the Winston Cup Series.

Robert Pressley, who had won ten races in the Busch series. But Pressley himself was replaced in the 1997 season by another young Busch standout, Jeff Green.

Although Bechtel's team has yet to reach its stride on the track, off the track Bechtel has helped NASCAR break into new markets by signing Ted Turner's Cartoon Network as his car's primary sponsor. The colorful stock cars, festooned with cartoon characters, have become favorites of the youngest NASCAR fans.

fourth Winston Cup start. Benson led the most laps in the 1996 Brickyard 400 but faded to eighth by the end of the race. Still, it was an impressive performance for a rookie in Winston Cup competition, and the young driver went on to finish the year with a remarkable total of six top-ten finishes.

Benson's smooth skills attracted the attention of team owner Jack Roush, who hired the driver to be part of a five-car Roush Racing team for 1998.

Geoff Bodine on racing in the Winston Cup Series:

"The great thing about our racing is that we have a variety of tracks that we run on, from Bristol—fast, high-banked, small—to a super-speedway like Talladega or Daytona and back to Martinsville, which is a half-mile [804.5m], flat, to two-road courses, two-mile [3.2km], mile-and-a-half [2.4km] tracks, one-mile [1.6km] tracks like Dover—they're all challenging and all different. I enjoy them all, and the tougher they are the better I like them. That's more of a challenge, and I think most race drivers feel the same way.

"If it was easy you could go out there and you wouldn't have to think. Qualifying is so close that we have a lot of good cars that don't make a race, and it's that way all over. Qualifying is that close everywhere, and it's because the tracks are all different and they're all challenging. If they were all easy and all the same we wouldn't have to adjust these cars, we wouldn't have to change springs or shocks, and a lot of the fun would go away.

"The tracks I haven't won at, people might think, 'They're the ones you don't like.' No, they're the ones I really like going to because I want to win there. They're the ones that are challenging to me now. They all are, but the ones I haven't won at are the ones I really want to go to and win at."

Right: **Longtime Winston Cup contender Geoff Bodine enjoys a great deal of respect in stock car racing thanks to his skills as a driver and his candor regarding the sport he loves.** Opposite: **Brett Bodine's Thunderbird hugs the inside of a road course turn in 1996 competition. Brett was an early member of a trend that began in the 1990s: Winston Cup drivers who own their own teams. While such ownership places pressure from sponsors squarely on a driver's shoulders, at least job security isn't a concern.**

BODINE FAMILY

Like the Wallace family of Rusty, Mike, and Kenny, the Bodine family has contributed three brothers to NASCAR Winston Cup Series competition.

Hailing from the Chemung, New York, area, the brothers all grew up surrounded by racing, as the family owned and operated a small speedway, the Chemung Speedrome.

The youngest brother, Todd (born 2/27/64), got his start with NASCAR stock car racing in the Busch Grand National Series in 1991 before making his first Winston Cup start in 1992. Despite driving for several teams and recording some strong performances, however, Todd was not able to find a Winston Cup team that he felt comfortable driving for. He returned to the Grand National Series and won several races through 1995, 1996, and 1997. His talent is undeniable, and a Winston Cup career is likely for Todd.

Brett (born 1/11/59) also used success in the Grand National Series to make the jump to Winston Cup. He started Grand National racing in 1985 and won three of his first thirteen races while still occasionally racing in the Modified division, where he'd gained his first profession-al racing experience. Brett's first Winston Cup start came in 1986, and his first full season came driving Fords for Bud Moore in 1988. After moving to Kenny Bernstein's team in 1990, Brett won his first Winston Cup race at Martinsville in his eightieth start. After one year driving for Junior Johnson in 1995, Brett started his own team.

Of all the Bodine brothers, it is Geoff (born 4/18/49) who has had the greatest success in Winston Cup racing. He, too, started out racing Modifieds and in the Grand National Series, with sporadic Winston Cup starts in 1979 and 1981. That led up to his first full season in 1982, when he was named Rookie of the Year.

Driving for Rick Hendrick in 1984, Geoff won his first Winston Cup race at Martinsville, then scored two more wins that year. In 1987, he won the International Race of Champions title and placed third in the 1990 Winston Cup points battle. Geoff also won the Daytona 500 in 1986. He drove for Junior Johnson in 1990 and 1991, scoring four wins, before moving to Bud Moore's team for 1992 and most of 1993. When Alan Kulwicki died in a plane crash in 1993, Bodine purchased the team and won three points races in 1994. Geoff is known for his refreshingly outspoken personality and will-ingness to comment candidly on any aspect of NASCAR racing.

In 1994, Geoff Bodine looked to have victory within reach at the inaugural Brickyard 400 when his brother Brett caused Geoff to crash on lap 101. In the aftermath, Geoff revealed this was the culmination of a yearlong feud between the brothers, showing that familial difficulties can carry over into the racing world.

BONNETT, NEIL

Neil Bonnett (born 7/30/49, died 2/11/94) was a driver who had as much bad luck on the racetracks of the Winston Cup Series as he did good luck. It seemed that every feat that led to victory was soon accompanied by a setback.

Bonnett was a member of the "Alabama Gang," a contingent of Winston Cup drivers from Alabama that also included brothers Bobby and Donnie Allison; Bobby's son, Davey; and Red Farmer. A track champion in the Birmingham area, Bonnett befriended the Allisons despite the fierce rivalries between them on the racetrack. Impressed by Bonnett's abilities, Bobby Allison hired Bonnett to race his short track cars when Allison was occupied with his Winston Cup duties. Bonnett would race up to one hundred times in a year all over the country, one year winning forty-two races on unfamiliar tracks.

Armed with those successes—and again aided by the Allisons—Bonnett broke into the Winston Cup ranks sporadically beginning in 1974, then more seriously in 1976 and 1977. He won twice in 1977 and through 1990 had won sixteen more times. But early in the 1990 season a bad crash at Darlington left Bonnett seriously injured.

While recovering from his injuries, Bonnett increased his television commentator work. But the lure of the driver's seat was too strong, and in the summer of 1993 Bonnett attempted a comeback in the July race at Talladega. Bonnett's return was less than successful—his car became airborne at 190 mph (305.7kph), crashing into the fence before bouncing back to the infield. Minutes later Bonnett, miraculously unscathed, appeared in the CBS broadcast booth to describe the crash.

Even that incident could not dissuade Bonnett from pursuing the sport he loved, and he planned his next comeback for the 1994 Daytona 500. It was not to be. Bonnett lost control in one of the early practice sessions for NASCAR's greatest race and was killed by the violent impact—one of two deaths to mar the Daytona activities that year. Bonnett's death

cast a pall over the race and hit the NASCAR world particularly hard coming so soon after the deaths of Alan Kulwicki and Davey Allison the year before.

BREWER, TIM

One of the most accomplished of today's active Winston Cup crew chiefs is Tim Brewer (born 1956), who has worked with many of NASCAR's greatest car owners and drivers.

Brewer began competing in the Winston Cup Series with Richard Childress in 1973. Winless in five seasons with the then-struggling car owner, Brewer found his first series win— and much more—when he moved to Cale Yarborough's team in 1978. Yarborough drove to ten wins and the Winston Cup championship that year, and Brewer suddenly found himself at the top of his profession.

Through the years Brewer has guided Winston Cup stars including Tim Richmond, Neil Bonnett, Bill Elliott, Darrell Waltrip, Terry Labonte, and Geoff Bodine. Brewer scored more than fifteen Winston Cup victories during an association with Junior Johnson's team between 1985 and 1992.

After working with young drivers Bobby Labonte, John Andretti, and Jeremy Mayfield from 1993 through 1996, Tim Brewer began the 1997 season with a move to the highly successful Morgan-McClure team and its driver, Sterling Marlin. But the performance of the

Opposite top: *Neil Bonnett crashes hard at Dover Downs International Speedway in September 1989. Bonnett hit the wall head-on in a crash that also involved four other competitors.* Opposite bottom: *After being removed from his car, Bonnett was transported to a local hospital.* Left: *After another terrible crash in 1990, Bonnett retired from racing and became a popular motorsports commentator. But he just couldn't stay away: in 1994 Bonnett was back in the garage area at Daytona International Speedway hoping to qualify for the Daytona 500. Tragically, he died in a crash during a practice session for the race.*

Ricky Rudd on racing on the high-banked .533-mile (857.5m) at Bristol:

"At Bristol, even though the speed is reduced compared to a super-speedway, it's a little bit more challenging than, say, a Charlotte, because things do happen so quickly. You unload your cars and you get on the racetrack for the first time, and things do happen so quickly at Bristol I've often caught myself wondering, 'Am I on the front stretch or the back stretch?' at least for the first ten laps of practice until you get oriented. Charlotte has much bigger straightaways, and you've got a chance to relax just a little bit.

"Bristol, with the concrete, it hasn't become a two-groove racetrack yet. Back in the days when there was blacktop, it was two grooves and for many years there was a lot of room at Bristol even though it looks very small at the speed we're running. With the concrete, it's a lane and a half wide. When passing, sometimes you really have to use a lot of patience there. Your chances of an accident there are a lot greater than anywhere else we go. It can be a little bit frustrating and a little bit intimidating.

"You have to hope that everybody takes the same discipline and realizes that we're at a difficult track. You're sort of at the mercy of the competitors who are running around you to determine the kind of race you're going to have."

team was a disappointment, and Tim Brewer left the team halfway through the season.

BRISTOL MOTOR SPEEDWAY

A racetrack nestled in a valley between two mountains—that is the essence of eastern Tennessee's Bristol Motor Speedway, affectionately known by the fans as "Thunder Valley."

For the drivers of the Winston Cup Series, Bristol is unlike anything else on the circuit, and affection may not be the best word to describe how they feel after five hundred laps rocketing around Thunder Valley.

A relatively tiny track, .533 mile (857.5m) in length, Bristol's turns boast the steepest banking in NASCAR racing: an astonishing 36 degrees. The forces encountered as a Winston Cup car powers through those turns leave drivers with aching muscles for days after a race. Lap speeds exceed 125 mph (201.1kph), and for a track with straightaways of just 650 feet (198.1m), that is a mind-boggling velocity.

Bristol's annual Saturday night Winston Cup race in August—run under the lights since 1979—has become the hottest ticket for NASCAR fans. The sight of more than 100,000 fans watching the brightly lit cars navigate the tiny oval at the foot of towering grandstands is a memorable one.

After purchasing Bristol Motor Speedway in 1996, track owner Bruton Smith hinted at the possibility of someday constructing a roof over the Tennessee racetrack. Smith has already leveled much of the mountain visible in this photograph to make way for hospitality areas and enormous parking lots.

Since the speedway's inception in 1961—with 22-degree banking that was reshaped to its current steepness in 1968—Darrell Waltrip has been the master of this fastest of short tracks, winning twelve races.

In 1996, after being purchased by Bruton Smith's expanding empire of racetracks, Bristol Motor Speedway saw an end to its valley status, as the mountain that once towered over the backstretch was leveled as part of an effort to make Bristol into a state-of-the-art modern speedway. Smith has even looked into the possibility of building a giant roof over the track. With the arrival of the glitz and luxury boxes, Bristol lost some of its character. Still, unless Smith decides to make a tri-oval out of Bristol, as he has done with Atlanta Motor Speedway, it will keep its reputation as the most hair-raising oval in the Winston Cup Series.

BURTON FAMILY

Brothers Ward (born 10/25/61) and Jeff Burton (born 6/29/67) are key members of the influx of young, talented drivers who have contributed to Winston Cup racing in the 1990s.

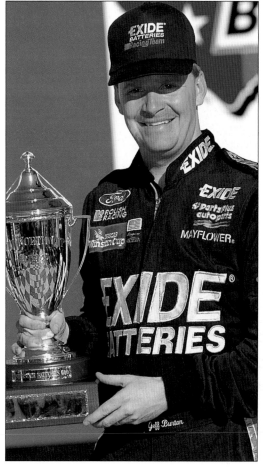

Above: **On his way to his first victory, Jeff Burton benefited from swift pit stops directed by crew chief Buddy Parrott.** Left: **Burton has become one of NASCAR's brightest stars, finishing in fourth place in the 1997 Winston Cup championship battle.**

Below: *Geoff Bodine is
one of the drivers who
has won the all-star
Busch Clash race. In
1992, while driving for
Bud Moore, Bodine start-
ed near the front for the
race's final segment, and
drove to victory after
passing Rusty Wallace's
Pontiac.* Opposite: *Before
the Busch Clash gets
under way, the cars are
lined up under the
Florida sunshine at
Daytona International
Speedway. It's a sight
that signals the beginning
of a new season of
Winston Cup competition.*

Both Virginia drivers cut their racing teeth on short tracks of the South, mainly at the historic speedway in South Boston, Virginia, near their home. And both made names for themselves in the Grand National division before moving up to Winston Cup racing.

Each brother entered competition full-time in NASCAR's elite division in 1994. Ward moved up from Busch competition with his Dillard Motorsports team, while Jeff began his Winston Cup career with the established Stavola Brothers team. But both drivers moved to new teams before reaching victory lane.

Ward, driving a Pontiac for Bill Davis, was the first Burton to win in Winston Cup, when he held off Rusty Wallace to win at North Carolina Motor Speedway in October 1995. Jeff, driving for owner Jack Roush since 1996, dominated the race at Texas Motor Speedway in April 1997, winning the track's inaugural event.

Having won once, Jeff Burton found he had a taste for victory. Jeff's team led in the majority of the races in the 1997 season and chalked up additional wins at tracks including New Hampshire International Speedway and Martinsville Speedway.

BUSCH CLASH

After a long off-season beginning in November, NASCAR Winston Cup fans are anxious for racing action as the month of February arrives.

The Busch Clash provides a welcome return to racing as the first event of a new racing year.

Like the Winston (the all-star race held at Charlotte Motor Speedway), the Busch Clash is a race that does not count in the Winston Cup points standings. The annual event marks the first time Winston Cup cars take to the surface of Daytona International Speedway to race in the days leading up to the Daytona 500. The field is made up of the fastest qualifiers from the previous season, and as such is made up of the cream of the Winston Cup crop.

The Busch Clash also provides an early barometer of which teams look to be particularly strong in the Daytona 500, and it is not uncommon for the winner of the Busch Clash to win the Daytona 500 the following week.

BYRON, ROBERT "RED"

Red Byron (born 3/12/15, died 11/11/60) played an important role in the history of NASCAR's earliest competition.

Byron was one of the first men to race under NASCAR's rules, and he emerged victorious in the very first NASCAR-sanctioned event, the Winter 160 Modified division race held on the beach course at Daytona on February 15, 1948. Although it was the stock car division that would bring NASCAR its greatest success, Byron's win in this first NASCAR event played a key role in the inception of the racing that has evolved into today's Winston Cup Series.

CALIFORNIA SPEEDWAY

NASCAR has always been very sensitive to marketing issues, and as the 1990s dawned it was clear a Winston Cup race in the lucrative Southern California market would be a gold mine. The problem was that there was nowhere to race. In fact, the annual road race at the Sears Point track north of San Francisco was the Winston Cup Series' only California entry in the season since the Riverside road course had been closed in 1987.

A major problem blocking the construction of a track in southern California was the tough environmental regulations builders would face. It took the discovery of an old steel mill in Fontana and the determination of Roger Penske to make it happen. In fact, once plans were

Jimmy Spencer on learning from Travis Carter to curb the tendency to run all-out all the time:

"I used to do that, and it's a mistake that Travis Carter helped me fix. He made me learn that you don't drive 500 miles [804.5km] right to the outer limits. You have to drive 400 miles [643.6km] at a pace that you feel the car will be comfortable at and you're comfortable at and you can finish at. The last 100 miles [160.9km] you can do what you need to do to win the race. It's so hard to learn that. That's what makes the crew chief so critical. That's what makes the team so critical. They're the ones who help the driver. It's not all the driver, it's [the input of all those people that makes the] thing work. It's not like a short track race where I'll burn the tires up in thirty-five laps and ain't got nothing to worry about. If you burn the tires up in thirty-five laps in Winston Cup, the next thirty-five laps they come around and lap you."

Travis Carter has helped numerous drivers to succeed in Winston Cup racing. Many drivers have natural racing talent, which they display in other series, but success in NASCAR's top division usually requires time spent with a motorsports mentor like Carter.

under way for the construction, NASCAR took two unprecedented steps that demonstrated how important this market is. First, it awarded a coveted Winston Cup date in 1997 to a track that wasn't even built yet. Second, it loaned NASCAR executive Les Richter from the sanctioning body's Daytona Beach offices to the speedway organization to help move things along.

In design, the track could not have had a better model, as it is based on Michigan International Speedway. MIS is a driver favorite, and California Speedway took into account spectator wishes by raising its backstretch to improve fan visibility. The turns are banked at a shallower angle than Michigan's, at 14 degrees as opposed to 18 degrees.

The Winston Cup race teams showed how seriously they took this new market, as many stopped at California Speedway for test sessions in May on the way home from the annual Sears Point race—despite having to race at Talladega in just six days.

The inaugural California 500 at California Speedway took place on June 22, 1997, and was won by Jeff Gordon, who stretched his fuel mileage to the limit to win the first Winston Cup Series race at the new speedway.

CARTER, TRAVIS

Travis Carter (born 11/21/49) has more than thirty victories in a lengthy career as a crew chief for drivers ranging from Benny Parsons to Cale Yarborough.

Carter started his own Winston Cup team in 1990 and began an alliance with driver Jimmy Spencer; then financial and sponsorship problems led to the team ceasing operation early in 1992. Carter formed another team in 1994 with sponsorship from R.J. Reynolds, again with Spencer as his driver. By 1997, the team was consistently placing in the top ten at Winston Cup events.

CHARLOTTE MOTOR SPEEDWAY (CMS)

Located in the town of Concord to the east of the city limits of Charlotte, North Carolina, Charlotte Motor Speedway is one of NASCAR's most historic tracks and a speedway that has reflected the growth of the sport of stock car racing.

Hosting its first race in 1960, as the first wave of superspeedways was constructed, this 1.5-mile (2.4km) tri-oval has served as the home base of the stock car racing community. With 24-degree banking in its turns, lengthy 1,952-foot (594.9m) angled frontstretch, and 1,360-foot (414.5m) back straightaway, Charlotte is a fast track that regularly sees laps approaching 190 mph (305.7kph). While some tracks have been dominated by a single driver, Charlotte has rolled over for several, with Darrell Waltrip and Bobby Allison each winning six times and Dale Earnhardt claiming five wins through 1996.

Charlotte has become known for what goes on around the track as much as for the competition that takes place on the track. Owner Bruton Smith and his partner in speedway development, Humpy Wheeler, have always been men who dream big. Seeing the influx of luxury boxes at football and baseball stadiums throughout the country in the 1980s, Smith and Wheeler saw no reason why such amenities could not be introduced to Winston Cup racing. Charlotte Motor Speedway became their test track, as sky boxes and even luxurious condominiums appeared at the top of CMS's grandstands. Some may have laughed when the idea of living at a racetrack first surfaced, but the condos quickly sold out to private investors and corporation heads who saw the value of entertaining clients at Winston Cup events. In addition, the speedway installed a costly lighting system to run events at night—a move that has proven tremendously popular with race fans.

Charlotte has also long been known for its elaborate prerace events, including such odd spectacles as daredevils leaping over exploding vehicles or large-scale military combat operations being demonstrated in the normally serene grass area between the frontstretch and pit road.

Charlotte Motor Speedway's flowering into a glistening high-tech sports palace has paralleled Winston Cup racing's ascension to the ranks of America's most popular sports, and the track's innovations have served as models for other racetrack owners.

CHARLOTTE, NORTH CAROLINA

Despite the fact that NASCAR's office is located in Daytona Beach, Florida, every race fan knows that the true heart of stock car racing beats in and around Charlotte, North Carolina.

With the hills of the state being the site of many of the great moonshiner chases that led to the development of legalized stock car competition, it seems only natural that the Charlotte area would acquire unofficial headquarters status. And as stock car racing has grown, Charlotte has benefited immensely, with millions of dollars of annual commerce directly traceable to racing.

Most of the teams that compete in the Winston Cup Series have their race shops located in the area. Many people, who are well aware of the number of fans who travel to see

Charlotte Motor Speedway on race day. One of the outstanding venues in Winston Cup racing, the speedway is considered home base for many of the Winston Cup teams. Competition is intense at the track for the bragging rights that come with a win here.

where the cars are prepared, have opened museums and gift shops to capitalize on the fans' fascination. A growing number of teams even offer tours of race shop activities.

And a majority of the drivers themselves have settled in the Charlotte vicinity, with many living around the shores of Lake Norman, just to the city's north.

While the city benefits from these high-profile residents, much of the economic advantage derived from stock car racing comes from the array of smaller businesses involved in racing activities. Ranging from souvenir distributors to racing parts manufacturers, the Charlotte area's racing merchants can fulfill every diverse need of the sport from the region's geographically centralized location.

CHILDRESS, RICHARD

Richard Childress (born 9/21/45) made an incredibly successful transition from Winston Cup car driver to team owner, winning six championships with driver Dale Earnhardt between 1986 and 1994.

Although everything seems to come easily to him now, Childress did not have his success handed to him. As an independent driver, Childress struggled from 1969 to 1981, starting 285 Winston Cup races with a total of just six top-five finishes to show for it. His best-ever finish was a third-place showing.

In 1981, Childress turned over his driver's seat to a young Dale Earnhardt. Dale managed two top-fives in the eleven races he ran for Childress, but at season's end Earnhardt was offered a ride by respected veteran car owner Bud Moore. Childress advised him to take the ride, and Dale did, winning three races in the process.

Meanwhile, Childress helped Ricky Rudd establish his career in 1982 and 1983, with Rudd beginning a string of at least one victory each season, with two wins for Childress in 1983. In 1984, Childress and Moore swapped drivers, and Richard began his second association with Earnhardt—one that would become legendary.

In six championship seasons, Earnhardt drove Childress stock cars to thirty-nine Winston Cup victories. In fact, in the decade from 1984 to 1994, the duo won just about every conceivable Winston Cup race except for the Daytona 500—a race that as late as 1997 seemed beyond Earnhardt's formidable reach.

In 1997, Richard Childress started a second Winston Cup team after seeing the success that fellow car owner Rick Hendrick had with his three-car operation.

COPE, DERRIKE

Nobody expected Derrike Cope (born 11/3/58) to win the 1990 Daytona 500. After all, Dale Earnhardt, in the first race of a season that would see him win his fourth Winston Cup championship, had a strong car and a comfortable lead going into the race's final lap. But Cope saw something most of the fans didn't immediately notice—Earnhardt's tire was failing after running over a piece of debris on the back straightway of Daytona International Speedway. When the tire finally blew—with Earnhardt just two turns away from winning NASCAR's biggest race—Cope passed the crippled black car, holding off Terry Labonte's charge in the final turns and winning the Daytona 500.

It was the culmination of a dream for the driver from Washington State, who was track champion at his local speedway in Yakima before making the move to NASCAR Late Model Sportsman and Winston West Series competition.

Cope's first Winston Cup entry came in 1982, but it wasn't until a 1989 association with car owner Bob Whitcomb that Derrike could mount serious challenges in competition. In addition to winning the Daytona 500 in 1990, he also was victorious in the June race at Dover Downs.

But Cope went through a difficult period after Whitcomb abruptly closed his operation on the eve of the 1993 season. Thereafter, Cope drove for a number of different teams, including those of Bobby Allison and Cale Yarborough.

In 1997, though, Cope moved to Pontiac with a new team and began putting together a

string of competitive finishes. Cope's plans to drive for Bahari Racing in 1998 bode well for his future in Winston Cup racing.

CRAVEN, RICKY

One of the most promising drivers to enter NASCAR Winston Cup competition in the 1990s is Ricky Craven (born 5/24/66). After beginning his motorsports career on the short tracks of his native Maine and the surrounding

Derrike Cope on making the transition to NASCAR Winston Cup competition and representing the sport to fans:

"First of all I think you have to put things in perspective. I'm sort of a realist and logical person and if you think about Winston Cup being the highest form of auto racing, we're one of forty people. You just think about all the series that there are and I'm just fortunate to be one of those lead drivers.

"That's what you work for when you're coming up through the ranks and you win championships. You win rookie of the year in Winston West, you win those races—I think it's just a steppingstone, an apprenticeship that you go through. And when you get to Winston Cup it's just the same thing all over again, you have to serve an apprenticeship.

"It's kind of an evolution. The Earnhardts are there now, the Elliotts, the Darrell Waltrips—all those guys. And they were once the younger guys coming in and had to serve their apprenticeship, go through their hard knocks and win one a year, two races a year or not win any races a year for three years. That's just the way the evolution is.

"I've come in at a time when I was able to break through and get some experience and serve this apprenticeship. I've won races in Winston Cup racing—a lot of people come in and never do that. I feel like I have a place in history in this sport, I feel like I belong, and I feel like I can race with the best of them.

"When it's Derrike Cope's day and the car's good, he can win it. That's the way I look at things now. And as far as my ability outside the car, I just feel like I'm right among the top and that's part of being a Winston Cup race car driver. It's not just the driving of a race car, it's the whole thing. It takes a well-rounded individual to be a Winston Cup race car driver. You just can't come in anymore and be good at driving a race car and be a Winston Cup race car driver."

Ricky Craven

Previous page: *Race fans are thrilled when a Winston Cup driver wins his first race, but when that first victory comes in one of NASCAR's premier races the applause is especially enthusiastic. That was the scenario when Derrike Cope won the Daytona 500 in 1990.* Right: *In his "office chair," Ricky Craven sits securely surrounded by a protective driver's compartment. The window net to Craven's left was implemented as standard equipment after a bad crash suffered by Richard Petty in May 1970, and is designed to keep a driver's extremities in the car in the event that a car should flip or roll during a race.*

New England area, Craven began racing in NASCAR's Busch North Series and was division champion in 1991.

His success in the northern series inspired Craven to make the move to Busch Grand National racing, and in his second full season of driving in the highly competitive division, he was runner-up to David Green in the 1994 championship battle. Craven finished the season with two wins and eight top-five finishes.

Craven moved to the Winston Cup Series in 1995, driving for car owner Larry Hedrick. After four top-ten finishes as he learned the

tracks of the division, Craven was named Rookie of the Year. In 1996, he placed third in two races, fifth in another, and had two more top-tens to his credit.

Car owner Rick Hendrick noticed Craven's talent and hired him for 1997 to replace Ken Schrader in one of the Hendrick Motorsports Chevrolet Monte Carlos. Joining a team that already boasted past Winston Cup champions Terry Labonte and Jeff Gordon, Craven was poised to build his own career in some of the most competitive stock cars on the Winston Cup circuit.

DALLENBACH, WALLY

Wally Dallenbach (born 5/23/63) comes from a racing family and has shown flashes of the talent needed to succeed in the Winston Cup Series. He has driven for a number of teams while searching for the right ride to take him to his first NASCAR victory.

Having raced in SCCA Trans-Am, IMSA GTO, and IndyCar racing—and having won the Daytona twenty-four-hour road race four times—Dallenbach entered his first Winston Cup races in 1991 for car owner Junie Donlavey, a man who has given many NASCAR stars their starts.

Jack Roush hired Dallenbach to run the full seasons in 1992 and 1993, and Wally drove to four top-ten finishes in the second year before moving on to a brief 1994 stay with Richard Petty's team (driver Rick Wilson's association with Petty Enterprises had not worked out, leaving room for Dallenbach).

Dallenbach started only two races in 1995—both on road courses, his specialty—but ran the full 1996 season for Bud Moore. In 1997, Felix Sabates offered Dallenbach a chance to run selected races, an opportunity that the Colorado driver hopes will lead to greater Winston Cup success.

DARLINGTON INTERNATIONAL RACEWAY

Darlington International Raceway, located in the South Carolina town of Darlington, is one of NASCAR's oldest racetracks, and one with an ominous motto: "Too Tough to Tame." Also known as "the Lady in Black," Darlington is a racetrack that challenges drivers with every lap.

South Carolina peanut farmer Harold Brasington attended the 1948 Indianapolis 500 and, impressed with the spectacle of the great race, decided a similar event would work well in his home state—but with NASCAR's stock cars instead of the open-wheel IndyCars. Thus was born a Labor Day tradition, the running of the Southern 500.

The newly completed track hosted its first Southern 500 race on September 4, 1950, with an immense starting field of seventy-five cars. Four hundred laps later, Johnny Mantz took the

Wally Dallenbach is just one of many drivers who have succeeded in other racing series and always longed to compete in the Winston Cup Series. Dallenbach nearly won a race in 1995, and given the opportunity to run a full season might one day become a serious threat in Winston Cup competition.

victory in a Plymouth. In the decades since, David Pearson has had the greatest success at Darlington, with a total of ten wins during his career.

Known as a speedway where drivers race the track itself as much as each other, the evidence of the frequent contact that racers make with the outside walls of Darlington's treacherous turns has received its own nickname: "the Darlington Stripe." The scrape marks running the length of cars that have received a Darlington Stripe are largely the result of the racetrack's unusual egglike shape. Race teams that have their cars set up perfectly for turns one and two find the cars handle poorly in turns three and four, and vice versa. In addition to the turns being of a different radius, the banking also differs from 25 degrees at one end to 23 degrees at the other end of the 1.366-mile (2.1km) oval. Still, lap speeds at Darlington exceed 170 mph (273.5kph) despite the difficulties faced in setting up the cars.

In 1993, NASCAR vice president Jim Hunter left the sanctioning body to return to his home state of South Carolina to lead the track through a series of modernization efforts. Chief among these was moving the start/finish line to opposite sides of the speedway to accommodate grandstand renovations. Still, no matter where the start/finish line is, Darlington International Raceway will always be one of the most challenging tracks that a Winston Cup driver will ever face.

DAVIS, BILL

Arkansas' Bill Davis (born 1/18/51) used the success he had enjoyed in the trucking industry to pave the way for his entry into NASCAR Busch Grand National racing in 1988. Over the next four seasons, the Davis team won six times in 104 starts and had twenty-six top-five finishes.

In 1991, Davis teamed up with an exciting young driver named Jeff Gordon, who was eager to break into stock car racing after a record-setting career in open-wheel USAC racing. Together the team had accounted for numerous top-five and top-ten finishes, as Gordon claimed Rookie of the Year honors. Gordon won three times in 1992 and started from the pole a record eleven times. There was great optimism on Davis' part that the success with Gordon would continue the next season with a move to Winston Cup.

Then Davis was hit with a bombshell—Gordon signed with Rick Hendrick to drive

Chevrolets, leaving Davis' Ford team behind. But the Bill Davis Racing team rebounded from its disappointment by signing another talented Winston Cup rookie, Bobby Labonte, and made the move to NASCAR's elite division as scheduled, in 1993.

In 1993 and 1994, the team learned the ropes of Winston Cup racing, and when Bobby Labonte left the team to drive for Joe Gibbs' operation, Davis was quick to sign young Virginia driver Ward Burton. In 1995, the Davis team logged four top-five and five top-ten finishes, but more important, Burton drove the team's Pontiac to victory lane for his and the team's first Winston Cup win, at Rockingham on October 22.

With the redesigned Pontiac Grand Prix in 1996 and 1997, the Bill Davis Racing team quickly developed into one of Winston Cup racing's better teams.

DAYTONA 500

Simply put, the most important race in the NASCAR Winston Cup Series is the Daytona 500. Held each February since Big Bill France opened Daytona International Speedway in 1959, the Daytona 500 is now the crowning event in several weeks of racing activities known as Speedweeks.

The first running of the Daytona 500 has become a legend. On February 22, 1959, after 199 laps of competition, the cars exited turn four on the final lap and charged through the frontstretch toward the finish line. Joe Weatherly's Chevrolet, a lap down, was on the high side, near the wall. Next to Weatherly were the two leaders, Lee Petty and Johnny Beauchamp. Beauchamp's Thunderbird was at the bottom of the track, nearest the infield, and Petty's Oldsmobile was sandwiched between the two other cars. They flashed across the finish line in a dead heat.

NASCAR officials declared Beauchamp the winner of the debut Daytona 500, but protests from the Petty crew and other observers moved France to declare the result unofficial pending a review of photography and film evidence. It took sixty-one hours, but eventually France announced that Lee Petty had won the race. The thrilling end to the race and the fact that the two finishers represented two automotive giants, Ford and General Motors, meant that NASCAR was immediately blessed with the most desirable thing any startup competition could hope for: tremendous publicity.

Today, teams begin preparing for the Daytona 500 months in advance. That the most important race of the Winston Cup season is also the first race may seem odd, but the scheduling allows teams to spend the few

The high speeds of competition at Daytona International Speedway give the cars a graceful appearance while racing, but the racetrack is the scene of tremendous power barely held in check; when something goes wrong it can lead to spectacular accidents like Johnny Roberts' 1967 crash, pictured here.

Above: *Daytona International Speedway was built to replace the chaos that often was found on the old beach and road course.*

Opposite: *In 1959 NASCAR replaced the stretch of highway and strip of hard-packed sand that had served as a racing course with a superspeedway that was built to promote high speeds and safe competition. Now, reaching the track's victory lane after winning the Daytona 500 is the dream of every Winston Cup driver—a dream realized by Derrike Cope in 1990.*

weeks of the off-season, from November to February, preparing for Daytona.

Qualifying for Daytona takes place in several stages. The two cars that will start the great race in the first row obtain their coveted positions through a normal qualifying session, but the starting slots of the cars that start behind the two fastest are determined by how well the cars perform in one of two 125-mile (201.1km) qualifying races. Those who don't get starting slots assigned by the qualifying races then start at the back of the field based on regular qualifying lap speeds. But the number of cars trying to get into the Daytona 500 is always greater than the number of starting positions available, and there is no worse way to start off a Winston Cup season than to miss the cut for this race.

Despite the addition of other such high-profile events as the Brickyard 400, the Daytona 500 is still recognized as the epitomy of what stock car racing is all about. Victory in this race generally means more to a driver than any other career milestone.

DAYTONA INTERNATIONAL SPEEDWAY

If there is one race that people who have never even watched a NASCAR event recognize, it is the Daytona 500, held every February at the legendary Daytona International Speedway. But as impressive as the track is today, people found it absolutely astonishing when it was built in the months leading up its first stock car race ever, held February 22, 1959.

Originally planned to open in 1955, a nagging series of delays prevented Big Bill France from realizing the dream of his superspeedway until 1959. But when it finally did open, competitors were amazed at the facility. At a time when many of NASCAR's drivers were still used to competing on bullring-size dirt tracks, the sight of a high-banked, 2.5-mile (4km) paved superspeedway was hard to comprehend. With a 3,600-foot (1,097.2m) back straightaway and turns banked at 31 degrees, the drivers immediately began racing at speeds far higher than they had ever attained before.

High speeds have always characterized racing at Daytona, with Bill Elliott holding the track record of 210.364 miles per hour (338.5kph), achieved while qualifying for the Daytona 500 in 1987. Since NASCAR instituted the use of engine manifold restrictor plates the following year to reduce velocity, the cars have been slower at Daytona—if you consider speeds in excess of 190 mph (305.7kph) to be "slow."

But regardless of the speeds, the competition at Daytona is what has made the track remarkable. The annual running of the Daytona 500 and the track's summer race, the Firecracker 400, have always given the fans in the grandstands—and those watching on television—plenty to talk about.

Two of the most unforgettable Daytona finishes have involved the legendary Richard Petty. In the 1976 Daytona 500, as Petty and David Pearson came off turn four in a side-by-side charge to the checkered flag, the two cars touched. They crashed, both vehicles suffering extensive damage before sliding to a stop in the infield just short of the start/finish line. Petty's motor was dead, but Pearson's was still running. Pearson got his Mercury in gear and eased across the start/finish line at the slowest speed ever to win a Daytona 500.

In 1979, in the first Daytona 500 ever broadcast live on CBS, Cale Yarborough and Donnie Allison were neck and neck in a heated battle for victory. Then the two drivers crashed in turn three of their final lap, allowing Petty—who was prepared to settle for third—to claim the win. When Bobby Allison stopped to check on his brother after the leaders crashed, a brawl ensued among the competitors. The live broadcast cemented the fight's status as a legendary television event while offering proof of how much a win at Daytona International Speedway means to the competitors.

While Richard Petty does hold the record for the most wins by a single driver at Daytona International Speedway, with ten victories, it is the elements of the unexpected and the unforgettable that have made this speedway the most hallowed in stock car racing.

DeHART, GARY

Gary DeHart is not the best-known of crew chiefs, mainly because he doesn't pursue opportunities to be interviewed. Instead, DeHart speaks loudest through the actions of his team on the racetracks of the Winston Cup Series. Witness the 1996 performance of his

Derrike Cope on the impact winning the Daytona 500 had on his Winston Cup career:

"As far as immediately, the thing really thrust me into a position of notoriety. When you win the biggest thing that happens to a person in stock car racing, the Super Bowl of auto racing, you're on a media whirlwind, and you're off to New York and you're doing satellite feeds from NBC all over the U.S. and you do Letterman. What that does, it goes throughout the entire year and it puts you in the spotlight. It just elevated my exposure...and I think I became more of a household word.

"Then when I started doing all these appearances..., people knew who I was and my face was recognizable, and it just seemed to do a lot for me.

"I'd worked very hard on the West Coast with the dream of winning the Daytona 500 and a lot of people said that I would never amount to anything. I told them that I would win the Daytona 500. A lot of great people helped me and just for us to win our first race in Winston Cup and [for it] to be that race..., it really took two goals that you set for yourself right off the top of the list. I think that it was an amazing moment coming down there—you just can't even fathom the excitement and the emotion and it stuns you. It really does. The magnitude of that race is incredible."

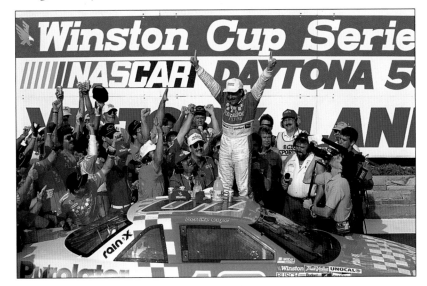

Hendrick Motorsports team with driver Terry Labonte, a season-long campaign that resulted in two wins, twenty-one top-five finishes, and the Winston Cup championship.

All of DeHart's experience as a crew chief has come while working for Rick Hendrick's organization, beginning with his employment as a metal fabricator in 1986. After four years

Above: *Darel Dieringer had much success in NASCAR racing throughout the 1960s.* Right: *Junie Donlavey started racing in 1949, when the term "stock car" was more literally applied to the vehicles that raced; the cars could have come right off the showroom floor and onto the racetrack.* Opposite: *The specialized designs of today's Winston Cup cars—shown here racing at Dover Downs International Speedway—would have been unimaginable to those who converted street cars into race cars throughout the 1950s and 1960s.*

working for Hendrick in various racing capacities, DeHart was given the opportunity to step up to the crew chief level in 1990. DeHart led the team and driver Greg Sacks to a second-place finish and two more top-tens in just thirteen races.

Hendrick promoted DeHart to lead Rick Rudd's team in 1992 and 1993, and the team won in Winston Cup competition each season. When Rudd departed and was replaced by Terry Labonte, some wondered if Labonte still had the competitive edge he had shown when he won the championship in 1984. Labonte and DeHart answered those doubts with three wins in each of the 1994 and 1995 seasons, leading up to the Winston Cup championship run of 1996.

DIERINGER, DAREL

Darel Dieringer (born 6/1/26, died 10/28/89) was one of NASCAR's top drivers in the Grand National (now Winston Cup) division throughout an intense period of growth in the 1960s. It was a time when drivers like Richard Petty, Cale Yarborough, David Pearson, and Fireball Roberts began to become recognized as genuine sports stars. Dieringer's talent was such that he could compete on an equal footing with these legendary names of stock car racing.

Dieringer started in 181 races in NASCAR's top division, winning seven times in his peak period of activity, from 1963 to 1967. Among his victories was the 1966 Southern 500 at Darlington.

DONLAVEY, JR., W.C. "JUNIE"

After beginning his involvement with racing as a driver in 1949, Junie Donlavey (born 4/8/24) quickly realized he preferred the view from pit road to the view through the windshield. In 1950, he began a career as an owner, building and fielding race cars. In the decades since, he has launched the careers of some of NASCAR's best drivers.

Although a Donlavey car has won in the Winston Cup Series only once—when Jody Ridley won the Mason-Dixon 500 in a Donlavey Ford at Dover in 1981—Junie has become known as a car owner who will give a chance to a young driver trying to begin a Winston Cup career. Many of those drivers have gone on to become NASCAR stars, including Ricky Rudd, Ernie Irvan, Chad Little, Ken Schrader, Mike Wallace, and Harry Gant.

Donlavey's Virginia-based operation continues to field cars in the Winston Cup Series, and even though the team has not racked up large numbers of top-ten performances, the contributions of Junie Donlavey to NASCAR are immeasurable. Those contributions were recognized in 1997, when Donlavey and fellow longtime car owner Bud Moore were presented with the Bill France Award of Excellence, one of the sport's greatest honors.

DOVER DOWNS INTERNATIONAL SPEEDWAY

Dover Downs International Speedway is located just to the north of Dover, Delaware. The high-banked oval has one of the more fearsome nicknames of the Winston Cup circuit: "the Monster Mile." It's a name that is justified.

The 1-mile (1.6km) track is known as one of the more grueling sites of stock car competition. The 1,076-foot (327.9m) front- and back-stretches aren't a problem—it's the steep, 24 degree banking through the turns and the narrow exits from those turns that cause drivers fits. The Monster Mile collects a number of cars in a big wreck at the exit of turn two in almost every race at the track.

The first Winston Cup race held at Dover was in 1970. Bobby Allison and Richard Petty share the record for the most victories, with seven each.

Five hundred laps around this track make for a demanding afternoon. The gravitational forces encountered in the steep turns are made

Ted Musgrave on the differences between Bristol Motor Speedway's concrete surface and the one at Dover Downs International Speedway:

"Dover did a better job. After what they went through at Bristol as far as how to lay these concrete surfaces down, Dover learned a lot and didn't [make the same mistakes]. Anytime that you do something for the first time, you find a better way to do it later. Bristol was the first time anybody ever poured concrete on an angle with the thirty-six-degree banking.

"Dover did a little better job, but don't get me wrong—I'm not a fan of concrete at all! But I think Dover has more room than Bristol. Bristol is a tight half-mile [804.5m] where Dover is twice as big, so you've got a little more room to maneuver. I've got to say that I hope they don't concrete any more racetracks."

While all of the drivers certainly noticed that they were racing at higher speeds than ever before, some drivers noticed something else. When they pulled up behind another car running down the long Daytona straightaway, it felt like the second car was being pulled along by the car in front. These drivers had discovered the draft.

The vacuum created behind a car running at high speed can be used by a car following if that second car tucks right up behind the first. Both cars will consume less fuel and run faster than a single car running alone.

Because of that, drafting and how to use it are important on many of the NASCAR Winston Cup speedways—although it's crucial at Daytona and Talladega. If two cars are far ahead and racing side by side, a group of cars running nose to tail can slice through the air faster and catch up with the other cars.

Modern Winston Cup drivers study how their cars run with other brands of Winston Cup cars to determine whether it's advantageous to be in front of such a car or faster if they follow. Often teams will set up informal agreements during a race if an especially effective drafting partner is found.

EARNHARDT FAMILY

When Ralph Earnhardt (born 2/29/28, died 9/26/73) began racing in NASCAR's top division in 1956, he probably never imagined what his sport would one day evolve into—and the incredible impact that his talented son would have upon it.

In various Sportsman and other NASCAR Series races, Earnhardt won more than 350 events as he competed full-time from his home base in Kannapolis, North Carolina. He built his own cars, and though his own career in NASCAR's top division was limited to just fifty-one starts in Grand National (now Winston Cup) racing, he made his mark as a tough driver. Though he never won in competition against the likes of Ned Jarrett and Junior Johnson, he did rack up five top-five finishes in his brief Grand National foray.

Helping Ralph Earnhardt prepare his cars on many occasions was his son Dale (born 4/29/51). So it seemed a natural progression when Dale followed in his father's footsteps and began a NASCAR career.

At nearly 200 mph (321.8kph), the wind resistance faced by Winston Cup cars is a very real concern. To minimize the force needed to cut through the air, drivers frequently "draft" behind other cars. The mandatory restrictor plates installed on today's NASCAR cars tend to keep the cars close together, and the entire field will sometimes remain this close, lap after lap.

all the more draining by the high speeds, as the cars turn laps at more than 150 mph (241.3kph). And when the track was switched from pavement to a concrete surface in the 1990s, many drivers were wincing after roaring along on the harsh surface.

Even with a recent move toward shortening Dover's races from five-hour, 500-mile (804.5km) marathons to more television-friendly 400-mile (643.6km) events, Dover Downs International Speedway is still one of the most intimidating of the Winston Cup racetracks.

DRAFTING

"Big Bill" France's huge Daytona International Speedway was the biggest track any of the Grand National drivers had ever seen when they first competed on the 2.5-mile (4km) speedway in 1959.

Dale's first Winston Cup start came in 1975, but it wasn't until 1979—when he was awarded the Rookie of the Year honors driving for car owner Rod Osterlund—that Earnhardt began making his mark upon the sport of stock car racing. He won once that season, then five times in 1980 to win the Winston Cup championship in just his second full season on the NASCAR circuit.

After collecting three wins for Bud Moore in 1982 and 1983, Dale began an association with car owner—and former racer—Richard Childress. The collaboration of the two men has been remarkable, with Childress providing exceptional vehicles and Earnhardt piloting those vehicles with his brilliant racing talents. Together they won the Winston Cup championship in 1986, 1987, 1990, 1991, 1993, and 1994, winning thirty-nine races in those years alone.

Dale Earnhardt has amply demonstrated that he can win on any kind of track, be it short track or superspeedway, high-banked track or road course. Earnhardt is also known for his willingness to help fans and other drivers, although his hard-nosed image and his nickname, "The Intimidator," would seem to indicate the opposite.

Fellow driver Derrike Cope on Dale Earnhardt's driving style and Dale's nickname, "the Intimidator":

"As far as intimidation goes, I think Earnhardt has been probably the most effective as far as being able to go in and root on somebody and manipulate the air on somebody. I think that...he's had some superior equipment and Dale Earnhardt is an incredible talent when it comes to all the faculties that he has as far as the variables in racing.

"Manipulating the air around the car, as far as manipulating the race car—if the race car gets loose he can get out of a spin. He's just an incredible talent and he's been doing it for a long time too.

"And he's not afraid to go in there and root you out of the way. I think that that kind of intimidation, he's implemented that before and people let him get away with it.... As far as intimidation goes, I just try to set a precedent. If you mess with me, you get messed with. I want to race you clean, I want to race hard, but if you're going to mess with me then we're going to play, that's the way I look at it. I'm not intimidated by Dale Earnhardt."

If anyone symbolizes the intense competitiveness of modern Winston Cup racing, it is Dale Earnhardt. Many insist Earnhardt is the best stock car driver ever, a claim backed up by seven Winston Cup championships.

Perhaps most remarkable is Earnhardt's ability to deal with adversity. After a terrible 1996 crash at Talladega Superspeedway—one that saw Dale's Monte Carlo reduced to an unrecognizable heap of scrap metal—Earnhardt emerged from the car and, despite severe injuries, insisted on walking to the ambulance, waving to the crowd in acknowledgment of their concern. Two weeks later, in extreme pain, Earnhardt qualified his car on the pole at Watkins Glen and then finished sixth in the road course race.

Late in the 1997 Daytona 500, Dale's car was involved in another violent wreck, which

Dale Earnhardt on winning the Winston Cup championship in 1993 after wrapping up the title in the last race of the season:

"For me, coming from a racing family—from Ralph and Martha Earnhardt and Kannapolis, North Carolina—I never thought, I never dreamed I would be in Winston Cup racing. I look back at what we've done, what we've accomplished, and it's unbelievable. To go back home to Kannapolis, I'm just one of the guys. It's really impressive to think about what somebody from Kannapolis, a small town, can do and accomplish.

"I'm proud of it, I'm proud of the team, I'm proud that Ralph Earnhardt was my dad, I'm proud of my race team. Richard Childress and all of those guys did a super job, and worked hard all year. We had a tough year at times, we had a great year at times. It was a real sad year losing our champion Alan Kulwicki and our great friend Davey Allison. It's just a tough year to review and think about. It's great to end it on a super note with winning the championship....

"Every man dug a little deeper and worked a little harder and that's the part of it that made our team turn around."

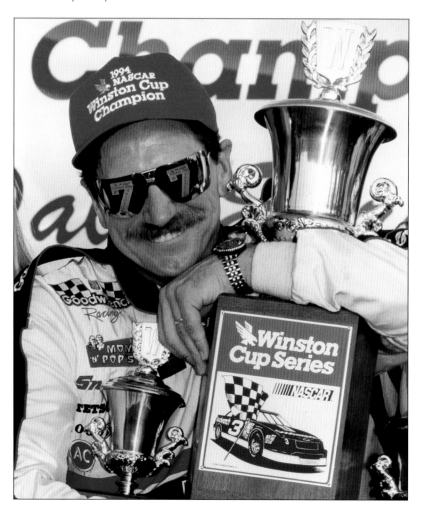

saw the Chevrolet become airborne and then crash violently. After climbing from the car, Earnhardt started to enter an ambulance as safety crews prepared to tow away the damaged vehicle. Taking one last look at his Monte Carlo, Dale decided his car didn't look too damaged to run. He stepped away from the ambulance, climbed back into the stock car, drove to pit road for repairs, and then re-entered the race.

If anyone deserves to beat Richard Petty's record of seven championships—a record Earnhardt tied in 1994—surely it is Dale Earnhardt.

ELLIOTT, BILL

In more than two decades of Winston Cup competition, Bill Elliott (born 10/8/55) has had a major impact on both the NASCAR record books and fans of Winston Cup racing.

Elliott and his brothers raced on short tracks near their home in Georgia, eventually setting their sights on the Winston Cup Series.

Images from the making of a legendary career. Left: *Entering Pocono International Raceway's treacherous first turn, Dale Earnhardt suffered this devastating crash in 1990. Fortunately, Earnhardt emerged from the wreckage with only a broken kneecap.* Opposite: *Happier times include the winning of a seventh Winston Cup championship in 1994, tying Earnhardt with Richard Petty for the most championships won by a single person in NASCAR history.* Below: *Many race fans will never forget the legendary on-track battles staged in the 1980s by Darrell Waltrip in car number 17 and Earnhardt in his famous number 3.*

Bill Elliott on fans and Winston Cup racing:

"I guess I'm going to sound a little cold here, but a fan ought to be a person who's with you through thick and thin. If I walk out on a racetrack and a guy walks up to me and he says, 'I'll pull for you if you never win another race'—that's what makes you feel good. When you walk out there and some guy says, 'If you don't win I ain't gonna pull for you no more'—fine! You don't need to be pulling for me anyway.

"Everybody wants to be for a winner, but the way this business is there's going to be ups and downs, there are going to be cycles, there's going to be people winning and people losing—but there is always going to be more people losing than there are winning. That's just the way this business is. And I can't control a lot of the circumstances that go on. I'm going to go out there and do the best job that I can, I'm going to try to race people as clean as I can. That's my style, and if people don't like that, fine. I can't help that."

9 Thunderbirds were a threat to win any race they entered. The team's climb passed through numerous lofty milestones—including eleven wins in 1985 and a NASCAR record qualifying lap of 212.809 mph (342.4kph) at Talladega in 1987—on the way to claiming the Winston Cup championship in 1988.

Elliott is also the only driver to claim the $1 million bonus posted by R.J. Reynolds for any driver who can win three of four "crown jewel" events in one season. When Bill captured the Southern 500 at Darlington in 1985—adding to his wins earlier in the season in the Daytona 500 and Charlotte's Winston 500—Elliott picked up a new nickname: "Million Dollar Bill."

After the 1992 season, Elliott left the legendary Dawsonville, Georgia-based team to drive for Junior Johnson. But the expected NASCAR domination of the collaboration never fully materialized, yielding six victories over three full seasons. "Awesome Bill from Dawsonville" returned home to race for Elliott-Hardy Racing in 1995. Although the new team

Bill Elliott sits behind the wheel of the Melling Ford Thunderbird. With this team, Elliott had his greatest success and became one of the most popular drivers in the sport's history.

Elliott Racing—with Bill behind the wheel and brothers Ernie and Dan handling car preparation—first began Winston Cup racing in 1976, meeting with moderate success for the next five years. But in 1982, the family-owned team came under the wing of manufacturer Harry Melling—and within months the number

went through growing pains, Elliott's car was competitive through the 1996 and 1997 Winston Cup seasons.

Through 1996, the soft-spoken Elliott has been voted Most Popular Driver eleven times. His 500th Winston Cup start was registered at Bristol, Tennessee, on April 13, 1997.

Left: *Bill Elliott closes in on victory at Dover Downs International Speedway in June 1988. Elliott fell nearly two laps behind in this race but made up the deficit on the way to his first win of what ultimately became a championship season. Below: Elliott's crew in action at Dover. This kind of swift team-work helped account for the team's six wins in 1988.*

ENERGY CRISIS

As a sport fully dependent on the consumption of fossil fuels, stock car racing faced one of its greatest threats in 1974, with the arrival of the energy crisis.

With many Americans sitting in line for hours waiting to purchase gasoline and everyone being urged to conserve resources, NASCAR realized that it was vulnerable to attack from people who would want to know why they should have trouble buying gas to get to work while Winston Cup drivers were out roaring around Daytona's superspeedway.

As it has done before, NASCAR anticipated events and made a preemptive strike at the threatening situation. The result was the running of the "Daytona 450," with 10 percent of the Daytona 500's length eliminated to show racing's solidarity with President Richard Nixon's call for conservation. Other Winston Cup events in the 1974 season included a 360-mile (579.2km) race at Michigan, Charlotte's World 600 cut to 540 miles (868.8km), and a 361.6-mile (581.8km) race at Riverside, California.

By the end of the 1974 season, the race lengths were back to normal, but the entire incident proved to everyone that NASCAR had the ability to react well to any crisis that might confront it.

ENTERTAINMENT SPORTS PROGRAMMING NETWORK (ESPN)

While individual races broadcast on the traditional "big three" television networks marked NASCAR milestones as the sport grew, it has been the association of stock car racing with the cable network ESPN—Entertainment Sports Programming Network—that has helped make the Winston Cup Series become what it is today.

ESPN televised its first Winston Cup Series race on November 8, 1981, when Neil Bonnett eked out a win over Darrell Waltrip. Almost immediately ESPN executives realized the potential of the sport. It seemed perfect for television broadcasts, and covering the series would help the fledgling network with programming that would attract more viewers.

The alignment of the Winston Cup Series and ESPN worked to the advantage of both entities. More viewers turned to ESPN to watch race coverage and were exposed to the network. And the network's coverage of races that had not been televised live before exposed new fans to the week-to-week drama of the championship points battle.

While in recent years cable television's Turner Broadcasting and Gaylord Entertainment/The Nashville Network have

Opposite: *NASCAR's Winston Cup Series has unique attributes that mesh well with the needs of television sports coverage. On television, stock cars following nose to tail through banked turns seem to move with near balletic grace.* Below: *In contrast to the sinuous streaming of the vehicles, the frantic energy of a pit stop also provides the kind of visual impact needed to make motorsports a popular attraction on ESPN.*

Jeff Gordon on why he found success so quickly in the Winston Cup Series:

"Because Ray Evernham went with me. I think that's been the key to a lot of the success, that if you look at when I was winning races in Busch Grand National, Ray was there, and since I've been in Winston Cup, Ray has been there. He and I just really work well together. And I think that not many rookies can come into Winston Cup and have the type of cars and the type of equipment and the resources and the people that I've been able to have at Hendrick's.

"Ray is a lot like a coach; he's a great motivator and he's a good friend of mine. I don't think our team could be as successful without him. He's been in a race car before and knows how to relate to what I'm saying. He's just the perfect kind of crew chief for me, and not every crew chief would be able to work with me. Because I'm the type of driver where I know what I feel and just relate back to the crew chief what I'm feeling and what I need in the car instead of knowing that if I'm feeling this, I need this, this and this in the car. I don't have that much experience yet, so Ray and I really just complement each other."

increased their presence in motorsports broadcasting, it is ESPN that deserves the credit for being there first and performing a valuable service for the NASCAR Winston Cup Series.

EVERNHAM, RAY

Rarely has a crew chief entered the Winston Cup Series and had such an immediate impact as Ray Evernham (born 8/26/57).

When Rick Hendrick signed the young Jeff Gordon to drive for him in 1992, Gordon knew who he wanted as a crew chief. Together, Ray Evernham and Gordon teamed up to win the 1995 Winston Cup championship in just their third year of competition together. The championship was attained after a season highlighted by seven wins and eight pole positions.

Evernham has a long background in motorsports, both as a competitor and on the mechanical side of race vehicle preparation. He has six years as a driver in the tough Modified division to his credit, but he moved in 1984 to work for the IROC Series as crew chief and team manager of the cars used in the all-star competition. He worked as crew chief with

Opposite: *Crew chief Ray Evernham guided Jeff Gordon's team to Winston Cup championships in 1995 and 1997, a tremendous accomplishment considering the fierce competition found in NASCAR's elite division. As Evernham would agree, success as a crew chief involves dedication at the expense of nearly any outside interests or recreation.* Left: *Competition in NASCAR has always been intense, as seen here in the final feet of the 1963 Firecracker 400. Fireball Roberts just managed to hold off Fred Lorenzen for the win at Daytona International Speedway.*

Gordon as they competed on the Busch Grand National circuit in 1991, and later in 1992 he worked with Alan Kulwicki until being hired by Hendrick for a reunion with Gordon.

Ray Evernham has developed a deserved reputation as one of the most innovative and intelligent crew chiefs of the Winston Cup Series. That is borne out by the Gordon team's performance in the Winston Cup Series. By the end of 1997, Hendrick's team—anchored by Ray Evernham's behind-the-scenes work and Jeff Gordon's driving—had won a second championship.

FIRECRACKER 400

As is the case with many of the racetracks of the Winston Cup Series, Daytona hosts the race teams twice a season. Daytona's races are the season-opening Daytona 500 and the event that marks the beginning of the racing season's second half, the Firecracker 400.

Held each Fourth of July weekend, the summer Daytona event begins in the late morning to avoid the stifling heat of a midsummer afternoon on the Florida coast. Originally a 250-mile (402.2km) race in its first four runnings, since 1963 the length has been 400 miles (643.6km). In 1989, corporate sponsorship officially changed the race's title to the Pepsi 400, but the original explosive name refuses to disappear from conversations in the racing world.

"Explosive" is a good way to describe the competition in the race. All teams want to perform well at every stop on the Winston Cup Series schedule, but a win at Daytona is always special. Some of the most exciting finishes in NASCAR history have played out under the July sun in Daytona. One of the most thrilling took place in 1994, when Jimmy Spencer won his first Winston Cup race.

Spencer, driving for Junior Johnson, had placed his Thunderbird directly behind race leader Ernie Irvan in the final laps, and the two cars had drafted away from the second group led by Dale Earnhardt, Mark Martin, and Ken Schrader. Spencer tested Irvan several times, edging his car to the inside or outside of Irvan to keep Ernie guessing as to what strategy Spencer had in mind. Then Spencer made his move on the final lap.

As the cars ran through turn two, Spencer planted his car up high by the wall, building extra momentum. As he hurtled down the banking toward the back straightaway, Spencer got his car's fender alongside Irvan's right rear quarterpanel, then edged alongside Ernie's Thunderbird. The two cars roared side by side at nearly 200 mph (321.8kph) through the final two turns, gently bouncing off each other in a precarious charge to the checkered flag. Jimmy Spencer won by mere inches.

It's this kind of superspeedway excitement that keeps fans looking forward to NASCAR's own unique brand of fireworks each Fourth of July, which are now being staged at night under a huge lighting system, which was inaugurated during the 1998 season.

Below: *Tim (left) and Fonty Flock, two of the three racing Flock brothers, all of whom competed in the very first NASCAR race in 1949.*

Opposite: *To show how much stock car racing has changed since those early years, consider that today's Winston Cup cars run faster at the short Bristol Motor Speedway than the Flock cars did on the much larger tracks (the Darlington Raceway, for instance) of NASCAR's early days.*

FLOCK FAMILY

In the earliest days of NASCAR stock car competition, many of the races were dominated by three brothers—Georgia's Bob, Fonty, and Tim Flock. All three brothers competed in the very first NASCAR race of the division that would one day become the Winston Cup Series when they raced side by side at Charlotte Speedway on June 19, 1949.

Oldest brother Bob (born 4/16/18, died 5/16/64) won four races during the seven years he ran in NASCAR.

Fonty Flock (born 3/21/21, died 7/15/72) was even more successful. In nine years of NASCAR competition and 154 races, Fonty achieved victory nineteen times.

But the most famous of the Flock brothers was youngest brother Tim (retired, born 5/11/24). Tim Flock competed from NASCAR's first season in 1949 until 1961, competing in 187 races and winning an impressive thirty-nine times. That translates to a winning percentage of 21 percent, a NASCAR record that is unlikely to be broken.

Tim Flock was also justifiably known as a showman, once racing with a monkey sidekick named Jocko Flocko.

FORD MOTOR COMPANY

Ford won only one race in the first six years of NASCAR's history, but the automotive giant quickly began to make up for lost time. In fact, Ford and its Mercury division have developed some of the greatest and most legendary NASCAR vehicles.

During the "aero wars"—a time when the manufacturers labored as hard in the wind tunnel as they did at the track—Ford unleashed the fastback Torino Talladega and Mercury Cyclone to battle the winged creations of Chrysler.

Since the 1980s, though, Ford has relied on its dependable Thunderbird as its NASCAR weapon of choice. The Thunderbird has flown proudly in NASCAR competition. It still holds the record for the fastest lap ever turned, when Bill Elliott raced around Talladega Super speedway at 212.809 mph (342.4kph) on April 30, 1987. That's a record that will in all likelihood remain in the possession of Ford, as NASCAR has since taken steps to ensure that Winston Cup cars stay below the 200 mph (321.8kph) mark.

Between 1990 and 1996, the Thunderbird won an impressive eighty-eight races, but an announcement by Ford in 1997 that production of the Thunderbird would cease meant that the model's days in NASCAR's victory lanes were numbered.

FOYT, A.J.

A.J. Foyt (retired, born 1/16/35) is possibly the United States' most legendary race driver. The exploits that built this legend occurred while Foyt raced in a staggering number of different series. Foyt has won races in IndyCars, sports cars, dirt track cars, midgets, and stock cars.

While Foyt has never competed in more than seven NASCAR races in any one season (1967, 1971, 1975, 1985, 1988, and 1989) he has won seven times out of 128 total starts through 1994.

While A.J. will always be remembered for the feat of winning four Indianapolis 500 races, he also had great success in his runs in the Daytona 500 stock car races. After a top-five finish in the 1969 race and a disappointing thirty-second place in 1970, he placed third in 1971 driving a Mercury for the Wood Brothers. The next year he returned in the same make car for the same team and dominated the race, winning the 1972 Daytona 500 by almost two laps over Charlie Glotzbach.

Right: **The legendary A.J. Foyt.** Above: **Foyt competes in a USAC-sanctioned race at Dover Downs International Speedway on July 19, 1970. Foyt, driving the number 2 car, is ducking low to pass Don White in a Dodge Charger Daytona while Roger McCluskey trails in a Plymouth Super Bird.** Opposite top: **NASCAR founder Bill France, Sr., was not a fan of the winged cars built by Chrysler and wrote rules to force the exotic vehicles out of NASCAR racing.** Opposite bottom: **France's dream was to run races among cars similar to the showroom cousins that the fans drove. Daytona International Speedway—shown here under construction in 1958—helped make that dream come true.**

That Foyt, only an occasional stock car competitor, could so handily win NASCAR's most important race doubtlessly rankled some of his fellow drivers, but it stands as a testament to Foyt's all-around abilities driving any kind of competition vehicle.

FRANCE FAMILY

To a large extent, NASCAR's remarkable growth is due to the fact that the sanctioning body has had only two presidents—Bill France, Sr., and Bill France, Jr.

Bill France, Sr., moved to Daytona Beach, Florida, in 1934 with his wife, Anne, and their young son. When they had the opportunity, "Big Bill" and Anne promoted races both before and after World War II. But Bill dreamed of creating a national stock car racing championship. So in December 1947, France invited other promoters, drivers, and car owners to meet in Daytona Beach at the Streamline Hotel.

After three days of meetings, NASCAR made the transformation from dream to reality. Incorporated on February 21, 1948, with France as its president, NASCAR immediately began sanctioning competition.

At a time when racers were frequently taken advantage of by unscrupulous promoters, France made certain that NASCAR lived up to his high ideals regarding the payment of purses and the rules of competition. But France also had a good head for marketing, and he found ways to bring NASCAR racing events into the public eye and attract corporate involvement.

By the time control over NASCAR was passed to Big Bill's son, on January 10, 1972, Bill France, Sr., had overseen the growth of the sport to a point where races were televised and R.J. Reynolds had come aboard as sponsor of the Winston Cup Series.

Bill France, Jr., grew up surrounded by NASCAR and learned well the lessons offered by his father. Young Bill's marketing sense was even more fully developed than his father's, and he guided the sport into an age where every race—and nearly every qualifying

Brian France on NASCAR's future marketing opportunities:

"Once you have a certain size audience—and I would say NASCAR is certainly at this level of audience—your audience has to look a lot like America looks, and that means diversity. That doesn't mean you're not going to have pockets of strength; of course we do. But the reality is that once you get an audience the size that we have it, it crosses through a lot of diversity, and that's positive.

"The Cartoon Network and Hanna-Barbera, owned by Turner, another network, has a big play with NASCAR with their team sponsorship. That's important to us because it goes after the youth audience. We're going to be going after a number of audience demographics, no question about that."

session—is televised live. He has labored to increase the involvement of the nation's largest corporations in stock car racing, and kept in delicate balance all the elements of a sport that has grown quickly. But perhaps most important, Bill France, Jr., has never lost sight of a fact that his father stressed—NASCAR's success is due to the fans. As a result, the necessity of safe but thrilling competition is always the most important factor.

Currently Bill France, Jr.'s own son, Brian, is heading the marketing efforts of the sanctioning body, overseeing new business development in all aspects of NASCAR's operations.

While other sports are governed by contentious groups of owners who are often unable to come to terms with each other, NASCAR has thrived under a benevolent dictatorship that has helped, not hindered, the ascension of stock car racing's popularity.

Right: **Bill France, Jr., has
helped guide NASCAR
into its modern era.**
Bottom: **Through France's
efforts and great racing
by such competitors as
Harry Gant, it's now
common to see well-
known figures from other
sports in the garage area.**

GANT, HARRY

One of the most popular drivers ever to compete in the Winston Cup Series, Harry Gant
(retired, born 1/10/40) started his career racing
on the short tracks near his home in
Taylorsville, North Carolina.

His Winston Cup debut came in 1973 at
the wheel of a car fielded by Junie Donlavey—a
man who has given many Winston Cup drivers
their starts. Gant raced for a variety of teams
throughout the 1970s, but it wasn't until April
1982 that he finally won his first race, at
Martinsville. He won again at Charlotte later
that season.

Gant's consistency showed with a second-
place finish in the championship battle of 1984,
and he further proved his ability by winning
the International Race of Champions title in
1985. But his most improbable success was yet
to come.

After joining a team owned by Leo
Jackson, Gant won one race each season in
1989 and 1990 before hitting an amazing hot
streak in 1991. Gant won four consecutive
Winston Cup races in the fall of that season,
earning the nickname "Mr. September."

Although Gant was quickly gaining notoriety,
he modestly shied away from the publicity generated by his remarkable successes and concentrated instead on his hobbies of house building
and motorcycle riding.

Harry Gant's last win in the Winston Cup
Series came when he was fifty-two years of
age, on August 16, 1992, at Michigan, a victory
that made him NASCAR's oldest winner to
date. Gant retired from Winston Cup competition in 1994, although he did later compete in
NASCAR's truck series and briefly filled in for
an injured Bill Elliott in Winston Cup racing at
Charlotte in 1996.

GENERAL MOTORS

General Motors' proud NASCAR tradition
dates all the way back to the sanctioning
body's very first year, when five of the eight
races in the 1949 season were won by
Oldsmobiles.

Statistics show that GM cars have by far
won the most NASCAR events, although in
recent years the share has equalized with its
modern era rival, Ford.

As the 1990s dawned, GM teams were
fielding Chevrolets, Buicks, Oldsmobiles, and
Pontiacs in the Winston Cup Series. But the
NASCAR programs at Buick and Oldsmobile
were brought to a conclusion, with GM focus-
ing on the Chevrolet Monte Carlo and Pontiac
Grand Prix models.

The Monte Carlo is surely one of the most legendary of Winston Cup competitors. During the 1980s, the Monte Carlo dominated the win column until Chevrolet teams migrated to the Lumina in the 1989 season. But in 1995, the Monte Carlo made its return, both to NASCAR and to victory lane, with twenty-one wins.

GIBBS, JOE

Joe Gibbs (born 11/25/40) has benefited tremendously from his association with NASCAR racing, but Winston Cup racing in turn owes Gibbs a debt.

As a National Football League coach who led the Washington Redskins to three victories in four Super Bowl appearances, Gibbs had one of the highest profiles in professional sports. So when he announced his retirement as coach on March 5, 1993, much of the focus of the sports world's media shifted to Gibbs' Winston Cup team and his love of NASCAR. The sanctioning body of NASCAR couldn't have asked for better publicity than that.

Gibbs' Winston Cup team began operation in the 1992 season, with Dale Jarrett as driver and Jarrett's brother-in-law, Jimmy Makar, as crew chief. Despite some growing pains, the team managed a second- and third-place finish to complement a handful of other top-ten spots. Then in 1993, the team had fully matured. In front of several hundred thousand spectators—and with his father announcing the race's finish to millions of television viewers—Dale Jarrett won the 1993 Daytona 500, hold-ing off a determined challenge from Dale Earnhardt. It was the team's only win that year, but it came in NASCAR's biggest race. Gibbs' race team finished fourth in the Winston Cup championship standings.

Jarrett won once again in 1994, but the team's points standings had fallen to sixteenth by the end of the year. Jarrett left the team to substitute for the injured Ernie Irvan with Robert Yates' racing team. Meanwhile, Gibbs had noticed the talents of Bobby Labonte, who had been driving for Bill Davis in 1993 and 1994, and hired the young Texas driver for the 1995 season.

Gibbs' legendary eye for football talent obviously carried over into racing, for Labonte won three times in 1995, and his team wrapped up the season in tenth place. Labonte also drove Gibbs' car to victory in 1996 at Atlanta. Today, the combination of Gibbs' excellent racing team and Labonte's smooth style makes the outfit a contender every week.

As busy as Joe Gibbs has been since his retirement from the NFL, the Winston Cup team has not been his sole motorsports interest. Gibbs grew up fascinated with drag racing, so in 1995 he began fielding National Hot Rod Association (NHRA) race cars in addition to his NASCAR vehicles.

GLOTZBACH, CHARLIE

"Chargin' Charlie" Glotzbach (retired, born 6/19/38) competed in four decades of Grand National and Winston Cup racing.

Above: **Charlie Glotzbach**
helped bring the winged
Dodge Charger Daytona
into NASCAR competi-
tion, and served as one of
Chrysler's two lead test
drivers with Buddy
Baker. Being asked to
test, be it for an auto
manufacturer or tire
manufacturer, is general-
ly an honor reserved for
the most respected com-
petitors. Right: **Tony**
Glover is highly respected
in his own right. Not
many crew chiefs can
boast of three Daytona
500 victories.

Best known for his aggressive runs in Chrysler products in the 1960s and 1970s, Glotzbach was also a test driver for the automotive manufacturer in programs such as the development effort that led to the creation of the aerodynamic Dodge Charger Daytona.

Glotzbach drove to victory four times in his Winston Cup career of 124 starts, and near-ly won the 1969 Daytona 500. Glotzbach was passed on the final lap by LeeRoy Yarbrough.

GLOVER, TONY

The son of a champion in NASCAR's Sportsman division, Tony Glover (born 4/17/57) began working as a crew chief for his father at the age of thirteen. This experience helped lead to Glover's current status as one of the most successful crew chiefs in the Winston Cup Series.

Like many successful crew chiefs and mechanics, Glover learned a lot during a period spent working at Petty Enterprises. That experience led to the young man being hired by the newly formed Morgan-McClure team in 1983.

For more than a decade, Glover directed the Morgan-McClure operation on its slow but steady climb to Winston Cup prominence and respect. By 1988, with driver Rick Wilson, the team managed several top-five performances. But it was in 1990, when driver Ernie Irvan came aboard, that the team put all the pieces together. Glover directed Irvan and his team to their first Winston Cup victory in August 1990, and they finished the season with six top-five finishes.

In 1991, Irvan and Glover won the Daytona 500 and improved the team's consistency, reflected by the team's three wins in 1992. After a final win for Morgan-McClure in 1993, Irvan left the team to drive for Robert Yates. Irvan's replacement, Sterling Marlin, was a friend of Glover's, and the two got their professional relationship off to an outstanding start with a win in the 1994 Daytona 500. They repeated the feat in 1995.

Late in 1996, Tony Glover brought his tenure at Morgan-McClure to a close and accepted a position with the Felix Sabates team.

GOLDSMITH, PAUL

Paul Goldsmith (born 10/2/27) was a frequent competitor in NASCAR events before the top division was christened the Winston Cup Series. From 1956 to 1969, Goldsmith competed in 127 events and won nine races in Grand National competition.

Goldsmith's best season came in 1957, when he won four races while driving Fords for famed car owner and mechanic Smokey Yunick. Goldsmith won the last race on the famed Daytona beach/road course, held in February 1958. In 1966, Goldsmith won three times behind the wheel of the Nichels Engineering Plymouth, the flagship car of Chrysler's factory racing operations of the time.

GORDON, JEFF

At a time when NASCAR management began to show a shrewd regard for the power of marketing, along came a young superstar whose image meshed perfectly with the promotional direction the sport was following: Jeff Gordon.

Born in California, Gordon (born 8/4/71) began racing go-karts and quarter-midgets at the age of five. When it became apparent that Gordon was a natural-born driver, his family moved to Indiana, where he could further his on-the-job training in a variety of competition vehicles. As Gordon drove to win after win in USAC midget and Silver Crown open-wheel race cars, America's race fans got their first televised glimpses of the future NASCAR great on ESPN broadcasts of USAC series events. The young driver was not only an outstanding competitor, he was bright, poised, and well spoken. The open-wheel childhood chapter of Jeff Gordon's life closed with an outstanding record of 500 short track wins.

In 1991, Gordon made his much-anticipated move to NASCAR racing, becoming Busch Grand National Rookie of the Year in 1991, then winning three races and eleven poles as fastest qualifier the following year. Gordon set these marks driving Fords for team owner Bill Davis. Davis was under the impression that the team would make the move together to Winston Cup competition, but team owner Rick Hendrick expanded his two-car team to a three-car operation and signed Gordon to race Chevrolets in Winston Cup. Ironically, the young superstar's first start in the elite series came in the final race of the 1992 season, as Richard Petty brought his career to an end.

Gordon ran strong in 1993: the twenty-one-year-old won one of the 125-mile (201.1km) qualifying races for the Daytona 500 and claimed seven top-five finishes in his first full season. As his relationship with crew chief Ray Evernham developed in 1994, Gordon won the non-points, all-star Busch Clash at Daytona, then won his first official Winston Cup race by winning the 600-mile (965.4km) event at Charlotte in May. Weeks later, Gordon won the first Brickyard 400 as NASCAR racing made its long-awaited debut at the historic Indianapolis Motor Speedway on August 4, 1994. He and Ernie Irvan were locked in a thrilling duel late in the race until Irvan suffered

a flat tire. In 1995, Gordon won seven races and became the youngest Winston Cup champion of NASCAR's modern era at the age of twenty-four. Gordon nearly won the championship again in 1996—falling just short of the points total of Hendrick Motorsports teammate Terry Labonte.

Early in 1997, Gordon had a winning percentage of nearly 30 percent in races from the end of 1996 into 1997, including victory in the 1997 Daytona 500 and the inaugural California

Above: *Paul Goldsmith won the first spring race at North Carolina Motor Speedway—on March 13, 1966—despite making ten pit stops, including one for a missing gas cap.* Below: *Today's Winston Cup cars don't have gas caps, and if a driver like Jeff Gordon had to make ten pit stops he would never be in contention to win a race.*

Jeff Gordon reflecting on winning the 1995 Winston Cup championship:

"I think you can go out there and you can have a good day. You can hit it right on one day, and we feel like that was our day at the Brickyard. It was like it was meant to be, like a fantasy that came true because we wanted it so bad. But to win a championship you've got to do it throughout the whole year. You can't just hit it every once in a while, you've got to hit it all the time and have the consistency— you can't fall out of races.

"After last year and the year before I realized how difficult it is to win a championship. We're all the time trying to finish every race, finish as far forward as possible, knowing that the best we've done is eighth in the points in the past. To go out there and have a year like we did this year is amazing. I think other people look at it the same way. They think, 'OK, it's one thing for him to win races, but to be a champion, now that's something!'

"If you look back at how many people have won championships you see it's pretty hard to come by. Only the guys who have been the best have gone on to win championships."

500. By the end of the 1997 season, Gordon— on course for a second championship—became only the second driver ever to win the Winston Million when he added victories at Charlotte and Darlington to his Daytona 500 win.

Gordon's phenomenal success was attributed by some people to the use of traction control or another equally illegal device in his stock car, especially since his Chevrolet was often the only Monte Carlo in contention amid a flock of Ford Thunderbirds at the head of the field. But if anything, the rumors just resulted in NASCAR's keeping a closer eye on the number 24 Monte Carlo in inspections. No irregularities ever turned up, and it's likely that the team's success was simply due to a dedicated pit crew, a brilliant crew chief, and Gordon's tremendous skill behind the wheel. That skill translated to Gordon's wrapping up the 1997 Winston Cup championship at the season's November 16 finale at Atlanta Motor Speedway.

GORDON, ROBBY

After running in just two Winston Cup races for car owner Junie Donlavey in 1991, Robby Gordon (born 1/2/69) returned to Winston Cup racing in 1993 under difficult circumstances and in the glare of the media spotlight.

Thundering down the longest straightaway in the Winston Cup Series— the 3,740-foot (1,139.9km) front straightaway at Pocono International Raceway— Jeff Gordon's DuPont Chevrolet leads the charge.

When Davey Allison died in a helicopter crash in July 1993, car owner Robert Yates returned his team to competition with Robby Gordon behind the wheel at Talladega Superspeedway. The union was short and not so sweet, as Gordon took the Yates Thunderbird too low on the track. The car broke loose and careened across the track, and Gordon crashed hard.

While Gordon—who competed for Felix Sabates in 1997—has had difficulty establishing himself as a star in Winston Cup racing, his record in other kinds of racing has been more noteworthy. His resume includes off-road racing championships, victories in the CART IndyCar series, and a number of impressive wins in the twenty-four-hour road race at Daytona.

The late Davey Allison on why many Winston Cup drivers remain active in Busch Grand National competition:

"Probably the most important reason is that the best conditioning for a race car driver is to run as many races as you can in similar equipment. Busch Grand National cars are very similar to the Winston Cup cars in the feel and the response to chassis adjustments. The aerodynamics are very similar, so not only does it help to keep me in shape but it also gives me an opportunity to see what the racetrack is going to do on the following day. We can see what kind of things we need to be looking for with our Winston Cup car in the final practice session."

Robby Gordon's attempt to compete in the Winston Cup Series was a failure, showing that success in other motorsports series does not mean a driver will succeed in Winston Cup racing. Bearing the brunt of Gordon's failure was team owner Felix Sabates, who invested millions in Gordon's efforts and got little in return.

Gordon showed promise of a strong future in Winston Cup racing in 1996 when he finished second, after Mark Martin, in the International Race of Champions. But his 1997 season with Sabates was disastrous, and it is unclear whether Gordon can become a successful Winston Cup driver.

GRAND NATIONAL

As the sport of stock car racing progressed toward its current status, the name of its elite level of competition has evolved.

When NASCAR first began sanctioning events on the beaches of Daytona in 1948, the organization was concentrating on its Modified division, with rules that called for coupes with full fenders and windshields but allowed almost any other modifications.

But at the June 19, 1949, race at Charlotte Speedway, NASCAR sanctioned competition in a new division that would account for its greatest success, the Strictly Stock division. This division was for full-size U.S. passenger cars with complete bodies.

Before the 1950 season, NASCAR renamed this division Grand National, after England's

Two champions of the Busch Grand National Series, Steve Grissom (right, making a pit stop) and David Green (below, waving to crowd). Making the transition from Grand National to Winston Cup racing can be difficult. Even though a driver has been champion of the Busch series, he must generally start at the bottom in Winston Cup racing.

premier horse racing event. Soon after, the Grand National division eclipsed the Modified division in NASCAR's hierarchy.

When the R.J. Reynolds Tobacco Company began its involvement in the sport with sponsorship of NASCAR's elite division in 1971, the sanctioning body in 1972 changed the name of the Grand National division to Winston Cup in recognition of Reynolds' welcome influx of money to the sport.

Today, though, the Grand National name lives on in the Busch Grand National Series. This is the level of NASCAR competition just below the Winston Cup Series, where the up-and-coming talent of tomorrow gains experience driving cars that are nearly identical to Winston Cup cars.

GREEN, DAVID

Even an impeccable record in other racing series does nothing to ease the growing pains of learning to compete in the NASCAR Winston Cup Series. Kentucky's David Green (born 1/28/58) would probably be one of the first to attest to the challenge of moving to NASCAR's premier series.

Green began short track racing near his home in Owensboro, Kentucky, getting off to a good start by winning four of his first five races. When he moved to the NASCAR Busch Grand National division, Green won in his first season of competition and was runner-up to Jeff Gordon in the Rookie of the Year battle in 1991. The promise of a Busch Series ride for 1992 fell through, and Green spent the season

as a mechanic for Bobby Labonte's Busch effort. When Labonte moved up to the Winston Cup Series, Green took over as driver for the team. Green went on to win the series championship in 1994 and finished second to Randy Lajoie in 1996.

Aided by Kirk Shelmerdine—the crew chief who guided Dale Earnhardt to numerous Winston Cup championships—as advisor, Green began his Winston Cup career in 1997. Although the team struggled to qualify for races and had to deal with crashes and mechanical failures early in the year, the patient and intelligent driving style that led David Green to great success in the Busch Series bodes well for his Winston Cup future.

GRISSOM, STEVE

Another NASCAR Winston Cup driver who cut his teeth in short track competition in the state of Alabama, Steve Grissom (born 6/26/63) had to make a choice as a young man: to continue to develop his motorsports career or to accept a scholarship to the famed college football program at the University of Alabama. Racing won out.

The captain of his high school football team, Grissom still managed to find time for local racing competition. And after high school he moved through the ranks, testing his competitive abilities with a series championship in the NASCAR All-Pro Series for stock cars before moving up to the Busch Grand National ranks in 1987.

Grissom won the 1993 Busch Series championship and prepared to move up to Winston Cup full-time for the 1994 season. Driving for team owner Gary Bechtel, Grissom finished 1994 as runner-up in the Rookie of the Year battle to Jeff Burton. After driving all of 1995 and part of 1996 for Bechtel, Grissom moved to the team owned by Larry Hedrick in the hopes of winning his first Winston Cup Series race.

GURNEY, DAN

Dan Gurney (retired, born 4/13/31) may be best known as a competitor in other racing series, but the California driver found success in NASCAR's top division as well.

Gurney won one race each in the years 1963 through 1966, and won again in 1968 for a total of five victories in just sixteen starts. As evidence of his talents racing in sports car competition, all of Gurney's NASCAR victories came on the 2.7-mile (4.3km) road course in Riverside, California. Gurney's first win came in a Holman-Moody factory Ford ride, with the remainder claimed at the wheel of Fords prepared by the Wood Brothers.

HAMILTON, BOBBY

When "the King," Richard Petty, hung up his helmet and retired, Petty Enterprises went

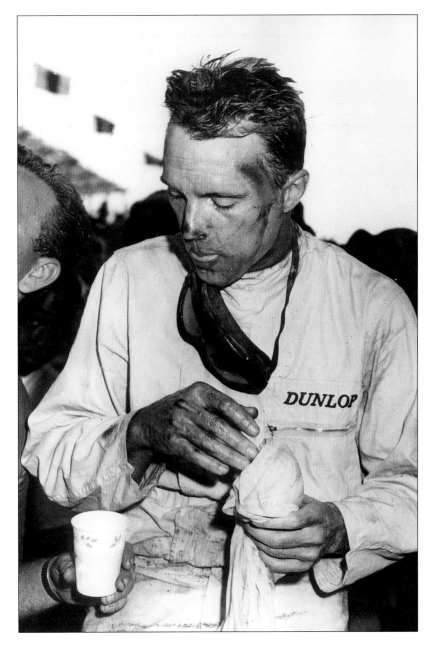

through a number of drivers searching for the right competitor to return the team's Pontiacs to victory lane. After suffering through a number of disappointing alliances, the team finally found the right combination with Bobby Hamilton (born 5/29/57) at the wheel.

Hamilton was born in Tennessee and grew up around race cars, as his father and grandfather prepared the stock cars raced in the Winston Cup Series by country music star Marty Robbins. Hamilton cut his teeth in racing at Nashville Speedway, where he was track champion. After Hamilton raced against Darrell Waltrip in a celebrity race in 1988, Waltrip recommended Hamilton to team owner Rick Hendrick, who was looking for drivers to pilot camera-carrying cars for the film *Days of Thunder*. Hamilton took the movie car to the lead from a fifth-place qualifying position before he was forced to park the unofficial entry by NASCAR.

Dan Gurney was well known for his skills on road courses, and his only success in NASCAR racing came on just that type of speedway. Here, Gurney has just won a sports car race, the type of motorsports activity he was best known for. Gurney drove a Lotus to victory in this December 10, 1961, competition in the Bahamas.

Bobby Hamilton on NASCAR's efforts to keep competition equal:

Bobby Hamilton on NASCAR's efforts to keep competition equal:

"I think they do a good job. Of course, you're so competitive that the first thing you're going to say is, 'Well, like it is right now, Ford's got this thing and General Motors can't keep up.' But it all works out down the road, when you really look at it. I remember Benny Parsons telling me they ran some stats and over a period of years that General Motors cars had won thirty-two races and Ford had won thirty-one races. So when you really get looking at the stats and the way it works over a season I think they keep it pretty even.

"They keep the cars safe, and when we qualify at Richmond or Martinsville the field is separated by half a second. That's a lot on a racetrack, but when you take a stopwatch and start it and stop it as fast as you can that's almost three-tenths of a second. It's real tight, so that shows me that they've done a good job on making everybody real tight and competitive."

Above: *Hollywood gave Bobby Hamilton the opportunity to show off his racing skills. Hamilton drove one of the movie cars in the film* Days of Thunder *at Phoenix International Raceway.* Top: *Years later, Hamilton won his first Winston Cup race at the same track.*

In 1991, Hamilton began racing in the Winston Cup Series full-time and narrowly beat Ted Musgrave for Rookie of the Year honors. Hooking up with Petty Enterprises for the 1995 season, Hamilton drove to ten top ten finishes as the team built consistency.

Considering Hamilton's *Days of Thunder* debut at Phoenix, it seems fitting that the 1-mile (1.6km) oval in the desert became the site of Hamilton's first Winston Cup win, on October 27, 1996, as Hamilton edged out Mark Martin and Terry Labonte. Hamilton won again

for Petty in 1997 at Rockingham, then announced late in the season his plans to compete for the Morgan-McClure team in 1998.

HAMILTON, PETE

Driving a winged Plymouth Super Bird as part of a two-car Petty Enterprises team, Pete Hamilton (retired, born 7/20/42) stunned the NASCAR Grand National world in 1970.

Never having driven a Super Bird even in practice, Hamilton wheeled the aerodynamic Chrysler to victory in the 1970 Daytona 500. Hamilton went on to sweep both Grand National Series stops at Talladega for three wins in that season. Teammate Richard Petty, who had hired Hamilton for the season, won eighteen times himself that season to give Petty Enterprises a grand total of twenty-one wins that season alone.

Cutbacks in Chrysler's corporate racing program dictated that Buddy Baker replace Hamilton at Petty Enterprises in 1971, and Pete moved on to drive a Plymouth for the Cotton Owens team. His fourth and final Grand National win came in one of the two qualifying races for the 1971 Daytona 500.

HAMMOND, JEFF

Vetran crew chief Jeff Hammond (born 9/9/56) has experienced tremendous success in more than two decades of prepping cars for Winston Cup racing.

After working on Cale Yarborough's team—during which time the South Carolina driver won Winston Cup championships in 1976, 1977, and 1978—Hammond began working with Darrell Waltrip as a crew chief in 1982. Hammond led the team to a dozen wins and the 1982 championship, and backed that up with a second championship in 1985.

After Waltrip moved to Rick Hendrick's multicar operation in 1987, Hammond followed. Hammond and Waltrip won once in 1987, then twice in 1988 before beginning an outstanding 1989 season by winning the Daytona 500. Waltrip won five more races that year, and the team finished fourth in the championship points standings.

In 1991, Darrell Waltrip formed his own team and, not surprisingly, hired Hammond as his crew chief. The team won three races over the next two seasons before Hammond left to work for Felix Sabates in 1993.

Reunited with Waltrip and his team in 1997, Jeff Hammond helped the legendary driver celebrate his twenty-fifth year in Winston Cup racing with renewed strength. Hammond also prepared cars that Darrell was able to bring home to top-five and top-ten finishes, a turn around after several years of relatively poor performances.

HEDRICK, LARRY

Larry Hedrick (born 12/12/40) entered competition as a team owner in the Winston Cup Series in 1990 and 1991, fielding stock cars in selected events that were driven by Larry Pearson, son of NASCAR legend David Pearson.

By 1992, however, Hedrick—who made his fortune in the auto auction business—had increased his involvement so that Larry Hedrick Motorsports stock cars competed in all of the Winston Cup Series events. Hedrick's team has relied on several talented drivers who have risen to the Winston Cup level after finding success in the NASCAR Busch Grand National Series.

Driver Joe Nemechek, who drove for Hedrick in 1994, won the Busch Series championship in 1992, while Ricky Craven was recognized as the Winston Cup Rookie of the Year after racing Hedrick cars in 1995. In 1997, Hedrick Motorsports turned to another successful Busch Grand National driver, Steve Grissom, who had won the Busch championship in 1993.

Pete Hamilton on the atmosphere of NASCAR stock car racing in the late 1960s:

"If you didn't have a Ford or a Chrysler factory ride you were wasting your time. I came into racing being used to winning and running really well, and went from being a reasonably big fish in a small pond to being a tiny fish in a big pond again....I just wasn't used to running even in the middle of the pack; I was used to running in the front of the pack. So you had to have a factory ride.

"My initial thought is that there were five or six factory teams on either side so you either had to have a Ford or a Chrysler product. I got involved with a fellow by the name of Jim Ruggles. He was the shop foreman at Nichels up in Indiana. He left them and managed a team in Tennessee and I drove his car, and that was my first involvement with the Chrysler engineering people. The first thing I drove for him was a Dodge Charger.

"In the middle of the year they changed that to a Charger 500 with the grille change and the back window—that helped the car a lot. It was basically a Charger but the grille change and the back window change helped the air flow over the front and helped the air attach to the rear, which gave it better downforce. I got in that car and I had only run about 163 mph [262.2kph] in a Sportsman car at Daytona. I got in that car [the Charger] and the first lap I ran was 187 mph [300.8kph]. So that was 24 or 25 mph [38.6 or 40.2kph] faster than I had ever been—on the first lap! So that was a big change—and I just knew that the first time I made that lap I was just committing hari-kari. I knew I was either going to make that lap or die, and that was the atmosphere."

Pete Hamilton celebrates in victory lane during the 1970 season. Hamilton took advantage of his status as a team driver for Petty Enterprises by driving his winged Plymouth Super Bird to numerous wins. Aside from providing aerodynamic stability at 200 mph (321.8km), the Plymouth wings obviously made good perches for celebratory photographs.

Jeff Gordon on making the decision to leave Bill Davis' team to enter Winston Cup competition with Hendrick Motorsports:

"Bill Davis and I don't have the relationship that we used to have. We got along real well, liked working together, but that whole situation happened because I was forced to make a decision. I wanted to go Winston Cup racing the next year; I felt like that was the year for me to move on.

"I was needing to make a decision right then because I had some offers coming in to me. But I wanted to stick with Bill Davis. He had helped me get a good start in Busch Grand National, and Ford Motor Company had helped me out. I had Ford Motor Company telling me, 'Hey, we'll put you in a Ford whether it's Bill Davis or somebody else.' And I said, 'Well, who are you going to put me with?' They mentioned some teams, and they weren't teams that I felt were winning and they weren't teams that I felt were going to really improve and be something that was a good move for Jeff Gordon.

"Then, with the Bill Davis situation, we were just waiting to get a sponsorship. It's tough when you're somebody who has no experience as a driver, who's only twenty or twenty-one years old, and you have no experience as a car owner. We weren't really getting any leads, we weren't getting any positive things to talk about. It just didn't seem like the sponsors were coming. I'd already been talked to by a couple of other Winston Cup owners. One of them was real positive, but when Rick Hendrick came along it just happened to be the right time. We were running out of time with Bill Davis, and it was a great opportunity that would have been difficult for me to turn down.

"Now I can say that I made the right decision and nobody can argue with me. But back then, it was the hardest thing I'd ever had to do."

HENDRICK, RICK

Rick Hendrick (born 7/12/49) has become one of the most influential race team owners in the Winston Cup Series, and the man whose faith in a multiple-car operation has changed the face of the sport in the 1990s.

The North Carolina native is owner of the Hendrick Auto Group, a multimillion-dollar company dealing in auto and truck dealerships as well as holdings in various other businesses. But it would be hard to imagine that anything gives Hendrick more satisfaction than his Winston Cup interests.

Hendrick's fascination with motorsports started when he was a youngster, and he was involved in drag racing as a teenager. From the strip his interest shifted to the water, and Hendrick became involved in drag boat competition. He established a quarter-mile (402.2km) record for propeller-driven craft of more than 222 mph (357.2kph), and his Nitro Fever team won three national championships in a row, from 1981 to 1983.

Hendrick's initial involvement in Winston Cup came in 1984, with a car sponsored by Northwestern

Above: *Rick Hendrick has done in the 1990s what Carl Kiekhaefer did in the 1950s—win big with a multiple-car team.*
Right: *Before the severity of his illness prevented him from attending races in 1997, Hendrick had struck the perfect balance of knowing when to get involved and when to just watch his teams work.*

Bobby Hillin—shown here in 1996—drove to his first victory at the always daunting Talladega Superspeedway on July 27, 1986. Hillin held off experienced drivers Tim Richmond and Rusty Wallace for the win.

Security Life and driven by Geoff Bodine. Hendrick established a winning tradition from the start, as the team won three races that inagural season, the first coming at Martinsville on April 29. It was not only Hendrick's first win, but also the first for Geoff Bodine as a Winston Cup driver.

The team went winless in 1985, but Hendrick was not discouraged and started a two-car NASCAR operation in 1986. He was rewarded with two wins from Bodine and seven wins from the flashy Tim Richmond. Hendrick figured that if two cars were good, maybe three would be better, so 1987 found Bodine, Darrell Waltrip, and Benny Parsons all driving for Hendrick, while Richmond won two races in a schedule limited by illness.

In 1988 and 1989, Hendrick's competitive stable solidified with Bodine, Waltrip, and Ken Schrader. The three drivers accounted for four wins the first year and eight wins the next. Ricky Rudd replaced Bodine for 1990 and was the only driver of the three to win that year. Waltrip left after the season, leaving Schrader and Rudd to get four victories in 1991 and 1992 before they were joined by the latest Hendrick acquisition, Jeff Gordon, in 1993.

In the years 1994 through 1996, the Hendrick lineup was Jeff Gordon, Terry Labonte, and Ken Schrader, with Schrader replaced by Ricky Craven in 1997.

Many in Winston Cup racing doubted the multicar concept that Hendrick has always championed, but those doubts were erased by the Hendrick Motorsports performances of the mid-1990s. Jeff Gordon won the Winston Cup championship in 1995, as did Terry Labonte in 1996. Hendrick teams won twenty-two races in those seasons, with Gordon's team alone accounting for seventeen of the wins.

After the 1996 season, Rick Hendrick was diagnosed with leukemia, and his drivers and crew member helped start a program in

NASCAR to raise public awareness of the need for bone marrow donors. Hendrick's illness could not prevent him from enjoying the results of the 1997 Daytona 500, as his cars finished first (Gordon), second (Labonte), and third (Craven), sweeping the event.

HILLIN, BOBBY

Texas-born Bobby Hillin (born 6/5/64) got his start in racing in 1977 at the age of thirteen, driving in mini-stock competition.

By 1981, he had won track championships at local speedways, so Hillin made the jump to NASCAR. He started his first Winston Cup race while still a high school student, just seventeen years old. Hillin's first win came with just his seventy-eighth Winston Cup start. At twenty-two years of age, Hillin won the 1986 Talladega 500 after becoming the youngest driver ever to run a 200-mph (321.8kph) lap.

After a lengthy stint with the Stavola Brothers team through the 1980s, Hillin has driven for a variety of teams in recent years.

HMIEL, STEVE

Crew chief Steve Hmiel (born 1954) began an association with driver Mark Martin in 1988. Soon after their team had a reputation as one of the most intelligent and tenacious in the Winston Cup Series.

Hmiel gained experience in Winston Cup racing through a stint with Petty Enterprises. After winning a championship in 1984 and races in 1985 and 1986 as crew chief for driver Terry Labonte and owner Billy Hagan, Hmiel was hired by Jack Roush to crew chief for Roush's new team and driver, Mark Martin.

In 1989, the team placed third in the Winston Cup points standings after winning

"It's had every kind of snout on it known to man and it's been wrecked a hundred times. It's a light car and it goes together real easy, which is a sign of a good race car. But a lot of times how good a car is has a lot to do with what the driver thinks about it, more so than what the materials are in it or the hardware that bolts to it. So the fact that Mark likes it is even better. That's why it's a good car."

Above: *No matter how carefully the cars are prepared, things can suddenly go wrong during the rigors of NASCAR competition. Here, Mark Martin makes solid contact with the wall at Dover Downs International Speedway in 1993.* Right: *Steve Hmiel can claim much of the credit for Mark Martin's ascension to Winston Cup stardom.*

one race and scoring more than ten top-five finishes. Hmiel and Martin almost won the 1990 Winston Cup championship, falling just twenty-six points short of Dale Earnhardt's total after winning three races in the season. The team's best year from a wins standpoint was 1993, when Hmiel guided Martin to five victories on a variety of NASCAR tracks.

Steve Hmiel left his crew chief duties in 1997, becoming the manager of Roush Racing's team operations.

HOLMAN-MOODY

When the racetracks of NASCAR acted as battlegrounds for a high-speed competition between Ford and Chrysler, both automotive giants had stock car headquarters that were the focus of racing operations. For Chrysler, it was the Indiana-based Nichels Engineering. Ford's operation was based in North Carolina, at the shops of Holman-Moody.

Formed in the late 1950s as a partnership between Californian John Holman and Massachusetts' Ralph Moody, Holman-Moody was based in Charlotte, North Carolina. Although Moody himself had competed in NASCAR racing, both men excelled in working as a team with the goal of building the strongest and fastest race cars.

Among the drivers who raced in Holman-Moody vehicles were Curtis Turner, Joe Weatherly, Fred Lorenzen, Dan Gurney, Tiny Lund, Fireball Roberts, Cale Yarborough, A.J. Foyt, Bobby Allison, Mario Andretti, Parnelli Jones, and David Pearson. As might be expected from this (partial) listing of prominent drivers, Holman-Moody found its way to victory at nearly every major NASCAR race during its years of operation through 1973.

HUTCHERSON, DICK

The career of Dick Hutcherson (retired, born 11/30/31) in NASCAR's top series was brief—just 103 events between 1964 and 1967—but the Iowa driver won an impressive fourteen races, including nine victories in 1965 alone.

How did Hutcherson claim so many victories in such a short period of time? It was a combination of his own talent and the awesome factory-endorsed Fords of the Holman-Moody team. Only Ned Jarrett won more races in 1965, and he too was at the wheel of a Ford. Hutcherson went on to win three more times in 1966 in just fourteen starts.

HYDE, HARRY

Crew chief Harry Hyde (born 1921, died 1996) began his racing career in the years immediately after World War II and was a model for today's Winston Cup crew chiefs. Hyde was also an outspoken and colorful character—so much so that his life inspired the role played by Robert Duvall in the film *Days of Thunder*.

Hyde's accomplishments on the racetracks of NASCAR came largely as a result of his willingness to try new things and his thirst for knowledge obtained from engineers, aerodynamicists, and others. Hyde applied this information to his racing operations, and he had great success with drivers like Tim Richmond, Buddy Baker, Dave Marcis, and Bobby Isaac, with whom he won the 1970 NASCAR championship. In all, Hyde-prepared cars won fifty-six races and eighty-eight pole positions.

Harry Hyde will be remembered both for the records his teams set on the racetracks of the Winston Cup Series and for his influence on modern approaches to race car preparation.

Harry Hyde on corporate involvement in NASCAR:

"I started racing right after the war—World War II, the big one—and I've been racing ever since. When NASCAR came to be I tore after it full-time about thirty years ago and I haven't let up yet. So I've lived a long time to see the changes made and I guess I can't forget the old days.

"It was a different thing going to a race then than it is now—the feeling then was a lot different than it is now. We had the big old Hemi and Ford had the big old 429 and we knew it was going be a hell of a race. But we knew we had the shit to get them with and they felt like they had the shit to get us with. Today, we hardly know if we're going to make the inspection. The corporate world got into it, and it's alright—I can't kick on it, racing's been good to me.

"But it's just not the same world we used to have. If the corporate world hadn't come into it we wouldn't be making the money we're making today and we wouldn't be drawing the crowds because the automotive people wouldn't be as interested in it. They wouldn't be able to promote it. But don't you see, back then you were in an era where they built those big, high-banked tracks and they were coming up all over the country, and we were hitting them with a hell of a strong motor and a hell of a strong car. It was a feeling then that was different. They say, 'Hell, this is the modern day, this is different.' Don't tell me that a little kindness wouldn't work in any time."

Above: **Dick Hutcherson** left a career as a driver to open a successful racing equipment business.
Left: *Harry Hyde stayed involved as a stock car racing participant for most of his life, turning wrenches and planning strategy for some of NASCAR's greatest teams.*

The start of the 1995 Brickyard 400. Though Indianapolis Motor Speedway has the overall length of such superspeedways as Daytona International Speedway and Talladega Superspeedway, the flat turns at IMS require a different approach to setting up a stock car for a competitive performance.

INDIANAPOLIS MOTOR SPEEDWAY

As legendary in open-wheel car racing as Daytona International Speedway is in stock car racing, Indianapolis Motor Speedway—"The Brickyard"—was always the site of a single race each year, Memorial Day Weekend's famed Indianapolis 500.

All that changed in 1993, however, when the speedway's Tony George and NASCAR's Bill France, Jr., made a shocking announcement: on August 4, 1994, the NASCAR Winston Cup Series would race at Indianapolis Motor Speedway in the inaugural Brickyard 400. The Brickyard 400 would thereafter be run each August.

Diehard fans of IndyCars were livid, viewing the invasion of the Winston Cup cars as blasphemy. The Winston Cup contingent was predictably thrilled with the news that they would be the first new type of race car to thunder around the 2.5-mile (4km) rectangular track since the present configuration started hosting competition back in 1909.

The first Brickyard 400 was one of the most heavily covered events in sports media history. What NASCAR hoped for was a race that would be fitting as a foundation for a new tradition and new legends. What they got was all that and more.

Jeff Gordon, the young superstar driver who grew up in Indiana, found himself dueling with Ernie Irvan for the lead late in the race. In a thrilling battle that had the 400,000 fans on their feet, Gordon's Chevy and Irvan's Ford swapped the lead back and forth as they roared through the 9-degree banking of the turns, running at lap speeds of more than 170 mph (273.5kph). Then, with just five laps remaining, Irvan suffered a tire failure. "Local hero" Jeff Gordon drove on to claim the race in the state that had become his adopted home. NASCAR could not have planned a more perfect finale to this first, crucial race.

In its short history, the Brickyard 400 has already approached the status level of NASCAR's most cherished races.

INTERNATIONAL RACE OF CHAMPIONS (IROC)

The idea behind the International Race of Champions is simple: take the best race car drivers in the world, put them in identically prepared race cars, let them race on several different tracks, and see who comes out on top.

The IROC series began racing in 1973 on road courses using Porsche Carrera RSR cars, but over the years models including Chevrolet Camaros, Pontiac Firebirds, and Dodge Avengers have also been used as the series moved toward a focus on oval tracks. But due to the format of the series, it's not so important which vehicle is being raced—they are indeed virtually exactly the same. What really matters in IROC are the racetracks themselves.

Although Winston Cup fans might not want to admit it, drivers from other series are often at a distinct disadvantage in IROC competition simply because the tracks that are used are Winston Cup tracks. A driver who races in the Winston Cup Series will certainly be more comfortable drafting down Daytona

International Speedway's back straightaway in a full-bodied car than someone used to competing in sports car competition.

But even though NASCAR drivers have an edge, the unpredictable does happen. In the 1993 IROC event at Talladega Superspeedway, Steve Kinser—a legendary driver from the open-wheel World of Outlaws Series—got the hang of drafting and proceeded to beat all of the Winston Cup drivers, finding himself in victory lane in just his second IROC race.

Among the champions of this elite series are the late Mark Donohue, Bobby Unser, A.J. Foyt, Al Unser, Mario Andretti, Bobby Allison, Cale Yarborough, Harry Gant, Al Unser, Jr., Geoff Bodine, Terry Labonte, Dale Earnhardt, Rusty Wallace, Ricky Rudd, Davey Allison, and Mark Martin.

INTERNATIONAL SPEEDWAY CORPORATION (ISC)

A separate entity from NASCAR—although intimately tied in with the sanctioning body's activities—International Speedway Corporation was founded by Bill France, Sr., and operates several of the tracks visited by the Winston Cup Series.

Of course, the first tracks under ISC were the speedways constructed by Big Bill himself: Daytona International Speedway and Talladega Superspeedway. Darlington International Raceway was acquired by ISC in 1982, and the corporation owns a large stake in the road course at Watkins Glen.

In addition to the racetracks, ISC also owns and operates Motor Racing Network (MRN). MRN is the premier motorsports radio broadcasting organization, presenting award-winning coverage of NASCAR competition.

While the France family owns all of NASCAR, the family owns roughly half of the ISC stock. ISC itself also owns a 12 percent interest in Penske Motorsports, the Roger Penske–founded company that operates several speedways under its own banner. ISC's move to align itself with Penske was seen by many as a shoring up of defenses after Bruton Smith and his Speedway Motorsports firm began an active period of racetrack acquisition.

IRVAN, ERNIE

It's a long way from Modesto, California, to the NASCAR Winston Cup Series—but Ernie Irvan (born 1/13/59) had the faith in his own talents necessary to make the journey, becom-

One of NASCAR's primary goals is close competition between the various brands of stock cars, but in the IROC series there is just one brand. The cars are identical, constructed and prepared in a race shop facility located in New Jersey. When the world's best drivers get behind the wheels of the IROC cars, the racing is always close.

Ernie Irvan on aggressive driving and the criticism that can accompany it after being involved in a crash during the Daytona 500:

"It reaches us and it bothers me. It bothers you any time anybody thinks you did something wrong if you didn't. I really don't feel I did anything wrong at that moment. Aerodynamics takes a big effect during the race and it did in that incident. People who know racing and really watch racing will look at the playback on the TV and figure out what they think happened. Everybody sees things different. Some people are going to think it's my fault, some people think it's the other's fault. It's just one of them deals—we don't like people to think it's our fault. If it was then we'd get out and say, 'Hey, it's our fault and we shouldn't have been in that position,' but that was a time when we were just racing for the lead.

"It's one of them deals when you get in that position you've got to be ready for whatever could happen and with the air you just don't know exactly what's going to happen until you get in there. If you don't ever stick your nose there and try to find out what it's going to do then you're going to be a tenth- or fifteenth-place car. The guys who win are the guys who get in there and react to what happens and keep on going.

"People pay $50 for a ticket, knowing when they leave that race-track they really felt they saw a great race and I was part of it. That sort of thing really makes me satisfied knowing that whether they like me or don't like me, there's fans up there who are satisfied with the race and they come back the next year."

ing one of the most respected Winston Cup veterans in the process.

As it happened, the Charlotte hub of stock car racing did not welcome Irvan with open arms. After all, when he first arrived in Charlotte in the early 1980s, his racing work consisted of building grandstands at Charlotte Motor Speedway. That would soon change.

Irvan began racing in his native California at the wheels of go-karts before advancing to local track stock car racing while in his teens. His father, Vic Irvan, helped Ernie build cars and gave him guidance.

Once Ernie arrived in North Carolina, he concentrated on building a reputation, racing everywhere from dirt tracks to Concord Motor Speedway. His winning record paved the way for his first Winston Cup start, on September 13, 1987, at Richmond.

Irvan drove for car owner D.K. Ulrich in the 1988 and 1989 seasons as he gained Winston Cup experience, scoring four top tens in 1989. After starting 1990 with Junie Donlavey, Irvan joined the Virginia-based Morgan-McClure team. That summer, on an August night in Tennessee, Irvan won his first Winston Cup race after a thrilling battle with Rusty Wallace at Bristol's high-banked half-mile (804.5m) speedway.

That first win was just the beginning for Irvan. He started off 1991 in grand fashion by winning the Daytona 500, then raced hard all season to finish fifth in the Winston Cup points standings. Despite his success with the Morgan-McClure team—including a victory in the 1993 Winston 500 at Talladega—Irvan decided an opportunity to drive for famed engine builder Robert Yates was just too good

Ernie Irvan accepts congratulations after his first Winston Cup win, at Bristol, Tennessee, in 1990. Irvan struggled to make his mark in the Winston Cup Series, and at one time he was only able to race thanks to sponsorship obtained from fellow driver Dale Earnhardt.

to pass up. After twenty-one races of the 1993 season, he joined the Yates team and won twice in the nine races that finished out the year.

Irvan stormed through the 1994 season, gathering three victories and lurking just a few points behind Dale Earnhardt in the Winston Cup championship quest. Then, in a morning practice session leading up to the August Michigan race, Irvan's car slammed into the outside wall. The impact was devastating, and Irvan was not expected to survive the fractured skull and other injuries he suffered.

But Irvan battled back through a lengthy program of rehabilitation. On October 1, 1995, at North Wilkesboro, North Carolina, NASCAR fans saw what many had believed would never happen again—Ernie Irvan taking the green flag in a Winston Cup race. He finished sixth that day and proved he was back by leading much of the Phoenix race and coming home seventh at Atlanta. Ernie Irvan won twice in 1996, settling any doubts about his comeback once and for all, and won again in 1997 before leaving Yates' team at the end of the season.

Ernie Irvan's driving style is an aggressive one. In fact, at one point in his career, his fellow drivers considered his actions to be unsafe. At a drivers' meeting before a race at Talladega in August 1991, Irvan asked to be given another chance.

With his aggression tempered by experience, Irvan is a constant presence at the front of the Winston Cup field. And in an emotional victory on June 15, 1997, Ernie Irvan won a Winston Cup race at Michigan International Speedway—the very racetrack where Irvan had nearly died three years earlier.

ISAAC, BOBBY

Bobby Isaac (born 8/1/32, died 8/14/77) was a soft-spoken, shy North Carolina driver who

*Above: **By the time Irvan moved to the Thunderbirds of Robert Yates' team he was a proven winner.** Below: **Winning the Winston Cup championship is certainly a goal Irvan will strive to attain in the future—a goal reached by NASCAR legend Bobby Isaac (seen here behind the wheel) in 1970.***

"If a car could win, he'd be out there doing it. He didn't ask any favors or get any. He was a real racer. He let his actions do all of his talking. He wasn't a flamboyant person or a headline-seeker or anything like that. 'Hey, just let me go drive my race car.' That was the way he was.

"The publicity, my personal opinion is that he didn't care one way or the other about it, but he deserved everything he got and he was a hell of a driver. Of course, in those days they didn't have the corporate stuff like you do now, where you have to go out and meet and greet—he'd go absolutely crazy today."

was able to balance the need to take care of his equipment during a race with the aggression needed for victory in NASCAR's top series.

The Grand National champion of 1970, Isaac was a driver who enjoyed challenging the tracks he raced on as much as he enjoyed running up against the other drivers. That would help explain his exceptional record of starting fifty races as the fastest qualifier in the 308 total events he competed in.

Bobby Isaac's first victory came in 1964, as he wheeled the Chrysler factory-backed Dodge of Nichels Engineering to victory lane in one of the two 125-mile (201.1km) qualifying races for the Daytona 500. Isaac's went on to win thirty-six more times in his career. Bobby Isaac's best seasons came in 1969, when he won seventeen races, and in 1970, when he was victorious

Legends Bobby Isaac (left) and Curtis Turner in the North Carolina Motor Speedway garage area in 1966. Stock car racing lore often tells of the wild nights and practical jokes of the NASCAR drivers of days gone by. But racing demands intensity, and the look on Bobby Isaac's face shows that focus was as important then as it is now.

Ned Jarrett finds himself dealing with a treacherous loss of traction while racing in the World 600 at Charlotte Motor Speedway in 1965. Don Hume passes safely to the high side. Jarrett recovered from the spin but finished in twentieth place because of engine problems. Jarrett was back in victory lane in the next race on the Grand National schedule, however, and well on his way to the 1965 NASCAR championship.

eleven times on his way to winning the 1970 championship.

Isaac also set numerous records at the famed Bonneville Salt Flats in an assault on world land speed record marks. The record runs were masterminded by Isaac's crew chief, Harry Hyde, and many of the records set by Isaac in a winged Dodge Charger Daytona still stand to this day.

Bobby Isaac died after collapsing after a race in 1977 at a North Carolina short track.

JACKSON FAMILY

Leo Jackson (born 7/8/33) joined Harry Gant to dominate Winston Cup racing in September 1994. The North Carolina team owner engineered the cars and built the motors that Gant raced to four consecutive Winston Cup wins, earning Gant the title "Mr. September."

Jackson and Gant accounted for a total of nine Winston Cup wins between 1989 and 1994. Leo Jackson sold his team to crew chief Andy Petree at the end of the 1996 season.

Leo's brother, Richard (born 1934), started in racing with his brother and eventually wound up forming his own racing team in the Winston Cup Series. Beginning in 1985, the younger Jackson fielded cars for drivers including Benny Parsons and his brother, Phil, Terry Labonte, and Rick Mast. The team's first win—while still in partnership with Leo Jackson—came in 1988, when Phil Parsons won at Talladega in May. The team went on to gather five top-five finishes that season.

With Rick Mast behind the wheel, Richard Jackson's Thunderbird claimed the pole position as fastest qualifier in the inaugural Brickyard 400 in 1994.

JARRETT FAMILY

Ned Jarrett (retired, born 10/12/32) was one of the most popular drivers of NASCAR's early years of growth, and the two-time champion's

Dale Jarrett on the incredible heat inside modern Winston Cup stock cars:

"That's the biggest problem that we have today. There's only so much that you can do in there, and you have to understand going into it how hot it's going to be.

"On a very hot day when we get into the middle of summer, you're going to get temperatures of 125 to 130 degrees [52 to 54 degrees C] in there—and that's just the temperature inside the car. The floor pans get a lot hotter than that.

"More now than ever before, with the aerodynamics playing a part, we try to keep air out of the inside of the car. Any time you do that you're keeping the hot air in there longer and making everything hotter. The headers that we use go right up under the car; we have to get them so close to the floorboard because of the frame heights that we run. We've got to get the cars as low as we possibly can. Therefore, to keep the pipes from dragging you have to run them up close to the floor pan and that just makes things hotter."

is fifty wins. He was NASCAR champion in 1961 and 1965.

After retiring from competition, Jarrett went into speedway promoting and then became a popular broadcaster for CBS and ESPN stock car television coverage.

Ned Jarrett's two sons, Glenn (born 8/11/50) and Dale (born 11/26/56), both followed in their father's racing footsteps.

Glenn only started in ten Winston Cup events between 1978 and 1985, and was more active in the Busch Grand National Series. In recent years, Glenn has developed an interest in broadcasting.

Dale's career in Winston Cup has matured to the point that he is a threat to win any event he competes in. Seriously entering Winston Cup competition in 1987, it took Jarrett until 1991 to find his way to victory lane. When he did, driving a Thunderbird for the Wood Brothers team, it came after a thrilling side-by-side battle with Davey Allison at Michigan International Speedway.

After moving to the new team owned by former National Football League coach Joe

Second-generation drivers like Dale Jarrett often face pressure to live up to expectations, particularly when the footsteps that must be filled are as imposing as those of father Ned Jarrett. But with a career that already includes two Daytona 500 victories, Dale has ensured his own place in the record books.

reputation as a gentleman has carried over into his work as a broadcaster.

Ned began competing in NASCAR events in 1958, although it was 1959 before Jarrett became a regular presence on the circuit by winning his first two races in seventeen starts. Thereafter Jarrett won in each season he competed in, until going winless in 1966, the year of his retirement. Jarrett won fifteen races in 1964 and thirteen in 1965, and his career total

Gibbs, Jarrett won the 1993 Daytona 500, holding off a determined charge by Dale Earnhardt. Father Ned thrilled millions of viewers as he called the exciting finale for the CBS broadcast of the race.

In 1995, Jarrett moved to Robert Yates Racing, filling in for the injured Ernie Irvan and then driving for a new, second Yates team in 1996. In that season, he claimed a second Daytona 500 victory and won the third running

Left: *Ned Jarrett wears the latest in crash helmets as he makes a point to fellow driver Joe Weatherly in the 1960s.* Below: *Firesuits were yet to be developed in the 1960s, and drivers often raced in jeans and T-shirts. That made situations like Ned Jarrett's 1965 pit fire at Riverside both frightening and life-threatening. Fortunately, Jarrett was not injured in the incident.*

After substituting for the injured Ernie Irvan at Robert Yates Racing, Dale Jarrett was asked by Yates to drive for a second team that Yates was forming. Jarrett responded by winning the 1996 Daytona 500 in the new Ford team's very first outing. In 1997, Jarrett narrowly lost the Winston Cup champonship, finishing second in the points standings to Jeff Gordon.

of the Brickyard 400 to highlight his four wins for the year.

His consistent yet aggressive driving style has made Dale Jarrett a fan favorite among the drivers of the Winston Cup Series.

JOHNSON, JUNIOR

Junior Johnson (retired, born 6/28/31) is a living legend of NASCAR racing. Both during his relatively brief racing career and during his years as a top car owner, Johnson's name has become irrevocably linked with the sport of stock car racing.

Johnson's heritage in the hills of North Carolina stretches back to the days of moonshiners outrunning federal revenuers, and Johnson even spent a brief period incarcerated as a young man as a result of activities involving an illegal still.

But once Johnson turned his focus to racing, he did so with a vengeance. He was a driver known for being tough and aggressive, not someone to back down. His first starts came in 1953 and 1954, although it wasn't until 1955,

when he competed in thirty-six NASCAR races, that Johnson made his mark with five wins.

In 1966, after a handful of starts in the season, Johnson quit driving with fifty wins to his credit in NASCAR's top division. Johnson's winning percentage over those years translates to one win for every six races he competed in—an enviable figure. Among his most prestigious wins were the 1960 Daytona 500 and the 1960 World 600.

His retirement from driving meant only that Johnson had shifted his interests to preparing race cars for other drivers who would compete under the Junior Johnson & Associates banner. Prior to the end of his active NASCAR involvement in 1995, Junior Johnson's record as a car owner consisted of 140 victories logged in 838 starts. This total includes two Daytona 500 victories, three Firecracker 400 wins, eight wins at Charlotte, ten wins at Darlington, and five wins at Talladega.

Often having a contentious relationship with NASCAR, the outspoken Junior Johnson elected to sell his race team interests at the end of the 1995 season in order to devote more time to his family.

Left: *Disaster struck in the 1964 Southern 500 at Darlington when Junior Johnson, in car 27, spun and was hit by Bud Moore in the number 45 Plymouth. The back end of Johnson's car collapsed under the impact. Junior was fortunate that a fire did not erupt in the aftermath of the crash.* Below: *Horace Smith, Junior Johnson, and Bob Auman (left to right) look over Junior's engine prior to a 1965 race at Watkins Glen. Johnson retired from driving the next year.*

JONES, PARNELLI

Rufus Parnelli Jones (retired, born 8/12/33) may be best known for his racing exploits in open-wheel cars at the Indianapolis 500, but Parnelli competed in thirty-four Grand National (now Winston Cup) races over a fourteen-year period.

His first of four NASCAR wins came on August 4, 1957, on a makeshift road course at an airport in the state of Washington. He won once in 1958 on a dirt track in Sacramento, California, and again in 1959 at the Ascot track in Los Angeles. Parnelli's final NASCAR win came in 1967 in the only Grand National race he entered that season, at the Riverside International Raceway road course race in California.

KRANEFUSS, MICHAEL

In the early 1970s, the major automobile manufacturers, which had been allocating tremendous resources to motorsports, suddenly closed their checkbooks. The great factory-driven racing operations that had supplied NASCAR teams—Nichels Engineering for Chrysler and Holman-Moody for Ford—were faced with the prospect of scrambling for parts.

Michael Kranefuss joined Ford Motor Company as assistant manager of Ford of Germany's competitions department in 1968, just before Ford's big NASCAR withdrawal.

Kranefuss, a strong believer in the value of motorsports activity for an automotive manufacturer, rose through the company and in 1981 became head of Ford Special Vehicle Operations (SVO). At the time Kranefuss began his SVO efforts, Ford's racing program consisted of one single-car program in the IMSA series. By the time of his retirement at age fifty-

Alan Kulwicki on making the transition from racing in the ASA series to the NASCAR Winston Cup Series:

"There's definitely adjustments to be made both in the way you drive your cars and just an attitude in the way you've got to handle yourself. The cars are different because they're bigger and heavier than anything else out there and they're not necessarily the easiest cars to drive. There are a lot of IndyCar drivers and sprint car drivers who have come out and tried their hand at this who didn't do very well at it. So there is an adjustment to be made in that the cars are quite a bit different.

"And then you also have to adjust your thinking. You can't go in there and be cocky, or think, 'I'll be one of you in a couple of weeks,' because it's not that simple. You go from being a big fish in a small pond to a small fish in a big pond. You just try to come in and be humble, respect the people who are already there and have been successful, and just do the best you can. I was accepted pretty well and no one really gave me a hard time.

"There are certain guys I would look to for advice, but I mean when it was all over and done with I pretty much had to do what I thought was right for me. Maybe Bobby Allison was one of the guys I used to look to a little for advice, and you know I would talk to all the guys who I had raced against in ASA competition in the Midwest. Rusty Wallace or Mark Martin, all the guys who had been there a year or two before me."

four in 1994, Kranefuss had guided SVO to the point that Ford was the only auto manufacturer involved in all of the four leading formats of auto racing—CART IndyCar, Formula One, World Rally Championship, and NASCAR Winston Cup.

A frequent presence around the Winston Cup garage area during his SVO tenure, Kranefuss showed his interest in NASCAR was genuine by starting his own Winston Cup team with CART car owner Carl Haas under the Kranefuss-Haas banner.

KULWICKI, ALAN

Alan Kulwicki (born 12/14/54, died 4/1/93) was one of the most unusual drivers ever to compete in NASCAR's Winston Cup Series— and one of the most heroic.

After establishing a name for himself in the Midwest-based American Speed Association stock car competition, Kulwicki packed what few belongings he had onto a truck to make the move from Wisconsin to North Carolina in 1985. Before he could hit the road, though, the truck caught fire. But this did not deter Kulwicki, who lived by a determined creed that symbolized his entire career: "Never give up."

When he arrived in the South, Alan found all of the problems that confront any new driver who attempts to break into the Winston Cup Series. But Kulwicki faced even greater obstacles. His goal was not to impress a car owner in the hopes of gaining a ride—Alan was

Alan Kulwicki's dream was to establish a career in Winston Cup racing, and he overcame all obstacles to succeed. Kulwicki's first full season was in 1986, when the team raced a Thunderbird with minimal sponsorship and mostly volunteer crewmen—and still managed to finish twenty-first in the season-long points standings.

After one of the most exciting Winston Cup races in history, Alan Kulwicki proudly stands as the 1992 Winston Cup champion. At the season's final race at Atlanta Motor Speedway there was a three-way battle for the championship between Kulwicki, Davey Allison, and Bill Elliott. But when Allison crashed with Ernie Irvan, Kulwicki took advantage of the opportunity and led the most laps in the race, picking up a five-point bonus. Although Elliott eventually won the race, Kulwicki finished in second and won the championship over Elliott by just ten points.

determined that he would succeed as that rare breed in NASCAR, the owner-driver.

Armed with a valuable racing weapon—his engineering degree—Kulwicki set about assembling an underfunded team that campaigned Ford Thunderbirds. To say that the odds were against such an outfit succeeding would be an understatement, but Kulwicki and his underdog team succeeded anyway.

In 1987, Alan captured his first of twenty-four career poles. He backed that up with his first Winston Cup victory at Phoenix in 1989. The unconventional driver celebrated in an appropriate way by turning his car around and circling the track in reverse—a rite of victory Alan dubbed a "Polish Victory Lap."

Kulwicki's greatest season came in 1992, when he captured the Winston Cup Championship by ten points over Bill Elliott. Elliott was driving for Junior Johnson, the legendary car owner who had offered a ride to Kulwicki. Alan turned down the offer and was promptly considered crazy by many in the garage area. In an appropriate touch, the Thunderbird Alan drove to the championship at Atlanta had a special name on the front grille—"Underbird."

Alan Kulwicki and four others died on April 1, 1993, when their plane bound for the race in Bristol, Tennessee, crashed in the night. Drivers still honor Kulwicki's memory by driving their own Polish Victory Laps.

Joe Ruttman in car number 26 feels the pressure from Terry Labonte in number 44 in a race at the old Richmond Fairgrounds Raceway in 1986. Labonte had been crowned Winston Cup champion just two years earlier, but after the final race of the 1986 season the Texas driver was mired in twelfth place.

LABONTE FAMILY

Hailing from Corpus Christi, Texas, Terry Labonte (born 11/16/56) has firmly established the Labonte name as one of the most important in NASCAR's modern era—and his brother, Bobby (born 5/8/64), looks to continue that trend for years to come.

Terry began racing quarter-midget cars when he was younger than ten years old, then progressed up through the ranks of more powerful and faster race cars. When Terry entered the Winston Cup Series he did it in style, placing fourth at the treacherous Darlington track in his very first Winston Cup race in 1978.

The demands that Darlington places on a driver are met with the skills that Labonte has relied on through his entire career. Nicknamed "the Iceman," Terry races with a cool awareness of everything taking place around him. He is considered one of the smoothest of all drivers, taking care of his equipment and ensuring that he'll be in a position to win as the laps of each race wind down. It's this calculating approach that made Terry NASCAR's Winston Cup champion in 1984 and 1996.

Surprisingly, Terry has raced for only four different car owners in his nearly two decades of Winston Cup racing. His most disappointing period was the years from 1991 to 1993, when a second stint with owner Billy Hagan fell far short of the championship standards set with Hagan earlier in Terry's career. Some in the NASCAR world even suggested that Labonte had lost his edge, but his association with Rick Hendrick—one that has resulted in a second championship for Terry—proved the fallacy of that speculation.

Terry Labonte's consistency is shown by one other racing milestone in his career—in early 1996, Terry Labonte broke Richard Petty's record for the most consecutive Winston Cup starts, 513. Since then, Labonte has been setting a new record with every wave of the green flag to start a Winston Cup race.

Bobby Labonte followed his brother's path to Winston Cup, starting in quarter-midget racing and progressing to the Busch Grand National Series in 1990. He was champion of that division in 1991 and made the move to Winston Cup by running the entire season for Bill Davis in 1993, gathering six top-ten finishes as he fell just short of winning the Rookie of the Year honors claimed by Jeff Gordon.

Bobby's own style on the racetrack is similar to that of Terry's, with an emphasis on con-

Left: *One of the happiest moments for the Labonte family came in November 1996. Bobby Labonte holds the trophy for winning the final race of the season, while brother Terry celebrates clinching his second Winston Cup championship.* Below: *Elmo Langley never won a NASCAR championship, but he was a strong competitor in the early years of NASCAR. Langley later became a car owner and gave some of today's top drivers a chance to compete.*

sistency and being in a position to win at the end of the race.

When Bobby Labonte switched to the Winston Cup team owned by former National Football League coach Joe Gibbs in 1995, he was rewarded with his first win, a high-profile victory in the 600-mile (965.4km) event at Charlotte. Labonte further established himself by winning both of the 1995 races at Michigan. He capped off the 1996 season by winning the last race of the year at Atlanta—a victory made all the more fulfilling as brother Terry won the championship in the same race.

LANGLEY, ELMO

Although Elmo Langley (born 8/22/29, died 11/21/96) was known to millions of Winston Cup fans as the driver of the Winston Cup Series pace car throughout the 1990s, many were unaware of Langley's record as both a competitor and a car owner in the series.

Elmo began competing in NASCAR's top division in 1954, and he raced on a sporadic basis throughout the 1950s. By 1965, though, when he competed in thirty-four races, Langley was an established presence among the competitors of the day. In 1966, driving his own Ford, Langley won his first big NASCAR race in

Spartanburg, South Carolina, on June 4. Just a month later, Langley won again, this time at Old Dominion Speedway in Manassas, Virginia. Although Langley placed second three times in the 1971 season, he never won another Winston Cup Series race.

Elmo Langley on the changes he witnessed during his years involved with Winston Cup racing:

"The money falls out of the sky to these people now—the drivers and even the crew chiefs. Back then, a year fifth in points making $40,000 in a total year, well that was actually a pretty decent year. Now they make that in a race, more than that in one race.

"Of course, we had no major sponsors or corporations involved in it back then. Racing started to turn around when Winston got involved in it in the 1970s, and people saw what we were doing. More corporate sponsors came into racing. We used to have a garage or a restaurant or a parts house that would give you a little bit of money, but that was about all anybody had. I was always hard-headed—I was the kind who wanted to do it on my own. We used to run sixty races in a year, and I did it with just me, one person and a helper. Tow the car to the racetrack, work on it, get it ready, qualify it, run the race with it, and then come back home that night.

"A lot of those 100-mile races [160.9km] only paid $1,000 to win. When I won at Old Dominion, I won the race by five or six laps. I sat on the outside pole, Bobby Allison was on the pole. He tore a transmission up or something and I won the race—four hundred laps on a ⅜-mile [603.3m] asphalt that paid $1,100 to win! That's how much it was different then, in 1965.

"Now I don't guess anybody other than Bill France, Sr., ever envisioned what racing was going to come to—I know I never did. And it hasn't stopped—it's still in a growing stage. A lot of the tracks we'd run the 100-mile races at, if they had six or seven or eight thousand people that would be a big crowd. Now you get 100,000 people. It used to be a redneck sport, but now business people come to it and there's just about as many women as there are men who come to our races. It's just been a complete turnaround for us in the demographics of the fans."

In the late 1970s, he started fewer races in favor of letting other racers drive his cars. Among the young drivers who got a break into the Winston Cup Series at the wheel of one of Langley's stock cars was Ken Schrader.

Langley's cars last competed in Winston Cup racing in 1987, and Elmo went on to work for Winston Cup race teams until he was hired by NASCAR. Although best known as the pace car driver of the series, Elmo was a respected presence in the garage area and was often sought out for advice by race team members.

Elmo accompanied the NASCAR officials and race teams to the exhibition race held at the Suzuka Circuitland track in Japan in November 1996. While giving Buddy Baker a ride around the track in the pace car in the days before the race, Elmo Langley suffered a heart attack. Baker managed to bring the car safely to a stop and summoned help, but Langley never regained consciousness.

LITTLE, CHAD

Chad Little (born 4/29/63) has a profession to fall back on should he decide to end his Winston Cup career, for in addition to his racing experience the Washington State driver has a law degree. But judging by the tenacity with which Little has chased a Winston Cup career, he looks to be part of the Winston Cup Series for some time to come.

Little began racing in the Spokane area, eventually moving up to the NASCAR Winston West series in 1986. After winning Rookie of the Year honors in that first season, Little stepped up the pace and won the series cham-

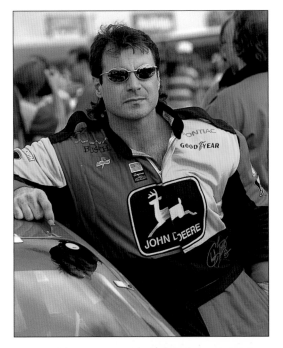

Chad Little offers a perspective on how the human body can react to a violent crash in stock car competition:

"I really don't have much of a memory of last Saturday. It's just one of those things associated with a concussion, that I'm going to have some memory loss. Some things are still kind of fuzzy—it seems like the wreck was a month ago, but it was just this past Saturday. But I remember things like going to the driver's meeting. I don't remember the race or making my first pit stop, or anything about the wreck.

"Really, the first thing I remember after the driver's meeting was being in the hospital. It's kind of strange how the mind works, but it's pretty much blocked out everything that happened so far. For the most part, it's all just blurry."

Opposite: *Driving the NASCAR pace car at Pocono International Raceway in 1995, Elmo Langley prepares to turn the Winston Cup cars loose for a 500-mile (804.5km) race.* Above: *Chad Little has survived several bad crashes in both Winston Cup and Busch Grand National competition.* Left: *When cars collide with walls as severely as in this 1996 crash involving Johnny Benson, it is a testament to the safety engineering of the driver compartments that injuries are rare.*

pionship in 1987. After a handful of starts for several owners from 1986 through 1989, Little fielded his own entries in 1990 and 1991 in forty-four starts. His efforts only resulted in one top ten finish, and Little moved to the Busch Grand National Series to regroup.

There, with a team owned by former Washington Redskins quarterback Mark Rypien, Little won six victories in 1995 and finished second in the championship standings. In 1997, Little returned with Rypien to the Winston Cup Series in the hopes of winning his first series race.

Then, late in 1997, team owner Jack Roush signed Chad Little to drive for one of his five teams during the 1998 season.

LORENZEN, FRED

Illinois' Fred Lorenzen (retired, born 12/30/34) became one of NASCAR's biggest stars in the 1960s, when he won twenty-six races between 1961 and 1967. In that time, Lorenzen—nicknamed "Golden Boy"—drove his Holman-Moody Fords to victories in the 1963 and 1965 World 600 races at Charlotte Motor Speedway and the 1965 Daytona 500. Seemingly at the peak of his career, Lorenzen unexpectedly retired from NASCAR competition in 1967.

But the lure of Winston Cup racing was too strong, and in May 1970 Lorenzen returned to the sport driving a winged Dodge Charger Daytona. Although he did come home with

Scenes from the return of Fred Lorenzen to NASCAR racing: the May 24, 1970, World 600 race at Charlotte Motor Speedway found Lorenzen driving a winged Dodge Charger Daytona to first place during the lengthy race. But engine failure eventually relegated Lorenzen to a twenty-fourth-place finish.

seven top-five finishes in the 1971 season, Lorenzen never won again in Winston Cup racing. He retired from competition once and for all in 1972.

LUND, TINY

Tiny Lund (born 3/3/36, died 8/17/75) was anything but tiny. A huge, imposing figure, Lund raced through NASCAR's top division and brought home five victories in 303 starts.

Lund's biggest NASCAR win was also his first, in the 1963 Daytona 500. Marvin Panch had been scheduled to drive the Wood Brothers Ford in the big race, but while testing a Maserati sports car at the track, Panch flipped the car. It burst into flames, and Tiny Lund was one of the people who rushed to the driver's aid. Too injured to drive in the Daytona 500, Panch asked the Wood Brothers to let Lund take his place. Lund won the race, narrowly beating Fred Lorenzen in the Holman-Moody Ford. The Wood Brothers figured out a way to make one fewer pit stop than the other competitors, and that was the margin of victory.

Tiny Lund died from severe chest injuries suffered in a terrible crash at the Talladega Superspeedway on August 17, 1975. After two years away from the sport, Lund was attempting a comeback to the Winston Cup Series.

MAKAR, JIMMY

Hailing from New Jersey, Jimmy Makar (born 3/24/56) moved to the South in 1977 to follow his dream of building a career in stock car racing. Now one of the best crew chiefs in Winston Cup racing, Makar has realized his dream.

He began to build the foundation for his current success by working as a mechanic for legendary names in NASCAR racing, including Harry Hyde, Buddy Parrott, and Junior Johnson. After working with crew chief Barry Dodson and driver Tim Richmond in 1985, Makar stayed with the team when Rusty Wallace became the driver. Highlights of the association include the 1989 Winston Cup championship and more than twenty victories.

When NFL coach Joe Gibbs decided to start his own Winston Cup team from scratch, the two most important components of his plan were driver Dale Jarrett and crew chief Jimmy Makar. Any crew chief will admit that building a team from the ground up is a daunting challenge, but Makar did an outstanding job for Gibbs beginning with the 1992 season. So com-

Left: *Long shadows are cast by the Fords of leader Tiny Lund, Fred Lorenzen, and Ned Jarrett as the 1963 Daytona 500 comes to a close. Lund won NASCAR's biggest race with an average speed of more then 151 mph (242.9km).* Below, left: *The personable Lund quickly became a fan favorite following his entry into NASCAR competition.* Below, right: *Crew chief Jimmy Makar has overseen the team of former Washington Redskins coach Joe Gibbs since its inception.*

petitive was the team that one year after it was formed Makar guided Jarrett to victory in the 1993 Daytona 500.

When Jarrett left the team in 1994, Jimmy Makar began an equally fruitful relationship with Bobby Labonte, guiding the young driver to his first Winston Cup win in the 600-mile (965.4km) race at Charlotte Motor Speedway in 1995. Labonte went on to win twice more that season, and Makar has helped the driver to the

It's a trip to victory lane for Dave Marcis at Talladega Superspeedway on August 8, 1976. Marcis passed Buddy Baker late in the race and then held on to win, benefiting from a fuel strategy devised by crew chief Harry Hyde. When Baker had to pit for more gas late in the race, Marcis' victory was assured.

top of the Winston Cup points standings in each successive season.

MARCIS, DAVE

Dave Marcis (born 3/1/41) has had one of the lengthiest Winston Cup careers—a fact illustrated by Marcis' habit of still racing in wing tips instead of high-tech racing shoes.

The Wisconsin-born driver became a short track champion in his native state, then first raced in Grand National competition in 1968. His first Winston Cup win came in 1975, driving for car owner Nord Krauskopf at Martinsville. Marcis went on to finish second in

the championship battle, with a season that saw him scoring more points than all the other Winston Cup drivers save Richard Petty.

Marcis won four more races thereafter, three of them coming in the 1976 season. Since starting his own race team, Marcis has gone winless, although he remains a fan favorite. One of the last of the independent drivers—accustomed to racing without the benefit of huge corporate sponsorships—Marcis has had to conserve his racing resources in recent years. Still, through the 1997 season Marcis had registered more than eight hundred Winston Cup starts, and rare is the race that he does not qualify for—often beating out far better-funded operations.

Marcis has been assisted with parts and equipment through his efforts in testing for the Richard Childress racing operations. His experience has further proved useful during his years as a lead test driver for the International Race of Champions series.

MARLIN FAMILY

Clifton "Coo Coo" Marlin (retired, born 1/3/32) began his Winston Cup career in 1966. The Tennessee driver was popular, although he never made the trip to victory lane in 165 starts through the 1980 season.

And for a long time, it looked as though Coo Coo's son, Sterling (born 6/30/57), just might suffer the same fate as a competitor. After gaining experience in short track racing in Tennessee, Sterling raced in ARCA competition and was late-model champion at the highly competitive Nashville Speedway in 1980, 1981, and 1982. Though Sterling competed in a handful of Winston Cup races between 1976 and 1982, his full-time entry to the series did not come until 1983, when he drove for Roger Hamby and won the Rookie of the Year title. But after that Sterling could only land part-time rides until he returned driving the entire 1987 season for Billy Hagan.

Marlin stuck it out with Hagan until the 1991 season, when Sterling switched to Junior Johnson's team. In 1993, he drove for the Stavola Brothers following his two years with Johnson. The end result of nearly two decades

of Winston Cup racing was no wins. But all that would change in 1994.

In his first race for Virginia's Morgan-McClure team, Sterling Marlin won his first Winston Cup race—the 1994 Daytona 500. Marlin held off a late charge by Ernie Irvan to win NASCAR's biggest race in a victory that was tremendously popular with race fans. Having developed a taste for victory, Marlin proceeded to win the 1995 Daytona 500 and

Above: *Coo Coo Marlin had a winless career in Winston Cup racing.*
Left: *His son, Sterling, suffered through a similar streak until he joined the Morgan-McClure race team. Sterling Marlin won two consecutive Daytona 500s at the wheel of the team's Chevrolets.*

Mark Martin after winning a Winston Cup Series race at Atlanta Motor Speedway:

"I was just waiting for something to go wrong today. When you get within six laps of winning one of these things—and they're so hard to win nowadays—and you've had a tire blow out like we have, you never think you're going to win one of these things until you do it. Man, I just didn't want anything to go wrong.

"After the race was over, I figured, 'Man, I sure don't want to mess up and give this thing away. I'll just take an extra lap to make sure they weren't mistaken about how many laps we'd run.' There's so much competition out there nowadays, you have to cherish every win you get."

Drivers in NASCAR's formative years were known for drinking and carousing. Mark Martin symbolizes the new breed of Winston Cup driver, aware of the importance of athletic conditioning to maintain endurance and concentration.

then won twice more that season, with two more wins coming in 1996. In late 1997, Marlin announced he would be moving to one of Felix Sabates' teams for a reunion with former Morgan-McClure crew chief Tony Glover.

Now a consistent threat to win any Winston Cup event, Sterling Marlin has added his family's name to the elite list of winners in NASCAR's most demanding division.

MARTIN, MARK

Tenacity is a good word to sum up Mark Martin (born 1/9/59), the NASCAR driver from Batesville, Arkansas, who first entered Winston Cup competition in 1981. Great success in the ASA series to back up high hopes for a successful NASCAR career didn't prevent Martin from getting the same rude awakening that greets many drivers beginning their careers in NASCAR's elite series. After three seasons of

mediocre success, Martin returned to his roots to regroup professionally.

When he returned to the Winston Cup Series full-time for team owner Jack Roush in 1988, it was with a renewed intensity. His first win came the next season, and in 1990 Martin finished behind Dale Earnhardt in the battle for the series championship by a scant twenty-six points. Since then, Martin has demonstrated his well-rounded abilities by winning on every type of track the Winston Cup Series races on. For the first time since 1988, Martin went winless for an entire season in 1996 but returned to victory lane by winning at both the Sears Point road course and at Talladega Superspeedway in May 1997. Martin finished third in the 1997 championship point standings.

Martin has also played a significant role in increasing NASCAR drivers' awareness of the need for athletic conditioning to successfully compete in modern Winston Cup racing. A devoted body builder, Martin authored a book on the importance of physical conditioning.

MARTINSVILLE SPEEDWAY

Martinsville Speedway, located in southern Virginia near the North Carolina border, typifies NASCAR's short track racing heritage. The historic track is only 0.526 mile (846.5m) in length, but in that short distance lies one of the more challenging tests of a driver's abilities.

This speedway is often described as being two drag strips separated by hairpin turns. Drivers rocket down the 800-foot (243.8m) straightaways, then must dramatically slow to make it through the exceptionally tight corners. Things are made more interesting by the fact that the straightaways are pavement while the corners are concrete.

Of all the variables in Winston Cup competition, at Martinsville there is one that is clearly more essential than the others: brakes. The cars approach 120 mph (193kph) on the straightaways, but an average lap speed is just more than 90 mph (144.8kph)—indicative of how much the cars must slow down to negotiate the turns. Conserving a stock car's brakes under competition at this track is difficult to do, but it is imperative. If a driver pushes his car too hard and wears his brakes out, he will find himself being passed as he is forced to reduce his overall speed to compensate for the lack of stopping power.

In all of the competition events since NASCAR racing began at Martinsville in 1949,

Richard Petty has won the most races of 200 miles (321.8km) or more, visiting victory lane fifteen times.

MAST, RICK

Virginia's Rick Mast (born 3/4/57) has been competing in the NASCAR Winston Cup Series since 1988.

His early interest in racing found young Mast trading a prize cow for his first race car; from that auspicious entry into motorsports Mast moved to the NASCAR Busch Grand National Series in 1984. Before moving up to begin his Winston Cup career, Mast won nine Busch Grand National races.

Although Mast had yet to win a Winston Cup race as the 1997 season got underway, he has demonstrated an ability to qualify well. His first pole came in 1992 in the last race of the season at Atlanta, and Mast was also fastest qualifier in the inaugural Brickyard 400 in 1994. His attitude and humor brought a much-needed note of levity to the pre-Brickyard onslaught of media coverage.

Mast nearly won the October 1994 race at Rockingham. He was passed late in the race by eventual winner Dale Earnhardt. After driving for Richard Jackson's team from 1991 through 1996, Mast moved to Butch Mock's Ford teams for 1997 in the hopes of scoring that elusive first victory.

MAYFIELD, JEREMY

As he grew up in Kentucky, Jeremy Mayfield (born 5/27/69) raced in a variety of classes, including go-karts, street stocks, and sportsman cars. In each series he excelled, and he moved up to ARCA stock car competition in 1993. The young driver proceeded to win Rookie of the Year honors with a season that included eight top-five finishes and ten top-tens.

His facility with the ARCA cars was noticed by legendary driver Cale Yarborough, who picked Mayfield to drive for his Winston Cup team in 1994. Mayfield helped improve the team's performance even as he learned the ropes of NASCAR's toughest division. In 1996 Mayfield had two top-five finishes.

Rick Mast's comments charmed hundreds of media members when he won the pole for the first Brickyard 400, in 1994, as the Virginia driver told a tale of how he traded a cow to buy his first race car.

Mark Martin on his opinion that Martinsville is the most challenging Winston Cup track:

"The one for me would have to be Martinsville, because you can only go as fast as your car will go and that's it. You can't drive hard like you can at other places and go faster than your car will go. You can't. I can't operate that way, because my car's not faster than everybody else's at Martinsville, and every time I try to hurry it up it doesn't do any good.

"If you just drive it as fast as it'll go and that's all you do is just drive it as whatever the car is capable of—I try to add something to my car. I try to take my car and add something to it. Instead of just taking it around the racetrack however fast it will go, I try to add something to that. But at Martinsville I don't have the knack to figure out what the car needs to be faster than everybody else. It doesn't come to me naturally like it does at some other places.

"It's the challenge of the narrow, sharp corners. It's not big and sweeping enough for where our sport is today, for thirty-five great race cars and drivers. It's too confining."

Late in the 1996 season, Mayfield moved to the Ford Thunderbird team formed by Michael Kranefuss and made several impressive runs to start off the 1997 season.

McCLURE, LARRY

One of the most successful NASCAR Winston Cup Series teams in recent years has been Morgan-McClure Motorsports from Abingdon, Virginia, formed by Larry McClure in 1983.

The team gave Mark Martin six starts in its first year of operation, then ran a full season in 1984 with Tommy Ellis, Lennie Pond, and Joe Ruttman all sharing the wheel. Others who drove during the formative years of McClure's team include A.J. Foyt, Rick Wilson, and Lake Speed. But it wasn't until the team hired Ernie Irvan that success became more frequent.

Irvan won his first race in his first year with the team after a thrilling battle with Rusty Wallace under the lights at Bristol in August 1990. Irvan got the 1991 season off to a good start for McClure by winning the Daytona 500, and he won once more that year. Irvan won again in 1993 but opted to leave Morgan-McClure to drive for Robert Yates, a spot that had become vacant in the wake of the aircraft accident that killed Davey Allison.

Morgan-McClure finished out 1993 with Jimmy Hensley, Joe Nemechek, and Jeff Purvis

The narrow turns of Martinsville Speedway play havoc with Winston Cup cars. Average speeds at the tight track are relatively low but the action is intense and contact between the cars frequent.

taking turns making Winston Cup starts. For 1994, though, McClure hired Sterling Marlin, a driver many felt was overdue to win his first race. Marlin justified McClure's faith by winning the team's very first race: the Daytona 500. For good measure, Marlin won the 1995 Daytona 500 as well.

The combination of Sterling Marlin and Morgan-McClure's superbly prepared stock cars has become one of the most potent in the Winston Cup Series.

McDUFFIE, J.D.

John Delphus McDuffie (born 12/5/38, died 8/11/91) set a Winston Cup record for futility— in 653 starts over a twenty-nine-year NASCAR career, McDuffie never made his way to victory lane. And during that time, he claimed only one pole position, when he was fastest qualifier at Dover Downs in 1978.

But J.D. McDuffie was a true fan favorite for his determination. Long after most Winston Cup drivers had accepted the necessity of major corporate sponsorship, McDuffie used what meager sponsorships he could scrape together to obtain enough parts to get his cars into the starting field of most races he entered.

J.D. McDuffie's career ended with his death at Watkins Glen in 1991, one of the few Winston Cup drivers to die in the modern era of competition. Entering the tight fifth turn, McDuffie's car suffered a suspension failure at nearly 170mph (273kph). McDuffie hit the wall with a violent impact and was killed instantly.

McGRIFF, HERSHEL

Rivaling Richard Petty in the length of his career, Oregon's Hershel McGriff (retired, born 12/14/27) competed in NASCAR from 1950 until his last Winston Cup start in 1993. Competing in a total of eighty-six races in NASCAR's top division, McGriff won four times—all in 1954.

Driving an Oldsmobile 88, McGriff's first NASCAR win came on August 22 at the San Mateo, California, track. Back east, he beat out Tim Flock and Lee Petty to win in Macon, Georgia, three weeks later. At the next race, held in Charlotte, McGriff got to the finish line ahead of Petty again, with Buck Baker taking third place. McGriff's hot streak in the last half of the season ended with a victory in the last race of the season, as he won out over Baker and Herb Thomas.

Above: *J.D. McDuffie was able to sustain a lengthy Winston Cup career without the benefit of a major corporate sponsor.* Left: *Today, though, much corporate support is necessary to be competitive, as evidenced by the numerous logos adorning the driving suit of Jeremy Mayfield in 1996.*

Although McGriff never again attained the level of success he had that one amazing ear, his active participation in many kinds of NASCAR competition continued for decades, particularly in the Winston West series, which races on the tracks in the western part of the United States.

McREYNOLDS, LARRY

Born in Alabama, a true hotbed of stock car racing, Larry McReynolds (born 1/10/59) turned an early love of motorsports competition into a career as a Winston Cup crew chief.

By the early 1980s, McReynolds had entered the world of NASCAR racing as a mechanic. As he worked through the ranks with such drivers as Neil Bonnett and Mark Martin, McReynolds caught the eye of drag racer Kenny Bernstein, who hired McReynolds in 1986 to be crew chief of the Winston Cup team he owned. Although the team had modest success in McReynolds' first two years calling the shots with drivers Joe Ruttman and Morgan Shepherd, it was in 1988 that McReynolds claimed his first win as a Winston Cup crew chief, when Ricky Rudd won for the team at Watkins Glen. The team won again with Rudd at the wheel in 1989, and then with Brett Bodine driving in 1990.

After starting the 1991 season with the Bernstein team, McReynolds was hired by Robert Yates to work with the tremendously talented Davey Allison. The result was five wins in 1991 and 1992 as McReynolds and Allison grew together. After a final win at Richmond in 1993, the Yates team suffered through the death of Davey Allison that summer. McReynolds was then faced with the challenge of building a winning relationship with new Yates driver Ernie Irvan.

In 1994, McReynolds oversaw three Irvan victories before Irvan was injured in a violent crash in Michigan. Dale Jarrett took over the car in Irvan's absence, winning at Pocono International Raceway in 1995. Irvan returned for two wins under McReynolds in 1996.

Larry McReynolds stunned the racing world when he announced that he would become Dale Earnhardt's crew chief for 1997,

moving from Yates' Ford team to Richard Childress' Chevrolet operation. Despite a rough beginning to the union, by midseason of 1997 McReynolds' meticulous preparation was beginning to show in Earnhardt's consistently strong finishes.

MELLING, HARRY

Melling Racing Enterprises became one of the best known Winston Cup teams when owner Harry Melling teamed up with an exciting young driver named Bill Elliott. Melling's stock cars made their way to the peaks of Winston Cup racing through the 1980s.

Melling first teamed up with Elliott's family-run operation for the 1982 season, when the new alliance got off to a solid start with eight top-five finishes. But the best was definitely yet to come.

Between 1983 and Elliott's departure from Melling Racing at the end of the 1994 season, the Melling Thunderbirds rolled to thirty-four victories. Elliott and Melling won the Winston Cup championship in 1988 and finished in the top five in the season-long points standings in every one of those years except 1989. In that season Elliott finished sixth—a position many drivers would be thrilled with.

In 1992 through 1994, Melling Racing suffered in the wake of Elliott's departure and competed in the Winston Cup Series on a part-time basis only. But by 1995, the Melling Thunderbirds were back, running the entire schedule with driver Lake Speed.

MICHIGAN INTERNATIONAL SPEEDWAY (MIS)

It's not very often that you will find almost all of the Winston Cup drivers in agreement about which track is their favorite to race on, but Michigan International Speedway is nearly always mentioned when the topic of good places to race is raised.

Located in Brooklyn, Michigan, this 2-mile (3.2km) rounded oval is close to the Detroit-area headquarters of the U.S. automobile manufacturers. As such, NASCAR drivers take pride in winning in front of the auto executives who often attend the Winston Cup events here.

Drivers love the Roger Penske–owned track because it's wide enough to race side by side on it all the way around. The straightaway banking of 12 degrees in the front and 5 degrees in the back gently blends into turns banked at 18 degrees—steep enough for average laps at speeds over 185 mph (297.6kph) but not so steep as to be jarring in the transition from straightaway to turn.

Crew chief Larry McReynolds on NASCAR's challenge to keep the Winston Cup cars from going airborne while still maintaining exciting competition:

"We try to look at it through their [NASCAR's] eyes as well. They've got a tough task in trying to slow these cars down, do it orderly, not hit one make harder than any other, make it a balanced situation, and also give the fans a good show as well.

"Yes, we all know they've got to slow down. Atlanta, Georgia—the cars go down there, they're probably running almost 195 mph [313.7kph] going into turn one. There's a set of grandstands sitting right there, and if one of these cars ends up in the grandstands this deal's over with.

"They're working feverishly trying to do things to keep the cars from flying when it flips around. That's the whole problem—to keep them from becoming airborne. NASCAR doesn't care how fast they run as long as they don't become airborne."

Safety is always a major concern during a NASCAR race, and as Larry McReynolds points out, airborne vehicles are a serious threat to that safety. This accident at Talladega on July 25, 1993, involving Neil Bonnett (31) and Ted Musgrave (55), actually damaged the catch fencing that protects the fans. Luckily, no spectators were hurt.

Since hosting its first stock car race in 1969, the Michigan International Speedway has been the site of memorable finishes in many of its events. One particular standout was the 1991 Champion 400, which saw Dale Jarrett capture his first Winston Cup win in a breathtaking battle with Davey Allison. The cars made contact numerous times and they vied for position in the closing laps, with Jarrett edging Allison by inches as the capacity crowd roared its approval.

Retired drivers David Pearson and Cale Yarborough hold the MIS records for most wins with nine and eight, respectively, though active driver Bill Elliott is closing in fast with seven wins through the 1997 season.

Richard Petty on racing before R.J. Reynolds' involvement moved the sport to the modern era:

"If we had to go back to it now it would be harder.... Now it's so much bigger a deal. We used to run a lot of 100-mile [160.9km] races, come sliding into town, come sliding into Philadelphia and run a race today and then load the thing on the truck and go up to Buffalo and run one tomorrow and stuff like that. Again, it's how you were geared up to take care of it.

"It was pretty serious because we were trying to make a living out of it, but it's pretty serious now because we're trying to make a living. I think the difference now is that you feel like you've got more pressure on you because you've got more sponsors, you've got bigger sponsors. Back then we didn't have STP, we just were doing our stuff on our own. Now we're obligated to some big people with big money to get the job done, and it's just different.

"The drivers now are no better than they've ever been. In other words, there have been some times when you come through and there's a lot of good drivers, and sometimes you come through and there's not. It'll always be that way.

"The difference now is the caliber of cars that the drivers drive. The cars are so much more competitive with each other now than...they used to be. You used to have six or eight really good teams and they won all the races. Now you've got six or eight teams that win all the races but you've got fifteen or twenty teams that are almost as good. They're not there, but they're almost as good. Then when one or two of them fall off that five or six then one of these picks up the pace. Before we didn't have anybody to pick up the pace."

MOCK, BUTCH

Starting with his own appearance in two Winston Cup races in 1978, Butch Mock (born 4/8/52) has been fielding NASCAR stock cars for twenty years—both in partnership with Bob Rahilly in the Rahmoc team and, since 1992, with his own Butch Mock Motorsports. After racing in two 1978 races, Mock concentrated on preparing stock cars for others to drive.

Mock's best seasons came during the Rahilly partnership years, when Neil Bonnett drove the team's cars to two wins each in the 1983 and 1988 seasons. Other notable Winston Cup drivers who have raced for Mock include Tim Richmond, Harry Gant, Kyle Petty, Joe Ruttman, Dave Marcis, Lake Speed, Morgan Shepherd, Phil Parsons, Dick Trickle, Todd Bodine, and Rick Mast.

MODERN ERA

The "modern era" of NASCAR Winston Cup racing is a distinct period in the sport's history.

When R.J. Reynolds teamed with NASCAR in 1971 to sponsor its top division of competition and financially reward the top twenty drivers of the season, only Grand National races of 250 miles (400km) or longer made up the Winston Cup Series. In 1972 the season schedule was shortened to eliminate the shorter races and all Grand National events became part of the Winston Cup Series. Richard Petty was the 1972 season champion, the first of NASCAR's modern era.

MOORE, BUD

Bud Moore (born 5/25/27) is a legend of NASCAR and of the Ford Motor Company's racing efforts. From his shops in Spartanburg, South Carolina, Bud Moore has fielded winners in NASCAR since his very first season.

Moore first entered NASCAR competition in 1961. Over the years, many of the legendary drivers—among them Joe Weatherly, Buddy Baker, Bobby Allison, Dale Earnhardt, Geoff Bodine, Ricky Rudd, and Morgan Shepherd—have logged seat time behind the wheels of Bud Moore Engineering's Fords.

In more than three decades of NASCAR racing, Moore's cars have won sixty-three times, capturing more than forty poles. He won the championship with Joe Weatherly in 1962

and 1963, and Bobby Allison drove a Bud Moore Ford to victory in the 1978 Daytona 500 —one of five wins for the team that season.

Not only is Bud Moore one of the most popular figures in the sport, but he was honored numerous times for his heroic actions in World War II. His racing contributions were recognized in 1997, when he and fellow long-time car owner Junie Donlavey were presented with the Bill France Award of Excellence, one of the sport's greatest honors.

MOROSO, ROB

Rob Moroso (born 9/28/68, died 9/30/90) seemed poised for tremendous Winston Cup stardom. The handsome Connecticut native

Ted Musgrave on the differences between racing on short tracks and superspeedways:

"Mentally, physically, there's a lot of things different. The only comparison I could say between racing at a place like Bristol and racing at Daytona, the only thing in comparison is that you're trying to win. There is a whole different style of driving, a whole different attitude of driving. Everything. Bristol is so short, so fast, so one-lane as far as traffic. Then you get to Talladega, run three or four wide, drafting comes into effect, fuel mileage is a factor—there's a whole different strategy and attitude. You have to change like going from AM to FM on the radio—you have to change from one to the other.

"On superspeedways, I guess the way you could put it in perspective is if you're flying in a commercial airliner. The airplane takes off, you're flying in the air and the plane moves around a little bit, but it's a slow-moving feeling. Take that airplane and crash it into the ground and you'll find out in reality how fast you're going.

"That's the same thing that you're seeing on TV, people looking at the in-car camera. Sure, the car's moving around a little bit because they're going so fast they're almost getting airborne—that's why they move. And it looks really smooth and slow. Well, that's only in relationship to the objects around you, which are the other race cars. You're only going about 1 mph [1.6kph] or 1½ mph [2.4kph] faster than the guy next to you. But in reality look at what's going on around you as the flagman goes flying by you and in a second you can't see him anymore. It looks easy, but I'll guarantee you it's not as easy as it looks!"

Top: **Rob Moroso won the Rookie of the Year title in 1990, but sadly it was awarded to him posthumously.** Right: **Ted Musgrave battled for Rookie of the Year honors with Bobby Hamilton in 1991, eventually losing to Hamilton by a handful of points.**

had great success in the Busch Grand National Series and moved to the top NASCAR division driving Oldsmobiles fielded by his father, Dick Moroso, in 1990.

The fact that young Moroso was just twenty-one years of age when he reached Winston Cup racing seemed to ensure that he had plenty of time to develop his considerable talent. But in the evening after racing at North Wilkesboro on September 30, Moroso had a few beers at a restaurant with his girlfriend and was involved in a highway accident in North Carolina on his way home. His car, traveling at a high rate of speed, went out of control and collided with another car. Moroso, who had turned twenty-two just days before, was killed, as was the driver of the other car. Moroso's girlfriend survived. Moroso was posthumously named Winston Cup Rookie of the Year.

The tragedy brought to a close a brief Winston Cup career—one that is remembered now for its unfulfilled promise.

MUSGRAVE, TED

The son of a racer, Ted Musgrave (born 12/18/55) is now a top Winston Cup driver.

Beginning his racing career on short tracks in his native state, Musgrave soon moved up to compete in the ASA stock car series. There, in 1987, his season's efforts netted him the Rookie of the Year title in the series.

After four seasons of learning the tracks of the Winston Cup Series, car owner Jack Roush—who had expanded his operation to a two-car team—called on Musgrave to drive his Thunderbirds. Since then, Musgrave has scored at least one top-five finish per season and has nearly won several Winston Cup events.

NATIONAL ASSOCIATION FOR STOCK CAR AUTO RACING (NASCAR)

The National Association for Stock Car Auto Racing (NASCAR) was founded by Bill France, Sr., at a meeting held in Daytona Beach, Florida, in December 1947. France realized that if stock car racing in the postwar era was to grow and prosper, it would require organization, and he summoned the top track promoters and other sport participants to the meeting.

The result of the meeting was the incorporation of NASCAR on February 21, 1948, with Bill France as president.

The success of the sport since then is truly remarkable. Annual attendance at NASCAR events is now more than 10 million people, and television viewership tops 120 million. The organization itself has more than fifty thousand members involved in a myriad of motorsports activities.

NASCAR now sanctions events at hundreds of racetracks across the United States in a dozen different divisions, topped by the Winston Cup Series. This premier division of stock car competition annually competes in more than thirty points races in a season that stretches from February's Daytona 500 into November. More than five million people annually attend Winston Cup events. These events have experienced the highest growth rate of any major league sport in the 1990s.

The current president of NASCAR is Bill France, Jr., who took over for his father in 1972. France has guided the sport into its profitable modern era through the presentation of exciting competition in a wholesome atmosphere.

The sponsorship logos of telecommunications corporations can be seen on Ted Musgrave's Ford Thunderbird as it races here in 1997. In the early years of NASCAR racing, sponsorship was more likely to come from a local garage or auto parts supply company.

NASCAR Winston Cup Series director Gary Nelson on his approach to policing a sport based on man interacting with machine:

"You have to look at our priority list. Obviously safety is number one and number two is close competition among various makes at the lowest cost to the team owners. So really what we're saying is, 'Yeah, there's a lot of technology out there, but it can be very expensive and it can upset the balance of competition.'

"So the number two thing, close competition, is constantly reminding us, 'Don't let the technology get too lopsided or too expensive for the owner.' That's become quite a problem when the auto manufacturers are pretty much technology-oriented. It's mostly engineers who are coming out of Detroit and working with these teams. So we've got a lot of areas that they can improve and work on, but we've restricted some areas completely like the computer technology or black boxes or on-board processors. By doing that it's made our job a lot easier.

"I look at [Ford and General Motors] like two equally matched boxers trading punches. One's on top for awhile, then the other, and then for awhile they're just even. So when you look at the whole season this year and you go back several years then you can see those patterns, the cycles, and it really is something that cycles up and down. So we look at it as it doesn't matter what cycle we're in, we're going to hear something from somebody.

"When you look at the win column and you see Ford winning a lot, but then you look at second and third and you see a General Motors car right there every week, how much help do they need? The fans may look at it as a win only and line up consecutive wins and say, 'Oh, this balance is off,' but all it would take is just an ounce of something and that one guy who's been up there consistently is going to win. Then Ford starts finishing second and it's the next cycle."

NELSON, GARY

In 1992, with NASCAR facing the retirement of Winston Cup Series director Dick Beaty, the sanctioning body turned to a surprising choice for a replacement—crew chief Gary Nelson.

Nelson had worked for several teams as crew chief, guiding his drivers to twenty-one wins, sixteen of which were with Bobby Allison driving. But in addition to his winning reputation as a crew chief, some suspected Nelson of developing intriguing and illegal "modifications" in his stock cars. In fact, in a 1988 article in *Grand National Illustrated,* Nelson created quite a stir when he openly discussed such items as a carefully hidden 5-gallon (18.9L) fuel tank and the release of buckshot hidden in a car's frame to lighten it after it is weighed in the prerace inspection.

NASCAR correctly figured the best way to make sure cheating came to a stop in the Winston Cup garage area was to hire somebody who knew all the tricks. So after a year spent working with Beaty, in 1993 Gary Nelson became the Winston Cup Series director. Nelson is credited with improving the inspection process to the point where it is extremely difficult for any rule bending to take place.

NEMECHEK, JOE

Joe Nemechek (born 9/26/63) brought immaculate credentials with him as he began his Winston Cup career in 1993.

The Florida driver first entered Busch Grand National competition in 1990 after gaining motorsports experience as a motorcross driver. Nemechek was named Rookie of the Year

"The new drivers are hungry. We have to do good. It's not a situation where we have long-term contracts. We want to win races and win poles as fastest qualifier.

"I'm a full-blooded racer. That's all I eat, sleep or drink. Whether it be in a Busch car or Winston Cup car, racing is what I want to do. I hope I can do it forever. For me to be able to live a dream, tickles me pink. There's no room for error, and if you make a mistake, there's no telling what it'll cost you."

Opposite: **NASCAR inspectors are seen here using templates to ensure that the car bodies are legal for NASCAR competition.** Far left: **Gary Nelson oversees the NASCAR inspection team.** Left: **Joe Nemechek showed great strength in qualifying with his Winston Cup car in 1997, but he also won an emotional victory in the Busch Grand National Series race at Homestead, Florida, in November—the track where his brother had died earlier in the year.**

in the Busch Series and won the series championship in 1992.

After driving for Larry Hedrick in 1994, Nemechek raced as an owner-driver with his own team in 1995 and 1996. But the pressures of ownership while trying to maintain a competitive edge grew too great, and after the 1996 season Nemechek sold his team to Felix Sabates. Nemechek began the 1997 season driving for the team and Sabates.

Joe Nemechek still competes in occasional Busch Series races. In May 1997, he scored an emotional win in the high-profile Grand National race at Charlotte Motor Speedway—a race Nemechek dedicated to his brother, John, who was killed just weeks before in NASCAR SuperTruck competition.

Nemechek also qualified on the pole at the inaugural race at California Speedway in June 1997.

NEW HAMPSHIRE INTERNATIONAL SPEEDWAY (NHIS)

Key to the Winston Cup Series' expansion in the 1990s was the ability to break into new markets. The New England area was one such market ripe for a date with NASCAR's elite series, and in 1993 New Hampshire International Speedway (NHIS) hosted its first Winston Cup race.

NHIS owner Bob Bahre had built a beautiful 1.058-mile (1.7km) oval in Loudon, New

Hampshire, and impressed NASCAR with how smoothly everything went when he hosted Busch Grand National races to christen the new facility in the early 1990s. The amenities for the race fans were first-rate, and the drivers enjoyed competing on the track, which features relatively shallow 12-degree banking in its turns.

When a Winston Cup race was announced for the 1993 season, New England fans showed their interest by making the race an immediate sellout. Rusty Wallace won the inaugural event, held on July 11, 1993, leading Mark Martin and Davey Allison to the checkered flag in what was to be Allison's final race. The son of former NASCAR champion Bobby Allison died the next week in a helicopter crash at Talladega.

Bob Bahre built the beautiful New Hampshire International Speedway with no guarantee from NASCAR that they would ever run the Winston Cup Series at the track. But NASCAR was so impressed with both the facility and the manner in which Bahre operated his track that the Winston Cup cars now make two visits per season.

NICHELS ENGINEERING

In the 1960s, Ford and Chrysler waged war on the racetracks of NASCAR, battling for supremacy in the belief that the phrase "Win on Sunday, sell on Monday" was a true reflection of the automotive sales market. As such, each of the automotive giants funneled huge amounts of money, labor, and equipment into NASCAR's top division during this time period.

While Ford's base of NASCAR activities was the Holman-Moody shops in Charlotte, North Carolina, Chrysler's racing center was in Indiana at Nichels Engineering.

Founded by Ray Nichels, who had been a NASCAR car owner as early as 1957, Nichels Engineering acted as a clearinghouse for Chrylser's competition parts. For example, when Chrysler developed the aerodynamic Dodge Charger Daytona to replace the Charger 500 in 1969, all of the sleek nosepieces and

wings necessary to convert the 500 to the new model were distributed through the Nichels Engineering shop to race teams running Chrysler product.

In NASCAR competition, Nichels' drivers included Cotton Owens, Darel Dieringer, Paul Goldsmith, Bobby Isaac, Charlie Glotzbach, Fred Lorenzen, and David Pearson.

NORTH CAROLINA MOTOR SPEEDWAY

North Carolina Motor Speedway (NCMS) in Rockingham, North Carolina, is one of Winston Cup racing's most unpretentious facilities. Despite the construction of a brand-new garage area in 1996 and other refinements, "the Rock" has a feel that complements its rustic location in the North Carolina Sand Hills region. It's an

nearly half the races he started during those years. Cale Yarborough is runner-up to Petty in the win-total category, with seven victories.

NORTH WILKESBORO SPEEDWAY

North Wilkesboro Speedway, a picturesque track located in the North Carolina town of the same name, is now notable not so much for its long history of NASCAR racing but because it fell victim to the greed and infighting that have occasionally characterized NASCAR's explosive growth in the 1990s.

Since its start as a host to longer NASCAR races, with a 200-mile (321.8km) event in 1961, North Wilkesboro epitomized the excitement of short track racing. Although the race cars themselves became more sophisticated as the years passed, the 0.625-mile (1km) racetrack remained a direct link to NASCAR's past.

But in 1996, the speedway was copurchased by Bruton Smith, head of Charlotte's Speedway Motorsports empire, and Bob Bahre, owner of New Hampshire International Speedway. Smith and Bahre bought their shares in North Wilkesboro for one reason: to get control of the track's Winston Cup dates. With NASCAR's approval, Smith moved the spring North Wilkesboro date to give his new Texas Motor Speedway a Winston Cup race for 1997, while Bahre awarded his New Hampshire track a second Winston Cup date.

Those moves were expected, as speculation had long centered on the possibility of tiny North Wilkesboro losing its dates as NASCAR expanded to new markets. But after Jeff Gordon won the final Winston Cup race at North Wilkesboro in September 1996, Bahre and Smith each refused to sell his half-interest in the track to the other man. By 1997, North Wilkesboro was slowly falling into disrepair, a sad fate for one of the very first tracks the Winston Cup Series ever competed on.

atmosphere that calls to mind the sport's early days, when the focus was on race cars battling on the speedway rather than corporate sponsorships and luxury boxes.

The 1.017-mile (1.6km) oval has hosted NASCAR events since Curtis Turner's 1965 win in the American 500, and has been in its current configuration—with turns banked at 22 degrees in one and two and 25 degrees through three and four—since 1969. The difference in banking, similar to Darlington's speedway, keeps drivers chasing the optimal setup for their race cars. Lap speeds approaching 160 mph (257.4kph) ensure they'll have their hands full during an afternoon at NCMS.

If anyone has mastered NCMS, it is Richard Petty. "The King" drove to victory lane eleven times during his career at the Rock, winning ten of those events between 1967 and 1979. With two races per season, Petty won

OWENS, COTTON

Born in South Carolina, Cotton Owens (retired, born 5/21/24) was one of the most prominent figures in NASCAR's early years. In just 160 career starts between 1950 and 1964, Owens had nine wins and eighteen second-place finishes.

Cotton Owens is seen here ready to race. Drivers of the modern NASCAR era would be horrified at the lack of protection afforded by Owens' clothing and primitive crash helmet. But in Owens' time, racing equipped with such gear was the norm.

Owens' best season came in 1964. In early March, he won at the dirt track in Spartanburg, South Carolina, holding off young Richard Petty after Junior Johnson's lead evaporated due to equipment problems. The same scenario played out in Hillsboro, North Carolina, a month later—leader Johnson ran into mechanical problems, Owens won the race, and Petty came in second. Less than three weeks later, Owens won in Columbia, South Carolina, this time beating out Ned Jarrett and Emanuel "Golden Greek" Zervakis. At the same track on July 20, Cotton led the way again, with Jim Paschal and Jarrett following Owens' Pontiac to the finish line.

In 1963, Owens—no fan of racing on pavement—started only one race. In 1964, he came back to run in two races on dirt. He won his first start, in Richmond, Virginia, on September 14, and less than a week later he placed second to Jarrett in Hillsboro, North Carolina. It was an impressive way for Cotton Owens to end his NASCAR driving career.

Owens' association with NASCAR continued as he became a successful car owner, fielding entries for drivers including David Pearson, Buddy Baker, Darel Dieringer, Charlie Glotzbach, and Pete Hamilton. His most successful year came in 1966, when his Dodges were wheeled by Pearson to fifteen victories and the series championship.

PAGAN, EDDIE

West Coast driver Eddie Pagan (born 8/1/18, died 8/1/84) competed in selected events in the early years of NASCAR. His best season was in 1957, when he won three races in Oregon and California out of a total of fifteen starts for the year. Pagan's last NASCAR entry came in the 1963 season.

PANCH, MARVIN

One of NASCAR's earliest stars, Marvin Panch (retired, born 5/28/26) was a consistent winner in stock car competition in the 1950s and 1960s. Out of 216 career starts between 1951 and 1966, Panch put his car in victory lane seventeen times.

Driving for Smokey Yunick in a Pontiac, Panch won the third running of NASCAR's biggest race, the Daytona 500, in 1961. His Yunick teammate, Fireball Roberts, appeared to have the race won until mechanical problems sidelined his Pontiac. Panch took over and was never challenged.

Panch's last win also came in one of NASCAR's most prestigious races, the World 600 at Charlotte Motor Speedway. Entering the 1966 running of NASCAR's longest race, Panch had been participating in a boycott mandated by the factory-backed Ford teams over NASCAR's rules of competition. But when Lee Petty offered Panch a Petty Enterprises Plymouth to race in for the Charlotte event, Panch did not hesitate to accept. He then made the most of the opportunity. Richard Petty drove Panch's car in the final laps in relief of Panch, who found that the seat in his car was aggravating an injury sustained in competition at Daytona several years before.

PARROTT, BUDDY

One of the most enduring crew chiefs of the NASCAR Winston Cup Series, Buddy Parrott (born 11/24/39) has been involved in racing for more than twenty-five years.

After first getting involved with stock car racing by working with racing tire supplier Goodyear, Parrott took an opportunity to work on the 1970 championship Winston Cup team

anchored by driver Bobby Isaac and crew chief Harry Hyde.

Five years later, working with driver Ferrell Harris, Buddy Parrott tried his hand as crew chief in a handful of races in 1975 and 1976. Parrott soon moved on and up through the Winston Cup ranks, guiding Darrell Waltrip to victories with the DiGard team from 1977 to 1980. Parrott's reputation as a winning crew chief was assured through Waltrip's twenty-one wins in that four-year span.

Parrott's next major accomplishment came as crew chief for Richard Petty in 1984, as he helped "the King" to his 199th and 200th wins in Winston Cup competition. Petty's win at Daytona International Speedway was to be his last in NASCAR competition.

In 1990, as crew chief for Derrike Cope, Parrott made a daring call to not change tires on the last pit stop of the Daytona 500. When Dale Earnhardt suffered a tire failure on the final lap, Cope was in position and won his first race in NASCAR's biggest event. The team won again later in the season in Dover, Delaware, proving that Daytona had been more skill than luck.

The value of Parrott's experience was shown once again when he joined driver Rusty Wallace in sweeping to ten wins in 1993 and eight in 1994.

After working with Steve Grissom in 1995, Buddy Parrott began working with another

bright young talent, Jeff Burton, in 1996. Parrott and Burton, running a Thunderbird for Jack Roush, raced hard but smart in the 1997 inaugural race at Texas Motor Speedway for Burton's first NASCAR Winston Cup win.

Right: *Todd Parrott took big strides toward creating his own legend when he led a brand-new Robert Yates Racing team to victory in the 1996 Daytona 500.* Below: *Benny Parsons in victory lane at Ontario Motor Speedway after winning the 1979 Los Angeles Times 500. Parsons won the same event a year later, after which the California speedway was closed.*

PARROTT, TODD

Displaying much of the same talent that has made his father a legendary Winston Cup crew chief, Todd Parrott (born 2/9/64) has made a dramatic entrance into the ranks of the NASCAR crew chief fraternity.

As a mechanic and chassis specialist, Parrott spent seventeen years learning the ins and outs of Winston Cup racing. During that time, he worked with a roster of drivers that includes Darrell Waltrip, Joe Ruttman, Morgan Shepherd, Richard Petty, Tim Richmond, and Rusty Wallace. While with Wallace, Parrott watched his father, Buddy, lead the team to seasons of ten and eight wins in 1993 and 1994, respectively.

In October 1995, the younger Parrott joined the Robert Yates race team, becoming crew chief for the 1996 season for Yates' new second stock car team. With the experienced Dale Jarrett at the wheel, Parrott wasted no time in making the most of his first opportunity to act as crew chief. The brand-new team won the 1996 Daytona 500 to get the season off to a tremendous start.

But Todd Parrott's Daytona 500 victory was just the beginning for the team. Jarrett's Thunderbird took the checkered flag first in the 600-mile (965.4km) race at Charlotte Motor Speedway, the Brickyard 400 at Indianapolis Motor Speedway, and the Goodwrench 400 in Michigan. By any standards, a season-ending third place in the championship points battle is a great accomplishment; that Todd Parrott achieved this success with a new team is even more remarkable.

PARSONS, BENNY

One of stock car racing's most popular television commentators, 1973 NASCAR Winston Cup champion Benny Parsons (retired, born 7/12/41) knows the sport he covers very well.

The North Carolina driver first tried his hand in NASCAR's top division in 1964 with one start in competition and in 1969 with four. Then in 1970 the young driver ran in all the events. One second-place finish to cap off an impressive twelve top-fives in his rookie season provided proof that Parsons had the necessary talent to succeed in Winston Cup racing.

Parsons' first win, driving a Ford for car owner L.G. DeWitt, came on the short track at South Boston, Virginia. But Parsons ran strong the entire season, finishing eleventh in the points standings. Parsons went winless in 1972, although the team climbed to fifth in the cham-

pionship standings, running near the front of the field all season long after switching from Ford to Mercury.

In 1973, the DeWitt team switched to Chevrolets, and although Parsons did not win until the July race in Bristol, Tennessee, consistency paid off for Benny as he won the championship by fewer than seventy points over Cale Yarborough.

After claiming his championship, Parsons went on to win nineteen more times for a total of twenty-one Winston Cup victories. Among those wins came high-profile victories in the 1975 Daytona 500 and the 1980 World 600 at Charlotte.

PASCHAL, JIM

Jim Paschal (retired, born 12/5/26) was one of the few drivers to build a racing career after competing in NASCAR's historic first Strictly Stock race. Paschal finished the June 19, 1949, race in Charlotte in twenty-third place. Over a period of decades, the Strictly Stock division became the Grand National division and then the Winston Cup division—and Jim Paschal raced through it all during a career that lasted until 1972.

In 422 NASCAR starts over twenty-three years, Paschal won twenty-five races. Among those were two victories in NASCAR's longest race, the World 600 at Charlotte Motor Speedway. Paschal's first win in the 600—dri-

ving a Plymouth as part of a two-car team with Richard Petty—came in 1964, in a race that was marred by the terrible crash that resulted in the death of Fireball Roberts.

Paschal barely escaped with his second victory in the 600-mile (965.4km) classic of 1967. Again driving a Plymouth, Paschal had a three-lap lead as the four-and-a-half-hour race finally neared its conclusion. But suddenly Paschal's stock car drifted up high—and into the wall. Paschal managed to regain control and made it to the pits while the caution flag flew. His car was repaired, but the three-lap lead was gone. In a stunning display of driving talent, Jim Paschal held off determined charges by both David Pearson and Bobby Allison to win his second World 600.

PEARSON, DAVID

Legend status is freely given in the world of stock car racing, but South Carolina's David Pearson (retired, born 12/22/34) is truly deserving of the title.

How legendary were Pearson's feats on the racetracks of NASCAR's Winston Cup Series?

*Left: **Jim Paschal is victorious in 1967 after winning NASCAR's longest race, the World 600, at Charlotte Motor Speedway. Paschal hit the wall during the race and lost a three-lap lead, but managed to hang on for the win.** Below: **David Pearson at the wheel of the famous Holman-Moody Ford. Any NASCAR Grand National driver of that era would have a smile as big as Pearson's if he, too, was driving for Ford's top team.***

David Pearson looks over the damage to the Wood Brothers' Mercury he drove in the 1976 Daytona 500. It's rare to see a car with this much damage in victory lane, but Pearson's focus in the race gave him the win in one of NASCAR's wildest finishes.

for 1966 after a season that featured fifteen wins. A relatively poor showing in 1967—with just two wins—was followed by another championship in 1968, a season that found Pearson in victory lane sixteen times after moving to the Holman-Moody Ford team. In 1969, Pearson won eleven times with forty-two top-five finishes on his way to a second consecutive championship.

By the time he climbed out of a Winston Cup stock car for the final time, after his last race in 1986, Pearson had won the World 600 at Charlotte three times, the Southern 500 at Darlington three times, three consecutive Winston 500 races at Talladega, and one Daytona 500.

Pearson's intelligence as a driver, his skill, and his craftiness are held in the highest of esteem. Perhaps in no other race were his talents more visible than in the Daytona 500 in 1976. Pearson had maneuvered his Wood Brothers Mercury to the front of the field and rode just behind race leader Richard Petty as the cars took the white flag to begin the final lap. Pearson got by Petty on the back straightaway, but Petty battled back. Side by side out of turn four, the cars streaked for the finish line—until they made contact and crashed. Both heavily damaged cars slid across the infield grass to a stop. But in the midst of the chaos, Pearson had the presence of mind to keep his motor running. David Pearson eased his damaged car into gear and won the Daytona 500.

The answer can be found in his win total, which is second only to Richard Petty's. In the 574 starts of his career, David Pearson won 105 times. He placed second eighty-nine times and third forty-nine times, and was fastest qualifier in 113 of the races he competed in.

Pearson first competed in the Grand National division in 1960, winning the Rookie of the Year title for racing in twenty-two events and coming close to winning with a season-best second-place showing. Proving he had the hang of NASCAR competition in 1961, Pearson won his first race in a Pontiac in the grueling World 600. He won the summer race at Daytona weeks later and capped off the season by winning in Atlanta in September. In just his second season, Pearson stood thirteenth in the final tally of championship points.

It did not take Pearson long to reach the championship. After mounting a charge that led to eight wins in 1964 and two more in 1965, David Pearson was crowned series champion

PEMBERTON, ROBIN

Rusty Wallace could be forgiven for feeling nervous when crew chief Buddy Parrott left his team after the 1994 season. After all, Parrott helped Wallace to eighteen wins in 1993 and 1994. Fortunately for Wallace, he was able to secure the talents of crew chief Robin Pemberton (born 8/15/56) to replace Parrott.

After working through the Winston Cup ranks with Bobby Allison, Neil Bonnett, and Mark Martin, Pemberton spent 1992 and 1993 with the Felix Sabates team and driver Kyle Petty. Although the team won three races in the two seasons, dissatisfaction among the parties led to Pemberton ending his association with the Sabates operation.

A brief period of employment with Roush Racing and the Ted Musgrave–driven Thunderbird preceded Pemberton's move to the Rusty Wallace team for the 1995 season. Pemberton led the Roger Penske–owned team to two wins in his first season, then more than doubled that tally for 1996 when Wallace won five Winston Cup races.

PENSKE, ROGER

After having been involved in NASCAR Winston Cup racing throughout the 1970s, Roger Penske (born 1937) returned to NASCAR activities in 1991 to begin a new venture with driver Rusty Wallace.

Penske has built a tremendous business empire in fields ranging from truck leasing to automotive retail centers to the development of new diesel propulsion technology. But despite his obvious business acumen, when Penske first became involved with Winston Cup ownership it was as a definite underdog, at least from the viewpoint of the car the team used—American Motors Corporation's Matador.

Still, Penske and his team—with drivers Mark Donohue, Dave Marcis, Gary Bettenhausen, and Bobby Allison—coaxed the Matador to five wins from 1972 to 1976. And before leaving Winston Cup racing, Penske fielded a Chevrolet in two races in the 1980 season for a young driver named Rusty Wallace, who drove the car to second- and fourteenth-place finishes.

When Penske began his second venture with Wallace, in 1991, the vehicle of choice was a more common one than the old Matador: the Pontiac Grand Prix, which the team used from 1991 to 1993. They switched to the Ford Thunderbird in 1994. But as one might expect from someone of Penske's motorsports stature, the bottom line using both models was a string of successful seasons.

In 1993 the team scored ten Winston Cup victories, and eight more in 1994. That's a good indication of the strength of the Penske organization, for 1993 was spent racing Pontiacs while 1994 marked the transition to Fords. For most team's, a model switch can be extremely difficult, but Penske and Wallace picked up right where they had left off. Although the team's win total dropped to two in 1995, five in 1996, and one in 1997, Penske and Wallace were expected to become championship contenders in 1998 with the new Ford Taurus–bodied stock cars.

PENSKE MOTORSPORTS

Roger Penske has always been known for his sharp business sense. The former competitor

and owner of Winston Cup and IndyCar teams has built a tremendous business empire ranging from trucking operations to manufacturing. Penske also owns the Michigan International Speedway and a smaller track in Nazareth, Pennsylvania, that hosts NASCAR Busch Grand National races.

So when Penske saw the success that fellow track owner Bruton Smith had with the public stock offering of Smith's Speedway Motorsports, it was just good business for Penske to follow suit with a similar operation. The result was Penske Motorsports.

Penske Motorsports is based on the Roger Penske racing empire, which includes not only the Michigan and Nazareth tracks, but the 2-mile (3.2km) California Speedway that opened in 1997 (the first new superspeedway in California since Ontario Motor Speedway ended its decade-long existence in 1980).

When a substantial interest in North Carolina Motor Speedway became available in 1997, Penske Motorsports outbid Smith's Speedway Motorsports for it. As a result, NCMS will in all likelihood continue to host Winston Cup races. Had Smith won out, specu-

Crew chief Robin Pemberton and driver Rusty Wallace on top of their race car transporter. The "hauler" serves as each team's headquarters in the garage area during a race weekend, and the view from the top provides a place from which to observe how well other competitors are running in practice.

Young Roger Penske built a reputation as a sports car driver, but soon after this photograph was taken in 1962 he turned his interests to building a business empire. But Penske never lost his interest in motorsports, and has been a team owner in numerous series.

racing, and by age sixteen Andy was working as a mechanic for local racers. When he built a short track car during his early exposure to motorsports, it was driven by a young man who also aspired to make Winston Cup racing his career, Dale Jarrett.

Working for Junior Johnson in 1981, Petree was able to take part in a Winston Cup championship season as Darrell Waltrip captured the series title. In 1982, Petree began an association with Leo Jackson, and as the Jackson team moved more solidly into Winston Cup competition, Petree came along as crew chief.

Phil Parsons drove the team car to Petree's first win as a crew chief in NASCAR's top division, capturing victory at Talladega Superspeedway in 1988. Working with Harry Gant as the Jackson driver from 1989 to 1992, Petree led the team to nine wins, including an amazing four wins in a row in 1991.

In 1993, Petree began the first of three seasons as Dale Earnhardt's crew chief for the Richard Childress–owned Chevrolet team. Petree helped account for fifteen wins in a three-year period and played a key role as Earnhardt captured his sixth and seventh Winston Cup championships.

Andy Petree returned to the Jackson team in 1996, with an agreement that he would become owner of the team at the end of the season. Since taking over, Petree lured driver Ken Schrader to the team and has set about the task of making his own team as successful as those he has worked for.

lation was that he would have closed the facility and redistributed the Winston Cup dates to other tracks in his empire.

Further solidifying the Penske Motorsports foundation and alliance with NASCAR is the fact that 12 percent of the operation was purchased by International Speedway Corporation, the France family's own speedway operations business.

PETREE, ANDY

When Alan Kulwicki won the 1992 Winston Cup championship, he started a trend of drivers becoming the owners of their own race teams. Andy Petree (born 8/15/58) hopes he will be the one to start a trend of championship owner–crew chiefs.

Seeing a race as a youngster at Hickory Motor Speedway hooked Petree on stock car

PETTY ENTERPRISES

While the Petty name is best known for the astonishing racing talent that has characterized three generations of the family, the outstanding record of Petty Enterprises as owners is equally important in the history of stock car racing.

As early as 1957, drivers other than father Lee, son Richard, and grandson Kyle have sat behind the wheel of Petty cars. That first year of fielding a two-car team—with Tiny Lund driving to a fifth-place best finish in six starts—would lay the groundwork for much greater success in the years to come.

One particularly notable Petty Enterprises driver whose last name is not Petty is Pete Hamilton, the driver from New England whose bold runs in NASCAR competition caught Richard's eye in the late 1960s. Brought aboard to drive Plymouth Super Birds in the 1970 season, Hamilton's hard-charging style complemented Petty's experienced approach. In fifteen races for Petty Enterprises, the young Hamilton won three times and collected six more top five finishes. Hamilton's victories consisted of both races at the Talladega Superspeedway as well as the Daytona 500 in February.

Buddy Baker took over Hamilton's seat in 1971, after Chrysler reduced its racing program, and won twice, with thirteen top five finishes over the two seasons he drove for the Petty clan.

Other drivers who at one time or another handled a NASCAR stock car for Petty Enterprises include Dan Gurney, Jim Paschal, Morgan Shepherd, Dick Brooks, Marvin Panch, Joe Weatherly, Darel Dieringer, and Jim Hurtubise.

In nearly five decades of NASCAR competition, Petty Enterprises cars have raced to victory lane 269 times through the end of the 1996 season, and Petty cars have taken the green flag almost seventeen hundred times. The sheer number of entries alone speaks volumes about the team's brilliant success in the Winston Cup Series, but the winning percentage of roughly one win for every six starts since 1949 says even more.

PETTY FAMILY

If there is one name that is as synonymous with stock car racing as NASCAR itself, it is the name Petty. From the sport's very infancy there has been a driver named Petty winning races and setting records.

Above: *A scene that took place two hundred times: Richard Petty celebrates a win in NASCAR's top stock car series. Here, Petty smiles after winning the 1975 World 600 at Charlotte Motor Speedway.* Left: *Richard's father, Lee, began the Petty domination of stock car racing with his own career in the 1950s. Lee Petty is seen here in 1956.*

Richard Petty on the importance of automobile manufacturer support in Winston Cup racing:

"There's always been two levels of support and there will always be two levels. No matter how many millions of dollars those people spend it's the same five or six teams that are the winning teams. There's just so much room at the top for any sport—just enough room for a few people. If you give everybody the same amount you're still going to have four or five of the same people who are going to win the races and if you take it away from those people they're still going to work hard enough to get it back. The factories will not determine the levels of competition.

"Financially it's pretty important. We get financial help and we get technical help. But if nobody gets technical help and nobody gets financial help then it still stays on the same level of competition. As long as they help some people it scatters out and if they don't help anybody then it's still just as fair."

Operating out of a barn behind his home in Randelman, North Carolina, and assisted by his family, Petty prepared an assortment of race cars and laid the groundwork for the legendary racing operation Petty Enterprises. Petty was Grand National (now Winston Cup) champion in the years 1954, 1958, and 1959, and among his achievements was victory in the first Daytona 500, in 1959. He was awarded the win after NASCAR spent three days analyzing photographs to determine if Petty or Johnny Beauchamp crossed the line first in one of the closest finishes in the sport's history. Petty retired from competition in 1964 with an impressive fifty-four wins in 427 starts. He still holds the record for the highest career average finishing position in NASCAR: 7.6.

While Lee Petty had carved himself a place in the NASCAR record books, his son Richard (retired, born 7/2/37) simply rewrote them. Richard's remarkable milestones—during a career that spanned from 1958 to his retirement at the season finale race at Atlanta in 1992—are nearly inconceivable, and many of his records will never be broken.

Richard Petty smiles in front of two of the Petty Enterprises winged Plymouth Super Birds in 1970. Although Dodge had built a winged Charger Daytona for racing in 1969, Plymouth had no interest in a winged car of its own—until Petty left Plymouth to drive for Ford in 1969. Plymouth built the Super Bird specifically to lure Petty back to the fold.

Lee Petty (retired, born 3/14/14) began his NASCAR racing career in 1949 at NASCAR's first race, the June 19 150-mile (241.3km) event at Charlotte Speedway. Petty came home in seventeenth position after crashing his Buick on lap 105. In that first year of NASCAR competition, Petty started just six races but won one and placed second in two others. It was a winning percentage that characterized his performance in NASCAR's early years.

In 1,177 starts, Richard won an even two hundred races for an astounding winning percentage of 17 percent. He was Winston Cup champion in the years 1964, 1967, 1971, 1972, 1974, 1975, and 1979, and won the Daytona 500 seven times. So important was Richard Petty that in 1969, when Richard left Plymouth to race for Ford, Plymouth developed the aerodynamic Super Bird specifically to lure the great driver back.

Richard's records set on the speedways of the United States were enough to assure him legendary status, but his actions off the track are equally well known. It is quite likely that Richard has signed more autographs than any other sports figure in the world. He has acted as an ambassador for the sport, giving countless hours of his time to shed a positive light on stock car racing. Always willing to speak with members of the media, Petty has offered his perspective again and again, in the process winning over many journalists who often considered stock car racing to be a sport of illiterate hicks. His last victory—at Daytona in July 1984—was witnessed by President Ronald Reagan and helped bring even more national attention to the sport as it began an intense decade of growth. In the long run, it is what Richard Petty has done out of the driver's seat that may be his most important legacy in NASCAR racing.

The Petty family's third generation of NASCAR competitors is Richard's son, Kyle (born 6/2/60). That Kyle was a Petty was demonstrated in his very first race on a speedway. Entered in the ARCA 200 at Daytona International Speedway in 1979, Kyle emerged from his car a winner.

Kyle's first Winston Cup starts came later in 1979, driving in Petty Enterprises entries through the 1984 season. Kyle then left the family team to drive for another legendary NASCAR operation in 1985. At the wheel of the Wood Brothers Ford, Kyle won his first Winston Cup race in 1986 at Richmond. After

Above: *Richard Petty in 1990, two years before his retirement from Winston Cup racing.*
Left: *Simply because he is the son of "the King," Kyle Petty faced expectations that were impossible to meet when he began his racing career.*

127

Above: *Kyle Petty's longest association with a team owner was his union with Cuban-born Felix Sabates, with Kyle behind the wheel of the number 42 Pontiac.* Right: *In 1997, Kyle formed a new team aligned with Petty Enterprises, PE2.*

one more win with the Wood Brothers in 1987, Kyle began a long association with team owner Felix Sabates that resulted in six wins. In 1997, Kyle formed a new Petty Enterprises team, PE2, and began to find a competitive consistency that has the potential to add more wins to the NASCAR record of the Petty family.

PHOENIX INTERNA-TIONAL RACEWAY (PIR)

As the cold winds of winter begin to blow, the NASCAR Winston Cup Series traditionally heads west to Phoenix International Raceway (PIR), located in Avondale, Arizona.

A 1-mile (1.6km) oval located in the desert country, PIR has a scrubby mount overlooking the track where tickletless fans who don't mind being removed from the action can observe from afar—as long as they don't mind sharing turf with a rattlesnake or two.

Those who prefer less adventurous seating get the best view of the track, which usually plays a crucial role in the late-season run to the Winston Cup championship. With turns one and two banked at 11 degrees and three and four at 9 degrees, the variation between the sets of turns requires a careful car setup. Lap speeds at Phoenix can exceed 130 mph

(209.1kph), which is fast for such a tight, relatively flat track.

The racing approach that drivers use at Phoenix is one that Davey Allison had much success with (the Alabama native won twice at the track after the Winston Cup Series began running at PIR in 1988). The first race at Phoenix International Raceway was a memorable one, as Alan Kulwicki won his first Winston Cup race—inaugurating both the speedway and the tradition of Alan's unique "Polish Victory Lap."

POCONO INTERNATIONAL RACEWAY

Pocono International Raceway, located in the scenic surroundings of eastern Pennsylvania's Pocono Mountains, presents a difficult challenge to the drivers of the Winston Cup Series.

Darrell Waltrip after winning by getting superior fuel mileage at Pocono International Raceway:

"It's a big win for us. We've been close on a number of occasions. Today things worked out for us perfectly.

"As a driver you really only have the fuel pressure gauge to go by. You've got to put that gauge out of your mind and if you make it you make it and if you don't you don't. I've had a lot of success here over the years. Every time someone asks about Pocono they say, 'That's a weird racetrack,' so I guess I just like weird."

Pocono's triangular configuration features a front straightaway that is the longest of the Winston Cup Series tracks, measuring in at 3,740 feet (1,139.9m). As the cars come off turn three, the drivers shift and then shift again in an attempt to build up the highest speed possible down the long straightaway, reaching nearly 200 mph (321.8kph) by the time they approach turn one.

At turn one, the drivers must quickly bring to an end the two-, three-, four-, and sometimes five-wide racing characteristic of the front straightaway in order to make it through the 14 degrees of banking. The cars then race down a 1,780-foot (542.5m) straightaway and into turn

two, which many drivers feel is the most challenging turn on the entire Winston Cup Series circuit. Banked at 8 degrees, its narrow groove has spelled disaster for many.

Another long straightaway—3,055 feet (931.1m)—connects turn two and turn three, which is banked at just 6 degrees. Making it through turn three completes the lap, run at an average speed of roughly 165 mph (265.4kph).

The dramatically different segments of the track make victory at Pocono something to be proud of. Darrell Waltrip, Bill Elliott, and Tim Richmond all share the track record with four wins apiece since the Winston Cup Series began running at Pocono in 1974.

Darrell Waltrip rolls through the sweeping, flat third turn at Pocono International Raceway. This turn is often the site of trouble as cars jockey for position to get a clear path down the long front straightaway.

Darrell Waltrip on how the introduction of radial tires has changed Winston Cup racing:

"Today's cars are smaller and that's gotten them faster. Radial tires are probably the biggest single thing that made our cars go faster. It's all in the corners.

"If you could clock straightaway speeds from cars fifteen years ago to cars today, the straightaway speeds aren't that much greater.

"But the corner speeds are incredible. Because the cars are smaller and they've got the radial tires on them, we run right on the bottom of the track. When in the '70s or even the early '80s did you see a car run on the bottom of the track? Nowhere.

"Today's cars have got power steering, radial tires, aerodynamics—we didn't even know what aerodynamics was. Those are the things that have changed the cars. They have made them incredibly fast and hard to drive, very difficult to drive because you work so hard in the corner. There's no rest period in these cars."

Crew members glue the lug nuts onto the wheels before a race. Having the nuts already on the wheels and ready to be tightened onto the studs during a pit stop shaves precious seconds off the time a stock car spends in the pit.

RADIAL TIRES

The tire is where a stock car meets the track, and no component in racing is more important. Developments in racing tire technology have helped improve the safety of the sport of stock car racing, especially when it comes to features like the inner liner developed by Goodyear—essentially a tire within the tire to help a driver maintain control if a blowout occurs.

A true revolution (so to speak) in racing occurred in April 1989 at North Wilkesboro, when Goodyear introduced the radial tire to Winston Cup racing.

Before radials arrived, the bias-ply tires in use were measured by the race teams to identify slight variations in tire circumference. The study of these variations became something of a science, matching a certain size tire to the optimum location on a stock car's four corners. This study of "stagger" was crucial to winning efforts, as putting larger-diameter right-side tires on a car helps it negotiate an oval.

With the new radials, though, tire size was much more uniform. A whole new art form developed as teams realized that the radials could be radically adjusted by changes in air pressure. In effect, the radial tires were considered part of the car's suspension system—more air made the tires stiffer; less air made them flexible.

Radials also differed in their wear patterns. Drivers like Dale Earnhardt, who were masterful at getting the most performance out of worn bias-ply tires, had to adjust their driving styles to the longer-lasting radials (although Earnhardt did win that first radial tire race). Stock cars do have a different feel to them when they race on radials, and as Goodyear introduced the new tires to all of the tracks between 1989 and 1992, virtually every Winston Cup driver went through a period of adjustment.

Left: *Dick Rathmann sits in the cockpit of an open-wheel race car at the new Daytona International Speedway in March 1959, after driving the car through a lap at more than 173 mph (278.3kph).* Below: *Later that year, a tired but happy Jim Reed stands in victory lane after winning the Southern 500. A crowd of seventy-eight thousand witnessed Reed win the event at an average speed of 111.8 mph (179.8kph).*

RATHMANN, DICK

In a short career that lasted only five seasons in NASCAR's infancy, California's Dick Rathmann (retired, born 1/6/24) managed to pull off thirteen wins in 128 starts. His first big NASCAR win came in 1952 at Martinsville Speedway in Virginia. Less than a month later, he won three consecutive races: Langhorne, Pennsylvania; Darlington, South Carolina; and Dayton, Ohio. Then he capped off the season in September with another win in Dayton. Rathmann won five times again in 1953 and reached a career-high third in the season-long points tally. He won three more races in 1954, with the last in his NASCAR career coming at Santa Fe Speedway in Illinois in July.

REED, JIM

New York's Jim Reed (retired, born 2/21/26) raced in NASCAR's top division from 1951 until 1963, but all seven of his wins came in 1958 and 1959.

Reed holds the record for winning the shortest race ever run in NASCAR's top division, a 25-mile (40.2km) event held on a quarter-mile (402.2m) paved track at Civic Stadium in Buffalo, New York, on July 19, 1958.

In spite of his success in such short races, Jim Reed also had the ability to perform well in larger events. His biggest career victory came

when he won the tenth running of the Southern 500 at Darlington; it was his third and final victory of the 1959 season and his last NASCAR win.

RESTRICTOR PLATES

As early as 1970, NASCAR had investigated the use of a restrictor plate to reduce engine power and slow stock cars down. The plates fit between the carburetor and the intake manifold, restricting the air and fuel mixture flow by forcing it through smaller holes.

Richard Petty on the realities of restrictor plate racing:

"There's no limit to how fast we can run—it's the rules that control how fast we can run. If they just turn us loose and say, 'Y'all do what you want to and see how fast you can run,' that's one thing, but if they keep us in the realm of NASCAR rules with restrictor plates to slow 'em down that's something else. If we just took the restrictor plate off and run wide open racing engines like we're using now we'd run 215 mph [345.9kph] at Daytona or Talladega.

"The drivers now have to take a lot more chances because you don't know when the time is right to pass. When you had open engines there were certain circumstances that you knew you could get by somebody so everybody waited and used those circumstances.

"Now, you're liable to go into a corner, the lower man or the outside man—the car's liable to catch the draft just right and you'll go by him. Now you could try to do that for fifty laps and nothing will happen. Then on that fifty-first lap, what you think is that same place won't be exactly the same—all of a sudden you go zipping by him. This makes these cats take chances more because they don't know just when they have to take a chance. So now they have to take more chances, where before we knew when to take chances. It makes it a lot more dangerous. The more cars you have running closer together the more chance you've got to have trouble."

Bill Elliott will quite likely retain permanent possession of the title "Fastest Man in NASCAR." After Elliott turned a lap of 212 mph (341.1kph) at Talladega Superspeedway in 1987, NASCAR determined that the Winston Cup cars had to be slowed down to less than 200 mph (321.8kph). NASCAR's solution to the problem was to enforce the use of restrictor plates on the engines of competing cars.

When Bobby Allison's Buick took to the air above Talladega during a race in May 1987, the catch fence in front of the grandstands was barely able to withstand the impact. Had the fence not held, the devastation a 3,500-pound (1,589kg) car moving at 200 mph (321.8kph) would have left in its wake would have been tragic. Add the fact that Bill Elliott had qualified for that race at more than 212 mph (341.1kph), and NASCAR had plenty of reasons to be desperately worried about the dangers such high speeds posed. The solution was the restrictor plate, the use of which is required on the superspeedways at Daytona and Talladega.

But the plates posed their own dangers. Every car tends to run at roughly the same speed, so it's not uncommon to see the entire field at Talladega stay nose to tail and side by side for lap after lap. If one driver makes a mistake under these conditions, widespread disaster can result.

Many of the competitors of the Winston Cup Series have been vocal about their dislike for "plate racing," preferring to try aerodynamic means of slowing the cars or even using smaller, less powerful engines at the large tracks.

Dale Earnhardt's suggestion? Make the tracks build higher protective walls and let the cars go fast.

RICHMOND, TIM

Tim Richmond (born 6/7/55, died 8/13/89) was a flamboyant young driver from Ohio who teamed up with one of NASCAR's legendary crew chiefs, Harry Hyde, and a new team owner named Rick Hendrick to make his mark in the Winston Cup Series. So successful was the result, and so unusual the combination, that the Richmond-Hyde-Hendrick team served as a model for the film *Days of Thunder*.

Richmond entered Winston Cup competition in 1980, but his first win came in 1982. By the time he teamed up with Hendrick he had four wins; with Hendrick, he grabbed seven more in 1986 and two in 1987 with Hyde guiding the team. But there the success story came to an end.

Richmond was ill with what was described as a flu that had blossomed into pneumonia as the 1987 season began. Richmond lost a lot of weight and was unable to return to racing until May, when he drove in Charlotte. On June 14, Richmond won at Pocono in an emotional victory, and incredibly won again the next week on the road course at Riverside. But his health was failing. Other drivers expressed concern to

NASCAR over his lethargic condition and appearance. Tim Richmond's final Winston Cup race came August 16, in Michigan.

A little less than two years later, on August 9, 1989, Tim Richmond died from complications due to AIDS. It was sobering proof that the deadly disease could strike anyone and helped change perceptions of the ravaging illness among racing fans.

RICHMOND INTERNATIONAL RACEWAY (RIR)

Richmond International Raceway (RIR) has had two incarnations on the Winston Cup Series schedule. From 1961 to 1987, the track was just a little more than half a mile (804.5m) in length, with the race cars at first competing on dirt and later on asphalt at the no-frills facility.

Then, in 1987, track owner Paul Sawyer unveiled a new RIR to Virginia and the Winston Cup world. This new track had grown to three-quarters of a mile (1.2km) in length, with banking of 14 degrees in the turns, a back straightaway 860 feet (262.1m) in length, and a gently curved frontstretch banked at 9 degrees.

The result of the redesign has been some of the most exciting competition in the Winston Cup Series. The stock cars are able to race side by side all the way around the track for lap after lap. And when masters of the sport like Rusty Wallace, Dale Earnhardt, and Ernie Irvan take advantage of the racing opportunities afforded by the track's configuration, the fans have unobstructed views of all the action thanks to the modern grandstands that ring the entire track.

Lap speeds at the reconfigured speedway run around 125 mph (201.1kph), compared to old track speeds of 90 (144.8kph) mph on pavement and 70 mph (112.6kph) on the old half-mile (804.5m) dirt track.

While all of the NASCAR drivers enjoy racing at Richmond, none has had more success on the new layout than Rusty Wallace, who has won almost half of the races since 1988.

ROBBINS, MARTY

Everybody's heard of singing cowboys, but singing stock car drivers? That is exactly what the NASCAR Winston Cup Series had between 1966 and 1982, as Marty Robbins (born 9/26/25, died 12/8/82), the well-known country singer, raced alongside Richard Petty, Buddy Baker, and other stock car stars.

Robbins placed ninety-four songs on the country charts of *Billboard* magazine and had at least one song on the chart every year of his career, from 1952, when he first recorded, until 1983, the year after his death.

Robbins' racing record was not quite as impressive. In a grand total of thirty-five starts, Robbins had one career-best fifth-place finish to cap off a total of six top-tens, all of which came during the years 1971 to 1974.

Still, Robbins was a popular addition to the Winston Cup Series. And in an interesting coincidence, the cars that Robbins raced were often prepared by the family of current Winston Cup

Top: *Tim Richmond brought an exciting flair to the sport of stock car racing.* Bottom: *Teamed with car owner Rick Hendrick and legendary crew chief Harry Hyde, Richmond was a frequent winner. A week after taking the 1986 Southern 500, Richmond won this race in Richmond, Virginia, on September 7.*

star Bobby Hamilton, who would grow up to drive stock cars for Richard Petty's team.

ROBERTS, FIREBALL

Even people who have never seen a stock car race recognize the name Fireball Roberts (born 1/20/29, died 7/2/64). The Florida driver from NASCAR's birthplace, Daytona Beach, did much to bring national attention to the upstart sport of stock car racing.

Edward Glenn Roberts started in only nine races in his first NASCAR season, but he won one of them. That the young Roberts won in just his third start, on August 13, 1950, at Hillsboro, North Carolina, proved to the other NASCAR drivers that a bold talent had arrived on the newly born stock car racing scene. It was through performances like this, the first of thirty-three career wins, that Roberts earned his nickname.

From 1950 to 1955, Roberts competed in only a handful of races, but in 1956 he won five of thirty-three starts. The next season his win total increased to eight. Among his biggest victories were the 1958 and 1963 Southern 500s at Darlington and the 1962 Daytona 500.

When Roberts won at Daytona, he virtually dominated the race and the events leading up to it. His Pontiac, prepared by famed mechanic Smokey Yunick, claimed the pole position with a lap of 156.99 mph (252.5kph). Fireball won the 100-mile (160.9km) qualifying race on February 16, then led many of the laps in the Daytona 500 on February 18 on his way to beating Richard Petty to the finish line by nearly thirty seconds.

Roberts began the 1963 campaign driving for well-known car builder Banjo Matthews, but by March of the young season he had switched to the number 22 Ford fielded by Holman-Moody, acting as teammate to Fred Lorenzen, who drove number 28. Roberts' last victory came on November 17, 1963, in Augusta, Georgia, on a 3-mile (4.8km) road course.

On May 24, 1964, Fireball Roberts started his last race, the World 600 at Charlotte Motor Speedway—a race he had never won. On the seventh lap, Ned Jarrett and Junior Johnson went into a spin on the backstretch. Roberts, who had started the race in the eleventh position, tried to avoid his two fellow drivers—but his car spun backward into a wall and exploded on impact. The intense flames were made worse by the fact that the race had just begun and the fuel tank was full. Jarrett raced to

Roberts' aid to help him out of the fully engulfed car, but Roberts was badly burned.

Just over a month later, on July 2, Fireball Roberts succumbed to his injuries. He was buried on July 5. More than one thousand people attended the funeral services.

ROOF FLAPS

One of the greatest safety advances in Winston Cup racing was borrowed from airplanes—and the NASCAR engineers actually used an airplane to make sure the safety measure would work.

In the early 1990s, a disturbing number of Winston Cup cars were taking off from the racing surfaces of superspeedways, becoming airborne at high speeds. Sometimes, when a stock car would turn sideways, the flow of the air around the car made it act like a wing. The car would rise into the air, slowly revolve horizontally, and then slam back to earth—usually in a series of rolls that sent parts of the car flying as the vehicle disintegrated. NASCAR officials began to actively seek ways to break up the airflow after Neil Bonnett took just such an ill-advised flight at Talladega, smashing into a fence (which luckily withstood the impact, preventing serious injuries to the fans behind it).

The strategy NASCAR decided to implement to prevent the worsening situation was to add a set of roof flaps to the cars. The flaps would be mounted on the car at the rear of and

*Opposite: **Crowds like this one packing the stands at North Carolina Motor Speedway are now common at every Winston Cup track.** Above: **Today's crowds might be less substantial had it not been for the heroics of drivers like Fireball Roberts, seen here in 1959 at the then-brand-new Daytona International Speedway.***

Roof flaps are the latest innovation in the effort to keep Winston Cup cars on the track where they belong. NASCAR mandates exactly where on the roof the flaps must be mounted.

flush with the roof. When a car did turn sideways, the force of the air would push the flaps up. This would vent the air trapped inside the cockpit, and the flaps themselves would disrupt the flow of air passing over the car and pushing the vehicle into the air. A later innovation was the addition of flaps to the back of the hood, to vent air that would become trapped in the engine compartment.

To test the flap theory, NASCAR took a car with the roof flaps mounted and backed it up to the sanctioning body's corporate jet. When the jet powered up its engines, the flaps popped up—giving the NASCAR engineers a good sense that they were on the right track.

Since the 1994 inception of the mandatory roof flap rule, the frequency of stock cars becoming airborne has decreased dramatically.

sion would soon be renamed the Grand National division (and later the Winston Cup Series), but the results of this first official stock car race found Jim Roper racing his 1949 Lincoln to first place, a showing that rewarded the Kansas driver with $2,000 in winnings. Strangely, Roper completed only 197 of the scheduled two hundred laps—he was awarded the victory when the car of race winner Glenn Dunnaway was disqualified for modifications to his car outside the rules of the Strictly Stock division.

Jim Roper's win at Charlotte came in the first of only two starts he made in Strictly Stock competition, with the other coming on August 7, 1949, in Hillsboro, North Carolina. In this second race Roper settled for a fifteenth-place finish.

ROPER, JIM

Much as Red Byron is known for winning the first NASCAR race—a Modified division event that took place in Daytona in 1948—Jim Roper (retired, born 8/13/16) has gone down in history for winning the first race of the division that has led to today's modern Winston Cup Series.

On June 19, 1949, the first race of the Strictly Stock division was held at Charlotte Speedway, a three-quarter-mile (1.2km) dirt track in North Carolina. The Strictly Stock divi-

ROUSH, JACK

Kentuckian Jack Roush (born 4/19/42) has become one of the most respected Winston Cup car owners and a man known for his loyalty to the Ford Motor Company.

CEO of Roush Industries—an international engineering and prototype development company servicing the automotive industries—Jack Roush has a long history of sports car racing, with more than twenty championships in various SCCA and IMSA road race classes. He began fielding a Winston Cup team in 1988 with driver Mark Martin, and his team was able to secure one second-place finish in its very first season. Martin has driven Roush Thunderbirds to more than twenty wins through the 1997 season, and Roush's team placed second in the Winston Cup championship standings in the 1990 and 1994 seasons.

Always an innovator, Roush started a second Winston Cup team in 1992 with driver Wally Dallenbach, a position Ted Musgrave took over in 1994. Roush Racing added a third team for driver Jeff Burton in 1996, and Burton grabbed his first Winston Cup win at the debut race at Texas Motor Speedway in 1997.

RUDD, RICKY

Ricky Rudd (born 9/12/56) has had a Winston Cup career that many drivers would envy. The Chesapeake, Virginia, driver entered Winston Cup competition in 1975 and has achieved a level of consistency that is astonishing.

Rudd first made his mark as Winston Cup Rookie of the Year in 1977 with ten top-ten finishes. Beginning with the 1983 season, when he won his first of two races that season for car owner Richard Childress, Rudd has had a win in every season of Winston Cup competition through 1997—an admirable demonstration of his consistency over the years.

One of the smoothest Winston Cup competitors of the modern era, Rudd moved on to drive for Bud Moore after his years with Childress, producing six wins for the South Carolina–based team. He then left Moore to drive stock cars for drag racer Kenny Bernstein's NASCAR team before beginning an association with Rick Hendrick.

In 1994, tired of driving in Hendrick's multiteam operation and having seen the success Alan Kulwicki had as an owner-driver, Rudd started his own team. Despite struggling early on, Rudd kept his victory streak intact, and his team has grown in consistency to be a solid threat on the Winston Cup circuit.

Ricky Rudd on why Winston Cup Series drivers like himself have made the move to owning their own stock car racing teams instead of being hired to drive for a car owner:

"I think it all depends on where we are at this time in NASCAR history. You know, in the old days drivers used to own their own cars and then they got away from that.

"I can't speak for anybody else, but for myself the reason I want to do it is that I was in my own car with my father for the first five years I raced. I know what's involved—a lot of hard work, a lot of dedication. There are some good Winston Cup teams that I could drive for, but this way I would control it. You know, whether I go up or whether I fail at least I had control of it."

NASCAR's 1977 Winston Cup Rookie of the Year, Ricky Rudd. Rudd started twenty-five races that season and logged ten top-ten finishes. The Chevrolets that Rudd drove were owned by his father.

Ricky Rudd leads Bill Elliott through a turn. Both drivers are at the wheel of Ford Thunderbirds. After the 1997 season, Ford ceased production of the Thunderbird and its race teams were faced with the challenge of making the Taurus model competitive in Winston Cup racing.

Known as a master of road course racing for his dexterity at the difficult dance of shifting, braking, turning, and accelerating required by the tracks at Watkins Glen and Sonoma, Rudd was also the title winner of the all-star IROC series in 1992.

SABATES, FELIX

Felix Sabates (born 9/9/42) would be the definition of an American success story regardless of his activities in the NASCAR Winston Cup Series. The story begins in Cuba.

In 1959, a Cuban immigrant and just sixteen years old, Sabates arrived in the United States with the clothes he was wearing, $25, and two boxes of Cuban cigars. Selling the cigars was the first building block of a foundation that has grown tremendously over the years.

Sabates wound up in the Charlotte, North Carolina, area selling used cars before moving to Top Sales, a company that represented manufacturers' products to retail outlets. Large catalog companies began to trust Sabates' recommendations of potentially lucrative products (including the early Atari video game Pong).

In 1983, Sabates personally invested in a talking teddy bear toy named Teddy Ruxpin. Teddy racked up sales of more than $100 million in its first five months on the market—and Sabates became a millionaire. Today his network of companies produces annual sales of more than $1 billion—and Sabates now owns Top Sales, the company he once worked for.

Sabates' sharp instincts guided him toward NASCAR racing and the tremendous growth potential of the sport. After getting his feet wet with a Busch Grand National racing operation in 1987, Sabates purchased Rick Hendrick's research and development team in 1988. The result of the purchase was the birth of Team SABCO.

With Kyle Petty driving for the team, Sabates saw his operation begin to win on the Winston Cup Series circuit. He was encouraged enough by his success to become one of the first owners to begin a two-car operation, beginning with two races in 1992 and then for the full season in 1993 with second driver Kenny Wallace.

Sabates has used his business knowledge and enthusiasm to profit from other sports: he has a partial interest in the Charlotte Hornets of the National Basketball Association and the Charlotte Checkers of the East Coast Hockey League.

In 1997, Sabates broke new ground by fielding an entry in the Indianapolis 500, qualified and driven by Robby Gordon.

SACKS, GREG

Greg Sacks (born 11/3/52) has driven for an unusually high number of teams in his more than ten years competing in the NASCAR circuit. Since entering Winston Cup racing in 1983, Sacks has driven for nearly twenty different teams.

The highlight of Sacks' career came in 1985. In July of that season, Sacks' Chevrolet beat the heavily favored Ford driven by Bill Elliott on the superspeedway at Daytona to win the Firecracker 400. The car he drove to victory was a research and development car with no sponsorship, overseen by crew chief Gary Nelson. In 1990 he had two second-place finishes. He also led briefly in the inaugural Brickyard 400 in 1994. Finally, Sacks was a driver and advisor for the filming of *Days of Thunder.*

SCHRADER, KEN

If any driver brings to mind the days when drivers would race anything, it is Ken Schrader (born 5/29/55).

The Missouri driver began his competitive career on the short tracks near his home, then moved on to drive in USAC midget, Silver Crown, and sprint car competition. It was a career path to the Winston Cup Series that Jeff Gordon would follow years later.

Once he arrived in the Winston Cup Series, Schrader made his mark by claiming Rookie of the Year honors in 1985 driving for Junie Donlavey. In the 1988 season, he began an association with car owner Rick Hendrick that would last almost a decade. Schrader's first Winston Cup win came that season at Talladega, and he also claimed the first of three consecutive pole positions for the Daytona 500. Later wins came at Charlotte, Atlanta, and Dover.

Left: *An American success story, Cuban emigre Felix Sabates has become one of the best-known Winston Cup team owners.* Below: *The thrill of an unexpected victory can be seen on the face of Greg Sacks, who has just won the 1985 Firecracker 400 in a Bill Gardner team research and development car. Current NASCAR official Gary Nelson was crew chief for the car.*

While competing in Winston Cup for Hendrick, Schrader maintained a dizzying pace of short track racing with a stable of race cars that he owned and maintained. It was not uncommon for Schrader to race somewhere in the United States almost every night of the week.

But by the mid-1990s, Schrader curtailed his demanding schedule so that he could concentrate on his Winston Cup efforts. After several disappointing seasons with Hendrick, Schrader left the team after finishing twelfth in the championship battle in 1996.

Schrader began racing in 1997 for the team owned by Andy Petree, the crew chief who masterminded Harry Gant's 1991 four-race winning streak and Dale Earnhardt's 1994 championship run. After a slow start at the beginning of the season, the team showed signs of becoming Winston Cup contenders.

SCOTT, WENDELL

Wendell Scott (born 8/29/21, died 12/23/90) was the first African American to compete in NASCAR's top division. He started 495 races from 1961 to 1973, winning his only race on December 1, 1963. The idea of an African American competing in a sport that at the time was viewed by many as the domain of "rednecks" convinced Richard Pryor to star in *Greased Lightning,* a film about Scott's exploits and tribulations.

Members of Scott's family honored his memory in May 1997 when they joined former basketball star Julius "Dr. J" Erving and football player Joe Washington in announcing the formation of a new minority-owned Winston Cup racing team, Washington-Erving Motorsports.

SEARS POINT RACEWAY

Sears Point Raceway is one of the more recent additions to the Winston Cup schedule. The track's Sonoma, California, location—near both San Francisco and Monterey—makes it a favorite stop on the itinerary.

NASCAR was in need of a California visit for the Winston Cup Series after the demise of the Riverside road course in Southern California and before the new California Speedway was ever imagined. The 2.5-mile (4km) road course at Sears Point fit the bill perfectly.

With five left turns and seven right turns, the Sears Point track offers the challenges that

Winston Cup drivers face only at the other annual road course race, at Watkins Glen in New York. Many of the same drivers who have mastered the subtle road racing techniques of shifting, braking, and accelerating at the Glen have transferred that knowledge successfully to Sears Point, as seen by the winners' roster, which includes Ricky Rudd, Rusty Wallace, Mark Martin, and Ernie Irvan. Lap speeds through Sears Point's twists and turns average approximately 92 mph (148kph).

In 1996, Sears Point Raceway was acquired by Bruton Smith's Speedway Motorsports firm, adding another racetrack to his growing collection of NASCAR tracks.

SHEPHERD, MORGAN

Morgan Shepherd (born 10/21/41) began his stock car career in one of the most challenging environments imaginable—racing at the Hickory Motor Speedway short track near his home of Conover, North Carolina. The lessons he learned battling at the tough little speedway have served him well in his Winston Cup career.

Like many Winston Cup competitors, Shepherd tested the waters of NASCAR's elite series with occasional appearances early in his career. After eight starts in the 1970s, Shepherd drove a full season in 1981—and scored a win

Ricky Craven on finding the Sears Point road course in Sonoma, California, to be his most challenging racetrack:

"In most cases in NASCAR racing, when you go to a place for the first time or even a place that you don't race a lot at, you reference another racetrack. You may reference one racetrack's entry to turn one, and then another racetrack's exit off of two. That's how I try to speed up the learning curve and accelerate through practice.

"With Sonoma being a road course, it's hard to adapt to and it's hard to reference because of our limited experience with road courses. That track would be number one with me.

"I honestly can't say that I would want to race thirty-one times a year on a road course, but I really enjoy what I do and I've been doing it for fifteen years. But it was only four years ago that I first went to a road course.

"Drivers are quick to form opinions of road course races. You either really enjoy it, which has an impression on how you perform, or you don't enjoy it. I don't think you can approach or enter an event with the attitude 'I'll make the best of it' and have any success— never ever, not in this league. The attitude of suffering through something doesn't apply. You have to be 100 percent. You have to have a nearly perfect day to win in Winston Cup."

Certain drivers seem to excel at the unique interplay of brake-clutch-accelerator that must be mastered to succeed on a road course. Seen here entering a turn at the Sears Point road course, Mark Martin's number 6 car is always a threat to win any road course event in the Winston Cup Series.

Jack Smith won at Concord Speedway in North Carolina in November 1961 by bumping Joe Weatherly's car out of his way. After apologizing, Smith was quoted as saying, "If Joe isn't satisfied with my explanation, I'm always ready to settle it with fists." That was the type of rough competition that characterized the first two decades of NASCAR racing.

at Martinsville driving for Cliff Stewart. At that point in his young career, Shepherd had already driven for six different car owners, and it was a trend that would characterize the years to come. Shepherd's longest stint with any team came during the years 1992 through 1995, when he won one event at Atlanta for the Wood Brothers team. In 414 starts in his first twenty-five years of Winston Cup racing, Shepherd gathered four wins.

Shepherd is now known as one of the most charitable and unpretentious of the Winston Cup drivers. His annual open house at his race shops is a favorite of fans, and Shepherd often donates his time to help those in need.

SKINNER, MIKE

Many drivers who compete in NASCAR series below the Winston Cup level dream of entering the elite series driving for a tremendously successful car owner who can provide a competitive car in each and every race. For Mike Skinner (born 6/28/57), that dream came true.

That isn't to say that Skinner didn't work to make that dream a reality. After racing in his native California, Skinner was told by his wife that he would have to either get serious about a racing career or give up on motorsports. Skinner got serious, winning on short tracks throughout the South after he and his wife moved east. Richard Childress noticed Skinner's talent and in 1994 hired him to drive his entry in the new NASCAR SuperTruck Series for pickups. Skinner rewarded Childress'

faith by winning his first-ever truck race in 1995. Skinner went on to win the inaugural series championship.

Childress, after winning six championships with Dale Earnhardt, decided to make his Winston Cup operation a two-car team for the 1997 season. Mike Skinner got the call to drive for the new team. He proceeded to claim the pole position as fastest qualifier in the Daytona 500 to start off his rookie season in the top division.

SMITH, BRUTON

Bruton Smith (born 1931), the head of Speedway Motorsports, is quite likely the most influential racetrack owner in the Winston Cup Series. His keen promotional sense—combined with his association with talented business people like the president of Speedway Motorsports, H.A. "Humpy" Wheeler—has changed the face of the Winston Cup Series.

A former army paratrooper, Smith built the Charlotte Motor Speedway in 1959. Financial woes cost him the track in 1961, but he built a financial empire in insurance and automobile sales that allowed him to reacquire that track and much more.

One of Smith's major contributions to the sport was the introduction of luxury services common in other sports arenas to NASCAR racetracks. He noticed that such amenities were a tremendous draw in baseball and football stadiums and was sure they would prove equally attractive in racing. With Wheeler's help, Smith's vision became reality: Charlotte Motor Speedway was transformed into a high-tech entertainment facility that seats more than 100,000, has a first-class restaurant overlooking the track, features thousands of enclosed luxury box seats, and even has condominiums overlooking the track's first turn.

This approach has been implemented at the other racetracks controlled by Smith's Speedway Motorsports entity, which now controls Atlanta Motor Speedway, Texas Motor Speedway, Bristol Motor Speedway, and the Sears Point Raceway in California. Smith's firm unsuccessfully attempted to acquire North Carolina Motor Speedway in 1997.

Some observers see Smith's acquisition of so many racetracks in the Winston Cup Series as a challenge to Bill France, Jr.'s control of NASCAR and major league stock car racing. Only time will tell if these moves will develop into an all-out war for control of the sport.

SMITH, JACK

Jack Smith (retired, born 5/24/24) finished thirteenth in the very first NASCAR stock car race on June 19, 1949, then went on to win twenty-one races in NASCAR's top division over the next fifteen years.

Smith's best season came in 1962, when the driver from Georgia won five races, had twenty-eight top five finishes, and finished up the season in fourth place in the championship points tally. Smith achieved that success driving his own Pontiacs.

Jack Smith's last season, 1964, saw him starting just four races, but he still managed a second-place finish in Savannah, Georgia, and a third-place finish in Jacksonville, Florida, among his few starts.

SOUTHERN 500

In a sport that has a strong regard for tradition, the annual Southern 500, run at the legendary Darlington International Raceway, is one of the most cherished institutions. Held each Labor Day, the 500-mile (804.5km) race is the oldest annual event on the Winston Cup schedule.

Its history, which stretches back to the sport's infancy, make Darlington's Southern 500 a race that every driver wants to win. The name of every legend of the sport appears on the roster of winners, and when a driver adds his name to that list he is in exalted company.

The very first Southern 500, held September 4, 1950, drew approximately twenty-five thousand people, a tremendous motorsports crowd for its day. The fans who packed the stands at Harold Brasington's new track saw an immense starting field ready to challenge the 1.366-mile (2.1km) speedway. Seventy-five cars had qualified for the race over a period of fifteen days. Bill France, Sr., was concerned about his NASCAR stock cars having to run 500 miles (804.5km), for prior to this date the longest race the young organization had sanctioned was 200 miles (321.8km).

Only one car did run the full 500 miles (804.5km): Johnny Mantz' Plymouth won by more than nine laps over Fireball Roberts' Oldsmobile. Still, more than one-third of the field was orbiting the track when the checkered flag fell, and that first Southern 500 proved to France that his drivers and their stock cars could handle the longer races that have now become the norm on the NASCAR circuit.

The outcome of the Southern 500 is frequently decided after the tricky Darlington racetrack has been misjudged by a driver, a mistake that often involves fellow drivers. Here, Junior Johnson in car 27, Darel Dieringer in car 16, and H.B. Bailey in car 04 all find trouble in the 1964 Southern 500. Dieringer alone was involved in four "incidents" during this race.

Jimmy Spencer on the pressures of breaking into the Winston Cup Series:

"I think that in the Busch Series a lot of people noticed me. I was pretty aggressive and I was doing pretty good in the Busch Series. But I think I came into the Winston Cup Series with the wrong attitude. I thought that I could beat these guys. I think that attitude hurt me a little bit for the simple reason that I could beat them, but it took time to beat them.

"I tried too hard in the beginning with Buddy Baker and the Heinz team. I was sixth in the points after about six races with the Heinz team, and I thought, 'Man, this is easy.' And Winston Cup racing is no different than racing for any track championship, any point championship in this country, whether it be dirt track or mini-stocks or whatever. The guy who prepares his team the best is going to win that championship. That's a simple plain fact, and Winston Cup is no different.

"But there is a lot more pressure, a lot more money, a lot more people to answer to in Winston Cup. I think that hurt me a lot. If somebody leaned on Jimmy Spencer I leaned back. It was like they said, 'We're going to teach this rookie something.' 'Well, I ain't no rookie—I can handle it.' And I'd push back on them. And I think my reputation of 'Mr. Excitement,' 'Mr. Aggressive' got out of hand. I think I crashed cars trying too hard to take a fifteenth-place car and put it in the top ten. That hurt me a lot."

SPEED, LAKE

A man with an appropriate last name for his profession, Lake Speed (born 1/17/48) came from Mississippi with an enviable background when he began racing in NASCAR competition. Speed's indoctrination into motorsports came at the wheels of go-karts, and so successful was Lake that he was the 1978 World Karting Champion—a title he won in competition in LeMans, France.

Back in the United States, Speed began his Winston Cup career with nineteen starts in 1980, and was good enough to secure five top-ten finishes. In the years since, Speed has driven for a variety of car owners, but his greatest success has come at the wheels of his own race cars. In 1988, Lake drove to victory at the demanding Darlington track, winning the spring event at the South Carolina speedway. After several seasons of sponsorship difficulties, Speed was poised to enter the 1998 with the funding necessary to be competitive in the Winston Cup Series.

SPEEDWAY MOTOR-SPORTS INCORPORATED

Speedway Motorsports was formed by Bruton Smith, owner of Charlotte Motor Speedway and Atlanta Motor Speedway. His goal was to raise capital for the planned 1997 opening of Texas Motor Speedway and for the acquisition of other properties.

Jimmy Spencer brought experience from a long career on the racetracks of the northeast United States to his Winston Cup efforts. But that experience did not ensure success in Winston Cup racing.

Starting out with both CMS and AMS already in its possession, Speedway Motorsports gained control of the track in Bristol and the road course at Sears Point, and secured half ownership of North Wilkesboro Speedway between 1995 and 1996. When combined with the then-completed Texas Motor Speedway, Smith's stock car empire had become enormous. Some felt that there may have been an ulterior motive behind the acquisitions: that Smith was perhaps planning some kind of challenge to NASCAR's stock car kingdom. Not surprisingly, Smith denied this charge vigorously.

Both Atlanta and Bristol have undergone extreme renovations to bring the tracks up to Smith's glitzy standards. Less fortunate was the North Wilkesboro track. Purchased by Smith and New Hampshire International Speedway owner Bob Bahre, North Wilkesboro was stripped of its two Winston Cup dates, one going to Texas Motor Speedway and the other to the New Hampshire track. Meanwhile, the venerable North Wilkesboro track has fallen into disrepair.

SPENCER, JIMMY

Jimmy Spencer (born 2/15/57) entered the NASCAR Winston Cup Series in 1989 as driver for Buddy Baker. Even then Spencer was known as "Mr. Excitement," a moniker given to the Berwick, Pennsylvania, driver based on his no-holds-barred career driving in Modified competition.

For the early part of his Winston Cup career, Spencer tried to apply the same "bang 'em up" philosophy that he'd used in other racing series—a rough strategy that did not win him many friends in the garage area. But as Spencer progressed with each passing season, he learned other strategies from associations with car owners like Travis Carter and Bobby Allison.

In July 1994, Spencer won his first Winston Cup race, beating Ernie Irvan to the line at Daytona in one of the most thrilling NASCAR finishes of the 1990s. Spencer backed up that win weeks later when he claimed victory at Talladega.

Reunited with Carter in 1995 and backed with sponsorship from R.J. Reynolds, Jimmy Spencer has matured as a NASCAR competitor, a fact that is demonstrated by his consistent top-ten finishes.

STACY, NELSON

Ohio-born driver Nelson Stacy (born 12/28/21, died 5/14/86) had about the best ride a NASCAR driver could ask for during his best season—the number 29 Ford fielded by the factory-backed Holman-Moody racing team.

Stacy's first NASCAR race was in 1952 and his second not until almost a decade after that. But when Stacy did get back into NASCAR in 1961, he won in his first start—the prestigious Southern 500 at Darlington. In 1962, allied with Holman-Moody, Stacy won again at Darlington, the World 600 at Charlotte Motor Speedway, and a 250-mile (402.2km) event at Martinsville Speedway in Virginia.

Nelson Stacy left NASCAR racing after his final start in 1965.

Nelson Stacy had never raced in the Southern 500 before, but that didn't stop him from winning NASCAR's prestigious Labor Day event in 1961. Mary Brennemer, Miss Southern 500, shows how impressed she is by Stacy's feat.

Top: *Driver Hut Stricklin
has driven for several
well-known team owners.*
Bottom: *Stricklin was
competitive at the wheel
of the Stavola Brothers
Ford in 1996 and 1997.
But for 1998, the team
planned to switch to
Chevrolet's Monte Carlo,
ensuring a challenging
first few races of the season for Stricklin.*

STAVOLA BROTHERS

Formed in 1983, the Stavola Brothers Racing Team—founded by brothers Mickey and Billy Stavola—has been a mainstay of the NASCAR Winston Cup Series for well over a decade. In that time it has provided competitive stock cars and top-notch crew support both for legends of the sport and for exciting up-and-coming contenders.

The team won a total of four races between 1986 and 1988, with one victory coming with Bobby Hillin behind the wheel and the remainder with Bobby Allison driving. In fact, the Stavola team swept both events at Talladega in 1986: Allison won in May and Hillin followed suit in July.

Sterling Marlin nearly won for the team again in 1993, before young Jeff Burton made his Winston Cup debut with a number of strong finishes for the team. Burton won the 1994 Winston Cup Rookie of the Year title driving the Thunderbirds of the Stavola Brothers team.

STRICKLIN, HUT

Hut Stricklin (born 6/24/61) had one of the best motorsports educations possible: growing up racing stock cars against the legendary Allison family on the short tracks of Alabama. The lessons he learned paid off with championship seasons in the 1982 and 1984 Winston Racing Series and the 1986 NASCAR Dash series.

Stricklin made his Winston Cup debut in 1987 at the now-closed North Wilkesboro, North Carolina, track. In the years since, Stricklin has raced for team owners including Rick Hendrick, Bobby Allison, Junior Johnson, Travis Carter, and the Stavola Brothers. Leading up to the 1997 season, Stricklin's best career finish in the Winston Cup Series was second place, a position he attained twice.

TALLADEGA SUPER-SPEEDWAY

The biggest and fastest track in the Winston Cup Series—and also the scariest—is Alabama's Talladega Superspeedway.

A 2.66-mile (4.2km) paved behemoth with turns banked at an intimidating 33 degrees, Talladega Superspeedway was Big Bill France's attempt to outdo his own creation at Daytona International Speedway.

Richard Brickhouse, winner of the first Talladega race in 1969, on why he did not join the boycott of the track:

"I remember Ronnie Householder—he was the head of Chrysler racing—he walked up that morning in the garage area. He pointed at the car and he told me, 'Either you run this car or somebody else will.'

"And those were his very words. That was coming from my boss. I was under Chrysler's thumb, so to speak, and whatever they said to do was what I was going to do. And they made it clear that I was going to drive that car."

Talladega Superspeedway, which has a reputation as frequent host of close, exciting racing, has also been the site of some of stock car racing's most frightening accidents. Here, Neil Bonnett is about to test the strength of the fence separating the cars from the crowd in July 1993. Fortunately for all, the fence did its job. Both Bonnett and the fans were unscathed, although the racing was stopped until the fencing was repaired.

Opened as Alabama International Motor Speedway in 1969, Talladega has always been a place where strange things seemed to happen. Its first event, held on September 14, 1969, was boycotted by most of the series regulars, who felt the track was unsafe due to its bumpy surface. France allowed a large contingent of racers from a lower NASCAR series to compete with the drivers who did stay to race. The troubled event was won by Richard Brickhouse driving a winged Dodge Charger Daytona in the aerodynamic model's debut.

Unfortunately, aerodynamics is a topic that often arises at Talladega, as a number of cars have been launched into the air after losing control at speeds nearing 200 mph (321.8kph).

Perhaps the most frightening was Bobby Allison's airborne excursion in May 1987, when his car took off and flew into the fence in front of the grandstands. Several spectators were injured, although things could have been much worse.

NASCAR officials, after pondering the potential consequences of the disaster that might have been and well aware that Bill Elliott had qualified for that event at the terrifying speed of 212.809 mph (342.4kph), issued new rules requiring the use of restrictor plates on manifolds to reduce engine power. Elliott's lap still stands as a NASCAR record.

The restrictor plate rule did not end danger at Talladega. With all of the engines producing

Right: *A typical sight at Talladega Superspeedway—a "freight train" draft, with long lines of cars running side by side at nearly 200 mph (321.8kph).* Below: *Marshall Teague smiles on February 11, 1959, just moments before he was killed in a crash of the "Sumar Special" at Daytona International Speedway. Teague had driven the car to a lap of 171 mph (275.1kph) during sessions before the accident.*

roughly the same horsepower, drivers find themselves running in huge packs at 190 mph (305.7kph), unable to pull away from each other. If one driver makes a mistake, many can suffer the consequences. Talladega has been the site of some of the most tragic wrecks in recent NASCAR history.

Talladega has also been kind to first-time winners, and it seems that restrictor plate racing offers dark horses a greater chance at competing with the favorites. Despite that, veteran Dale Earnhardt—who favors removing restrictor plates and letting the cars run just as fast as they'll go—has won the most races (seven) at Talladega.

TEAGUE, MARSHALL

Marshall Teague (born 2/17/22, died 2/11/59) got his career off to a great start in 1951 and 1952, but his life was cut tragically short.

Teague began the 1951 season by winning the season-opening race on the Daytona beach/road course in his "Fabulous Hudson Hornet" at an average speed of just more than 82 mph (131.9kph). Teague went on to win four more times that season and had two wins in his first four starts of the 1952 season in his "Teaguemobile Hudson" entry.

But the brilliant promise of the season's tremendous beginning was never realized, as Marshall Teague was killed in a racing test session.

TEXAS MOTOR SPEEDWAY

Texas Motor Speedway's debut in 1997 marked the return of the Winston Cup Series to the Lone Star State after a long absence. A market that NASCAR wanted to compete in, the Dallas area was chosen by Bruton Smith to be the site of a trioval clone of his Charlotte Motor Speedway.

On the surface, the Texas track did have much in common with Charlotte's speedway. But when competition began at the track on April 6, 1997, many drivers found quite a bit to complain about. For one thing, they charged that the racing surface was too narrow. The number of wrecked cars in the garage area by the end of the inaugural race certainly seemed to back up the heated opinions.

Still, the track does have the potential to become one of the NASCAR circuit's major attractions in the years to come. The physical amenities—including Smith's standard array of luxury boxes and condos—are first-rate, and as the competitors become accustomed to racing on the track and adjust to its unique demands, this 1.5-mile (2.4km) speedway will no doubt host its share of legendary battles.

THOMAS, HERB

In just 230 starts, Herb Thomas (retired, born 4/6/23) won forty-eight races during a career that stretched from NASCAR's first year of stock car sanctioning up to 1962.

Thomas was one of the thirty-three drivers to compete in the June 19, 1949, Strictly Stock race at Charlotte Speedway, the NASCAR race recognized as the predecessor to today's Winston Cup Series. Although Thomas finished twenty-ninth in this historic race, by the next year he was winning races in NASCAR's top division.

Herb Thomas was the division champion in both 1951 and 1953, driving in early Oldsmobiles, Plymouths, and fellow racer Marshall Teague's "Teaguemobile Hudsons." Thomas won thirty-nine races between 1951 and 1954, a span that encompasses his two championship seasons. Thomas left NASCAR competition after a single start in 1962.

THOMPSON, ALFRED "SPEEDY"

Speedy Thompson (born 4/3/26, died 4/2/72) lived up to his swift moniker, accumulating twenty wins in 198 starts.

Thompson first entered NASCAR competition by racing in a single event in 1950, but by 1953 he had won his first two races and was well on his way to a respectable career. His best season was 1956, when the North Carolina driver won eight races and drove for the respected Carl Kiekhaefer Chrysler team. And from 1956 through 1959, Speedy Thompson was in the top three spots of the championship standings, narrowly missing out on being crowned champion each year.

Herb Thomas leans on the hood of his Smokey Yunick–prepared stock car, traditionally emblazoned with the number 92. Thomas was a powerful competitor in NASCAR until he was gravely injured in a crash in October 1956 in North Carolina. He eventually retired in 1962.

Leo Mehl, Goodyear Tires director of competition, on the 1994 tire war between Goodyear and Hoosier:

"Prior to Hoosier's arrival our primary concern was economics for the drivers and the teams, and supplying a good-handling tire that would be consistent. When you have competition, your job is to win races. The competition is only beneficial to the tire companies. I said at the beginning that this was going to be great for the tire companies—they'd get lots of publicity, learn a lot of things technically—but I had serious doubts as to whether it was going to be good for the teams and the drivers.

"NASCAR has worked for several years to slow the cars down. Well, within six months of the tire competition all the speed they had taken off had been put back on—and a heck of a lot more. The result was that teams were spending more money on tires than they ever did, and the primary reason for that is that after the checkered flag falls every tire that they bought and didn't use is obsolete."

For now, the sight of no tire brands other than Goodyear in the garage area is a comforting one to the drivers of the Winston Cup Series because in general a tire war leads to reliability problems.

In 1957, Thompson won the Southern 500 at Darlington, driving his Chevrolet to victory in what was considered the most prestigious NASCAR race of that era.

Speedy Thompson died of a heart attack in 1972 while competing on a North Carolina short track.

TIRE WAR

If there is one thing that can strike fear in the drivers of the Winston Cup Series, it's the possibility of a tire war.

In the late 1960s, Goodyear and Firestone were both active in supplying competition tires to NASCAR's top drivers. But eventually Firestone retreated from competition tire development, and as NASCAR's modern era began—with the name of the top series changed from Grand National to Winston Cup in 1971—Goodyear basically had NASCAR's top division to itself. That continued until 1988.

Hoosier Tire Company had made a name for itself making tires for short track competition in the Midwest. When Hoosier's founder, Bob Newton, announced that his company would enter into Winston Cup in 1988, few people in the racing world took the announcement seriously. After all, NASCAR rules required that any company competing in Winston Cup would have to supply enough tires for the entire field at any race. But tiny Hoosier rose to the challenge, and Neil Bonnett finished fourth in the 1988 Daytona 500 on Hoosiers. The tire war was on.

The problem with a tire war is that not only are race team loyalties to longtime suppliers challenged, but as the companies strive to make a faster tire, reliability can suffer. A number of drivers were hurt as tires failed in 1988. Hoosier managed to win nine of the twenty-nine races that season, but it faced an uphill struggle against the giant Goodyear. In May 1989, Hoosier withdrew from Winston Cup competition.

Most observers thought they had seen the last of Hoosier's purple corporate colors in the Winston Cup Series, but they were wrong. In 1994, a tire war erupted again as Newton led Hoosier back into NASCAR's elite division. With Geoff Bodine as Hoosier's flagship race team driver, Newton watched as his tires rolled to just three wins. Just after the season-ending Atlanta race, Hoosier once again withdrew from the series. Expected financial backing that would have allowed Hoosier to compete with Goodyear in 1995 had fallen through—much to

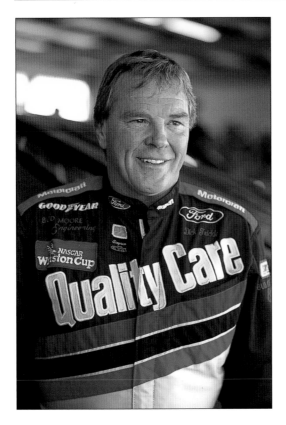

TURNER, CURTIS

After placing ninth in the very first NASCAR race of the Strictly Stock division—the class that led to today's Winston Cup Series—Curtis Turner (born 4/12/24, died 10/4/70) may have realized he had a future in stock car racing. His first win, in the fourth Strictly Stock race later in 1949, probably erased any lingering doubts about his career choice.

And from that first NASCAR stock car season of 1949 until he raced in his last NASCAR race in 1968, Curtis Turner had at least one victory in more than half the years he competed. He won four times in 1950, and three times each in 1951 and 1958. Turner was also victorious in the 1956 Southern 500 at Darlington, the annual event that was the most important NASCAR stock car race until the Daytona 500 appeared on the schedule in 1959. Turner had led the great Darlington race in the past but had never won. This time his Ford held off Speedy Thompson's Carl Kiekhaefer Chrysler.

Curtis Turner was killed in 1970 when his private plane crashed in Pennsylvania.

ULRICH, D.K.

Donald Keith Ulrich (retired, born 4/10/44) has had a lengthy career, not only as a driver, but also as a car owner who has given many aspiring young drivers a chance to enter Winston Cup competition.

the relief of almost all of the drivers because it brought an end to the tire war.

While Goodyear has rolled through the late 1990s with its Winston Cup tire monopoly intact, at any time another tire manufacturer could decide that the prestige of a winning tire in NASCAR justifies the development and manufacturing expenses. After all, Firestone just returned to IndyCar racing after an absence of decades. A new tire war in the Winston Cup Series could erupt at any time.

TRICKLE, DICK

Dick Trickle (born 10/27/41) is one of the rare drivers who was a legend before he ever climbed into a Winston Cup car.

The Wisconsin driver earned his fame in short track competition throughout the Midwest, where he has more than twelve hundred feature race wins to his credit, an astonishing total. That record includes sixty-seven wins in 1972 alone.

Trickle first competed in Winston Cup in his own entry in 1970, and thereafter he raced sporadically for owners including the Stavola Brothers, Cale Yarborough, Larry Hedrick, and Bud Moore. Trickle began an alliance with car owner Junie Donlavey in 1996.

Trickle has also competed in numerous Busch Grand National Series races, winning his first such event in 1997.

Kenny Wallace has faced the same problems that have dogged every young driver trying to break into the Winston Cup Series. Winning a pole in the 1997 season helped ease the transition.

Between 1971 and 1992, D.K. Ulrich competed in 273 Winston Cup Series races, with a record of one fourth-place finish in addition to fifteen more top-ten finishes. It may not be a record that rivals Richard Petty's feats, but keep in mind that many talented drivers never make the grade to compete in even one Winston Cup Series race.

Helping drivers who want to attain that goal has made Ulrich a popular employer for stock car racers who are just starting their careers in the Winston Cup Series. Sterling Marlin, Tim Richmond, Mark Martin, Rick Mast, and Ernie Irvan are just some of the drivers who have used seat time in Ulrich's cars to establish themselves in NASCAR's top division.

VOGT, JEROME "RED"

Jerome "Red" Vogt, a car builder from Atlanta, Georgia, is the man who gave NASCAR its name.

Red Vogt was one of the thirty-five men who met at the Streamline Motel on December 14, 1947, to hear Bill France's vision of a national stock car sanctioning organization. Vogt's cars had a reputation for being useful for running in early stock car competition and for running moonshine on back roads. Presumably, it's the reputation that his cars had generated when racing that moved France to extend an invitation to Vogt.

During the three days of meetings that led to the foundation of today's Winston Cup Series, the newly instituted competition board passed a resolution that the organization go by the name National Stock Car Racing Association, or NSCRA.

It was Red Vogt who pointed out that promoters in his native Georgia were already using that name. Vogt followed his comment with a suggestion for a name that race fans around the world have come to recognize: NASCAR, the National Association for Stock Car Auto Racing.

WALLACE FAMILY

The sons of a three-time track champion from St. Louis, Missouri, Kenny, Mike, and Rusty Wallace have become three of the largest "name" presences in Winston Cup fields—rivaled only by the three Bodine brothers.

The youngest of the Wallace brothers, Kenny (born 8/23/63), got started racing go-karts before moving to the ASA and NASCAR Busch Grand National Series. Kenny was Busch Series Rookie of the Year in 1989 and was championship runner-up in 1991. His first full Winston Cup season, driving for car owner Felix Sabates in a two-car team with Kyle Petty, came in 1993 with disappointing results. After regrouping in the Busch Series, Wallace became a force in Winston Cup with a full-time effort in 1997, which saw the youngest Wallace win his first pole in the April race at Martinsville.

Middle brother Mike (born 3/10/59) won hundreds of short track events throughout the Midwest as he gained experience on the path that led to his Winston Cup debut in 1991. Splitting his time between occasional Winston Cup races and several successful runs in the ARCA stock car series, Mike began full-time Winston Cup competition with car owner Junie Donlavey in 1994.

But the most successful Winston Cup Wallace to date is Rusty (born 8/14/56). Rusty used his ASA experience—including the series championship in 1983—to make his move into Winston Cup. After a handful of starts between 1980 and 1983, Wallace ran a full season for the first time in 1984. His first win came in 1986, and he won a second time later that season. In 1988, he won six times, and he repeated that feat in 1989—a win total that gave him the season championship over Dale Earnhardt by just twelve points. In 1993, driving for car

Rusty Wallace after winning ten races in the 1993 season but falling just short of Dale Earnhardt in the battle for the Winston Cup championship:

"I'd like to congratulate him on what he's done. Yeah, I'd like to win it myself but we'll work real hard on making all of these cars finish the whole 500 laps or 500 miles [804.5km] next year and hopefully be back up at the top and win that championship next year.

"I'd never have thought I'd win ten races and not win the championship. There's a chance that if I hadn't fallen out of those ones I fell out of—I mean I could be sitting here with fourteen victories. Very easily. I know that sounds wild but I had the lead in so many races. The list goes on about 'what ifs' but, hey, ten? Great! Buddy Parrott said, 'I'm gonna try and win ten races' and we all chuckled. Coming off a bad year it was unbelievable to think that, but we did it. It feels good to back up what you said."

Rusty Wallace is one of the veteran drivers of the circuit, respected not only for his competitive abilities but for his knowledge of race car setups and how a stock car chassis will react under any conditions.

owner Roger Penske, Wallace won ten events but lost the championship to Dale Earnhardt in a spirited season-long duel for the title.

Rusty is a master at race car setup, and his "hands-on" approach to preparing his car's chassis helps account for his outstanding success in Winston Cup competition.

WALTRIP FAMILY

Brothers Darrell and Michael Waltrip have each attained success in the Winston Cup Series, although Michael's career has been slower to gain momentum; Darrell's entry into NASCAR's top division was positively explosive.

Michael (born 4/30/63) was still searching for his first victory through the 1996 season. His career best was a second-place run in 1988, with a total of sixteen top-five finishes through 1996. However, Waltrip did win the May all-star race at Charlotte Motor Speedway in 1996. Winning the Winston Select does not entitle a driver to any Winston Cup points, but even though the race does not count as an official win, Waltrip still beat the best drivers in the Winston Cup Series that night in Charlotte.

Older brother Darrell (born 2/5/47) can be assured of his place in the Winston Cup record books. A winner of eighty-four points races, Darrell won twelve times in 1981 and 1982, sewing up the championships in those years. After more than fifteen years of trying, Darrell finally won the Daytona 500 in 1989. Waltrip's emotional victory lane celebration has made many NASCAR highlight films.

While Darrell was known for his outspoken behavior in his early career—earning him the nickname "Jaws"—he has matured to become one of Winston Cup racing's most important and thoughtful sources of perspective. After twenty-five years of competition, Darrell Waltrip had planned to reduce his race schedule to part-time status for 1998, but runs like his top-five finish at the Sears Point road course in 1997 showed that he still had a sharp competitive edge.

> **Kenny Wallace on how rookies—whose cars are required to carry yellow identification stripes across the rear bumpers—must learn to fit in with veteran Winston Cup drivers on the track:**

"This is a systematic type of racing deal where you've got to be in with the clique. It's a traveling type of circus every week, and if you're not in with the clique then you are out, out in left field.

"The first thing you do as a rookie in this series to get respect is to stay out of the way. No matter what you do, you're in the way. When a veteran comes up and sees that rookie yellow bumper, you're in his way and they don't like it right away.

"You need to race them clean. If they're behind you and they've caught you, you have to pull over and let them go. That's what you've got to do for a while, and if you don't you get burnt.

"A lot of the good racers, the veteran racers who run up front all the time, if somebody catches them you'll see them pull up, let them go by, and then pull back in. That's the way everybody wants to be raced. The biggest thing you have to do is earn their respect."

WATKINS GLEN

One of the two road courses visited each season by the Winston Cup Series, Watkins Glen—located in the town of the same name in New York—is one of the most historic racetracks in the United States.

The 2.45-mile (3.9km) course run on by NASCAR's stars features eleven turns with banking that varies from 6 to 10 degrees. The challenge presented by running on the track, which snakes around an expansive infield area, is one that some NASCAR drivers love and others despise.

NASCAR first raced at the track in 1957, returned in 1964 and 1965, and then made its visit an annual affair beginning

Mike Wallace has struggled to succeed in the Winston Cup Series. Like many drivers, he has had to fill in his schedule with ARCA and Busch Grand National races in between his sporadic Winston Cup starts.

with Tim Richmond's win at the "Bud at the Glen" in 1986.

While some drivers and fans feel that the Winston Cup Series has no business racing at a road course, the fact that the NASCAR-offshoot International Speedway Corporation has a financial interest in the track would seem to indicate that Watkins Glen will continue to be a stop on the Winston Cup schedule in the foreseeable future.

WEATHERLY, JOE

A two-time NASCAR champion, Joe Weatherly (born 5/29/22, died 1/19/64) entered stock car competition under the rules of Bill France's new organization and met with great success until his death in 1964.

In a classic illustration of how wins are commensurate with experience, Weatherly had just one win in 1958, none in 1959, three in 1960, and then nine in both 1961 and 1962. Weatherly won the championship in 1962, and even though his win total dropped to three in 1963, he repeated as champion. In 230 starts, Weatherly made his way to victory lane twenty-five times.

Sadly, Joe Weatherly never had the chance to go for three championships in a row. On January 19, 1964, Weatherly was racing in the NASCAR event at the Riverside, California, road course in a Mercury owned by Bud Moore. On lap 86, he lost control of his car and hit the wall with a glancing blow. Although the wreck did not look severe, rescue workers found Weatherly lifeless inside the car. His head had hit the retaining wall when the car made impact, and Weatherly's helmet was found to have cracked from the force of the blow. Joe Weatherly was credited with twenty-ninth place in his final race.

Darrell Waltrip in 1997, reflecting on his twenty-five years in NASCAR Winston Cup racing:

"It's different from the perspective that everybody did it on their own when I started. There was nobody with what you would call deep pockets. There was nobody wanting to get into Winston Cup racing to sponsor cars. There were four or five well-supported teams and then a bunch of what we called independents. You went around and scraped up as much money as you could and put together a car and part-time help would come in on the weekend and help you out. It was a lot of fun back then.

"Today, expectations are so much different. Drivers today who haven't even won a race or finished in the top ten in the points are getting $750,000 salaries to drive, and that's amazing to me....

"That's where the sport is today. It was just a whole lot more fun back then. It wasn't any easier. I drove my own truck and my own car with my wife and my dog. We went to a number of races that way, just Stevie and I and the dog. You wouldn't have much of a chance doing that today."

Darrell Waltrip at Daytona International Speedway in 1973. The young driver was just beginning his journey in the Winston Cup Series— a journey that would see him go from being an aggressive, outspoken driver nicknamed "Jaws" to becoming one of stock car racing's most respected sources of perspective.

WELBORN, BOB

When the first Daytona 500 was held on the huge 2.5-mile (4km) superspeedway in 1959, the drivers of the NASCAR Grand National Series had never seen anything like the track. And while many stock car fans know that Lee Petty won that first, incredibly close race after a lengthy review of the photo finish, many don't know that Bob Welborn (retired, born 5/5/28) won the first NASCAR stock car race on the track: the February 20, 1959, 100-mile (160.9km) qualifying race for the Daytona 500. Welborn drove his Chevrolet to victory at a speed of more than 143 mph (230kph) and earned the right to start the Daytona 500 from the pole position.

Bob Welborn first competed in NASCAR in 1952 and continued to do so each year until 1964. His highest ranking in the championship points standings was in 1955, when he placed fourth in the season-long tally. Welborn won nine races of the 183 he started.

WHITE, REX

One of NASCAR's earliest champions, Rex White (retired, born 8/17/29) won twenty-eight races in a career that began in 1956 and continued until 1964.

White's championship season in 1960 was marked by six wins and twenty-five top-five finishes, an impressive record of consistency. White's first win of the year came on a half-mile (804.5m) dirt track in Columbia, South Carolina, in early April, with the second in July on a 2-mile (3.2km) triangular course laid out on the paved runways of an air force base in Montgomery, New York. The difference between the two tracks demonstrates the wide variety of venues NASCAR drivers once had to prepare for.

Rex White's last NASCAR victory came in 1962 in the season-ending race at Atlanta International Raceway, as he held off Joe Weatherly, Marvin Panch, and Richard Petty for the win. It capped off a season in which White won eight races, finishing fifth in the championship points standings.

THE WINSTON (THE WINSTON SELECT)

The Winston (also occasionally known as the Winston Select, depending on which brand of cigarette R.J. Reynolds is promoting in any given year) is a non-points shootout among NASCAR's top drivers.

First held in 1985, the Winston was originally envisioned as an event that would take place at different speedways, but has since found a permanent home at Charlotte Motor Speedway.

The field of the Winston is made up of recent race winners and special qualifiers, and its current format consists of three race segments. After the first segment, the finishing order is inverted for the start of the second segment. The final segment is a ten-lap free-for-all with the winner claiming more than $250,000.

With such a high payout—complemented by the fact that the results of the race have no bearing on the championship points battles—Winston Cup drivers tend to go all out in the Winston.

Memorable moments from the Winston include Davey Allison losing control of his car after making contact with Kyle Petty as their cars flashed across the finish line under the checkered flag in 1992. Davey won the race but was knocked unconscious just seconds later by a violent impact with the wall. Dale Earnhardt once successfully pulled off an outlandish move, passing Bill Elliott by blasting across a section of the grass infield. It's become known as the "Pass in the Grass." Ernie Irvan tried the same move on Geoff Bodine in 1994's Winston and demolished his car.

Such risky moves would usually not be tried in longer races where championship points are at stake, but if any phrase can sum up the Winston, it's "Anything goes."

WINSTON 500

One of the oldest annual races of the Winston Cup Series, the first Winston 500 at Talladega Superspeedway was held on May 16, 1971.

Before the inaugural Winston 500, the track had been known as Alabama International Motor Speedway and had been hosting races only since September 1969. Although the track surface caused racing problems at the first events held on the huge 2.66-mile (4.2km) superspeedway, those difficulties had been ironed out by the time the Winston Cup cars competed in the first Winston 500.

Appropriately for a race held in the heart of Alabama, it was two members of the "Alabama Gang" who swept the top positions after leader Dave Marcis had mechanical problems late in the race. Donnie Allison drove his Wood Brothers Mercury across the finish line just a few feet ahead of his brother Bobby, at the wheel of the Holman-Moody Mercury. Buddy Baker trailed the two Alabama drivers in a Petty Enterprises Dodge.

In the years since that race, the Winston 500 has been characterized by tremendously close competition at hair-raising speeds. In fact, it was during qualifying for the Winston 500 in 1987 that Bill Elliott set the all-time NASCAR speed record of 212.809 mph (342.4kph). NASCAR soon instituted the use of restrictor plates under the carburetors to reduce engine strength and slow the cars to speeds under 200 mph (321.8kph).

WINSTON CUP

The Winston Cup, the trophy that symbolizes the annual championship of NASCAR's elite division of competition, first came into existence with the birth of the Winston Cup Series itself in 1971.

Images from the early years of NASCAR. Opposite, top: *Fireball Roberts (left) and Joe Weatherly with just a few of the many trophies won by the two drivers in their illustrious careers. Each driver had just emerged victorious in the qualifying races for the 1962 Daytona 500.* Opposite, bottom: *Bob Welborn poses proudly with his convertible stock car. NASCAR briefly sanctioned convertible racing.* Above: *Rex White leans from the window of his championship-winning 1960 Chevrolet, emblazoned with a hood that boasts "320 HP."*

Prior to 1971, NASCAR's senior division was known as the Grand National, and competition was spread throughout the country on nearly every type of racetrack imaginable—paved and dirt. But in 1970, the R.J. Reynolds Tobacco Company and NASCAR began one of the most successful alliances in sports history.

Much of the credit has to go to Ralph Seagraves, the head of Reynolds' sports marketing division. He recognized the potential of an alliance between his company and the sport of stock car racing. The result was the naming of NASCAR's top series after Reynolds' flagship brand of cigarettes, Winston.

Reynolds began its first season of Winston Cup involvement by providing $100,000 for a point fund to the top twenty drivers in the season championship hunt. With the sponsorship came a scaling back of the schedule to a more manageable thirty-race season. And Winston Cup events would not be run on dirt tracks.

In the years since Reynolds began its sponsorship, the financial rewards provided by the company to the drivers and teams of the Winston Cup Series have paralleled the sport's exponential growth. The point fund has grown from $100,000 with $40,000 earmarked for the champion to more than $4 million, with the champion's portion alone worth more than $1.5 million.

Winston has also instituted a series of other competition incentive programs for the drivers of the Winston Cup Series. Among these was the Winston Million. If a driver wins any three of four specified events in a season—the Daytona 500, the Winston 500 at Talladega, the Coca-Cola 600 at Charlotte, the Southern 500 at Darlington—that driver is awarded $1 million by Reynolds. Bill Elliott did it in 1985, garnering the nickname "Million Dollar Bill." In 1997 Jeff Gordon became the second driver to claim the huge paycheck.

For 1998, the Winston Million was replaced with the "Winston No Bull 5." Adding the Brickyard 400 to the four races of the Winston Million series, Winston makes any driver who finishes in the top five positions of the previous "No Bull 5" race eligible to gain a million-dollar bonus by winning the next special race. The announcement of the "No Bull 5" was met with great enthusiasm from the drivers, who now have a much greater chance at claiming the bonuses.

A side benefit of the Winston involvement is the sponsorship of the Winston Racing Series, where the NASCAR Winston Cup stars of tomorrow get their first experience on the short tracks of the United States.

Winston Cup driver Jimmy Spencer on the changes that the Winston Cup Series and R.J. Reynolds' involvement have brought to stock car racing:

"Years ago, before R.J. Reynolds even got involved and Bill France started NASCAR, this was for Saturday night racers. You could never make a full-time living out of it. Now, we've got ten cars back at the shop, twenty-five people working for us, tractor-trailers, sponsor commitments all the time—that's just incredible what this sport has done in twenty-five years.

"That's all because of sponsors and people like R.J. Reynolds. I mean, if it wasn't for Winston, I don't think this sport would be where it is. A lot of that is due to Ralph Seagraves—he's the one who started this. At one time RJR could have bought every racetrack, but they didn't want to do that. Instead, they just wanted to help and I just hope the fans realize that. If you talk to the champion, Dale Earnhardt, or if you talk to Richard Petty, who has been a seven-time champion, or you talk to Terry Labonte, they'll tell you how good RJR has been. I mean we get paid an awful lot of money to do what we're doing.

"When I first started racing I never dreamt—never dreamt!—that you could make the kind of money that I'm making for driving a race car. And I would drive it for free."

WOOD BROTHERS

Formed roughly fifty years ago, the Wood Brothers Racing Team has forged a history of legendary performances in NASCAR Grand National and Winston Cup Series racing.

Virginia's Glen Wood (retired, born 7/18/25) founded the team, racing throughout Virginia and the Carolinas until he moved up to Grand National (now Winston Cup) competition. He had four wins in sixty-two starts from 1953 until 1964. Glen then joined his mechanic brother, Leonard, in fielding the team's Fords for a series of legendary drivers, including Cale Yarborough, A.J. Foyt, Marvin Panch, Curtis Turner, Junior Johnson, Joe Weatherly, Dan Gurney, Parnelli Jones, Donnie Allison, David Pearson, Buddy Baker, and Bobby Rahal.

In recent years, the Wood Brothers' Thunderbird has been guided on the tracks of the Winston Cup Series by Kyle Petty (1985–1988), Neil Bonnett (1989–1990), Dale Jarrett (1990–1991), and Morgan Shepherd (1992–1995). Michael Waltrip took over the dri-

Opposite: *Jimmy Spencer slides sideways in the 1996 running of the Winston Select 500 at Talladega Superspeedway. Not only is this race sponsored by R.J. Reynolds, but Spencer's car is also sponsored by the company.*

Right: *Fifty years after NASCAR held its first race, Virginia's Wood Brothers are still involved in the sport.* Below: *Leonard Wood joined with his brother, Glen, to found the team whose racing roots stretch all the way back to the early 1950s, when Glen himself competed in NASCAR races.*

ver's seat in 1996, winning the Winston all-star race at Charlotte Motor Speedway.

Glen's children, Eddie, Len, and Kim, will one day officially inherit the racing operation from their father, but all three have been active in the team's activities and on-track performance since they were youngsters.

As the children grew up, they saw the family team build a track record that is the envy of just about every Winston Cup competitor. The team's total start count in NASCAR's elite division is nearing one thousand since they entered into competition in 1953, and they have nine-

ty-seven wins through 1997. That includes victories in the 1963, 1968, 1972, and 1976 Daytona 500s; the 1968, 1976, 1977, and 1981 Southern 500s at Darlington; and the 1974, 1976, 1982, and 1987 World 600s at Charlotte.

In fact, the only major accomplishment missing from the Wood Brothers' list of milestones is a Winston Cup championship. But it doesn't look like the legend of the Wood Brothers will be coming to a close any time soon, so that championship season could very well be waiting in the future.

WORLD 600

The World 600 is the longest race of the Winston Cup Series. Held annually since 1960 on Memorial Day Weekend at Charlotte Motor Speedway, the race's extra 100 miles (160.9km) of competition rewards a mixture of consistency and hard charging.

Following the craze of corporate sponsorship of events, in 1986 the race was retitled the Coca-Cola 600. But the change that concerned the competitors came in 1994. With a multimillion-dollar lighting system installed around the 1.5-mile (2.4km) track, the decision was made to start the race in the late afternoon, the finish taking place under the lights.

The difficulty of adjusting a race car as the track surface dramatically changes (due to the transition from sunlight to moonlight) makes this race a challenge for crew chiefs, race teams, and drivers.

YARBOROUGH, CALE

Cale Yarborough (born 3/27/40) is one of NASCAR's most legendary drivers, with a track record to match.

The South Carolina native started his first Grand National race in 1957 and struggled to break into the series. While seeking the racing success he longed for, Yarborough worked at logging and raising turkeys. Just as he was about to quit racing for good, he received a phone call from Jacques Passino, the director of Ford's racing program. Passino told Yarborough to report to the Holman-Moody shops—the elite front line of Ford's NASCAR racing program in the 1960s. Yarborough never looked back, racing and winning for such teams as the Wood Brothers, Junior Johnson, and Harry Ranier.

Cale Yarborough is the only driver to win the Winston Cup championship three years in a row, a feat accomplished while driving for Johnson in 1976, 1977, and 1978. He started and finished every race in the 1977 season and won fourteen pole positions as fastest qualifier in the 1980 season. Cale won four consecutive races in 1976 and was also voted most popular driver in 1967.

Cale Yarborough's last Winston Cup starts came in 1988, capping off a tremendous career that saw him win eighty-three times, fifty on superspeedways.

The end of Yarborough's racing career was not the end of his association with the Winston Cup Series. Cale kept his own team active after he retired from competition and, with young drivers Jeremy Mayfield and John Andretti, has guided the team into contention. Yarborough's team, with Andretti at the wheel, won at Daytona on July 5, 1997.

YARBROUGH, LEEROY

LeeRoy Yarbrough (born 9/17/38, died 12/7/84) was one of NASCAR's top stars throughout the 1960s, an important era of growth for the sport. It was a time when television executives were just starting to realize that stock car racing made an excellent subject for sports broadcasts; the hard charges of drivers like Yarbrough helped pave the way for the Winston Cup Series of today.

Left: *LeeRoy Yarbrough waves to supporters after claiming another NASCAR Grand National victory.* Below: *Cale Yarborough won often as a driver, but had to wait years for his first win as a car owner. John Andretti finally won for the team in 1997.*

Above: *Davey Allison makes a pit stop in the Robert Yates Racing Thunderbird during the 1989 season. Allison was poised to bring the team a championship when he was killed in a 1993 helicopter accident.* Right: *Yates later expanded his team to a two-car operation with drivers Ernie Irvan and Dale Jarrett. Winston Cup newcomer Kenny Irwin replaced Irvan for 1998.*

Yarbrough's best season was in 1969, when he won seven races. Driving for the Junior Johnson team, Yarbrough swept the most important races of the season: the Daytona 500, the World 600 at Charlotte Motor Speedway, and the Southern 500 at Darlington Raceway. Winning those four races was an accomplishment that, in modern

Winston Cup racing, would be worth a $1 million bonus from R.J. Reynolds.

With his last start coming in 1972, LeeRoy Yarbrough's 198 races resulted in fourteen wins for the Florida driver. The later years of Yarbrough's life were plagued by mental problems, and he died while under supervised care.

YATES, ROBERT

Robert Yates (born 4/19/43) is not only the owner of two of the top Winston Cup teams, but he is also an innovator in NASCAR engine development.

Rightfully recognized as a genius in the complex science of motor building, Yates' powerplants are considered by many observers to be the very best motors in Winston Cup racing—developing phenomenal power as his cars come off the corners of racetracks. Designing new features or enhancements under the tight scrutiny of NASCAR's rules is a challenge, one that Yates has consistently met over the years.

The North Carolina native became intrigued by NASCAR racing after attending the first NASCAR Grand National race at Charlotte Motor Speedway, in 1960. His first entry into the sport on a professional basis was in 1968, when he received a job offer from the legendary headquarters of Ford's NASCAR efforts, Holman-Moody.

By 1971, Yates was fully involved in motor work with Junior Johnson. He prepared the motors used by Bobby Allison in 1972, when the Alabama driver won ten races and claimed twenty-four top-three finishes.

Yates moved to the then-new DiGard racing team in 1976, building powerplants for the team for the next decade, in support of such drivers as Darrell Waltrip, Ricky Rudd, and Bobby Allison. Yates' motors propelled the team's stock cars to more than forty wins during this period of consistent success.

In 1986, Yates moved to the Ranier/Lundy racing team late in the season. In 1987, driver Cale Yarborough was replaced by a young rookie with an impeccable pedigree, Davey Allison, son of Bobby Allison. Davey took to the Yates motors almost immediately, winning his first Winston Cup race in May at Talladega. It was to be the first of many wins for the two.

In 1988, after Davey won twice more and finished second to his father in the Daytona 500, Yates bought the team from Harry Ranier. The Robert Yates Racing Thunderbirds became a threat to win any Winston Cup race.

From 1989 until the middle of 1993, Yates motors propelled Allison to fifteen victories, and the team nearly won the 1992 Winston Cup championship after crew chief Larry McReynolds came aboard in 1991. But tragedy struck in July 1993, when Davey was killed in a helicopter accident.

Late in the 1993 season, Ernie Irvan moved from the Morgan-McClure Chevrolet team to drive Yates' Fords, winning twice in just nine starts. But then Ernie himself was critically injured in a crash during practice in Michigan after starting the 1994 season with three wins.

Dale Jarrett came aboard to win one race in 1995, and Yates decided to operate two cars in Winston Cup racing when Irvan returned from his injuries late in 1995. Both Jarrett and Irvan won in 1996, with Jarrett claiming both the Daytona 500 and the Brickyard 400. Both Robert Yates Racing cars found victory lane again in 1997. Yates surprised the racing world when he announced he would replace Irvan with rookie Kenny Irwin in 1998.

YUNICK, HENRY "SMOKEY"

Smokey Yunick (retired, born 5/25/33) can best be described as an automotive innovator. Based out of his automotive garage (doing business under the name "Best Damn Garage in Town") in Daytona Beach, Florida, the colorful Yunick

fielded cars in early NASCAR Grand National competition for the likes of Mario Andretti, A.J. Foyt, Curtis Turner, Charlie Glotzbach, Bobby Unser, and Buck Baker. In his years as a team owner, Yunick saw his cars win eight times.

Yunick—who was also involved in numerous Indianapolis 500 entries—is known for his technological knowledge and for his outspoken opinions about NASCAR racing.

As one of racing's legendary characters, many yarns exist about Yunick's exploits. Perhaps the most infamous Yunick tale revolves around a disqualification. Sometime in the 1960s, Smokey's Chevrolet stock car failed an in-depth NASCAR technical inspection. Smokey proceeded to start up the Chevrolet and drive the vehicle away—despite the fact that the NASCAR inspectors had removed the car's fuel tank.

ZERVAKIS, EMANUEL

Emanuel Zervakis (retired, born 1/23/30) was a Richmond-based driver who competed in Grand National competition from 1956 until 1963. In those years, Zervakis—nicknamed the "Golden Greek"—started eighty-three races, winning twice. In the early 1980s, Emanuel returned to the sport as a car owner. Drivers Geoff Bodine, Mark Martin, Morgan Shepherd, and Dale Jarrett briefly took turns in the driver's seat of Zervakis entries in the Winston Cup Series.

NASCAR fixture Smokey Yunick seems to be pondering a new innovation in a NASCAR garage area in the 1960s. Yunick was a progressive and innovative crew chief— and he also had a reputation for tangling with NASCAR over interpretations of the sanctioning body's rules.

GLOSSARY

AERODYNAMIC BALANCE: A state of equilibrium between front and rear aerodynamic downforce.

AERODYNAMIC DRAG: The force resisting the motion of a body passing through air.

AERODYNAMICS: The science studying the effects or forces exerted by air or other gases in motion. Understanding this science is crucial to building stock cars that cut through the air with as little resistance as possible.

AIR DAM: A front-end aerodynamic tool used to create a low-pressure area beneath a stock car.

AIR FOIL: Usually wing-shaped, an aerodynamic tool used to create downforce.

APRON: The immediate area around the bottom or inside of a speedway.

ANTIROLL BAR: A bar used to create resistance to a stock car's tendency to have body roll through turns.

ARCA: Automobile Racing Club of America.

ASA: American Speed Association.

BACKSTRETCH: The straightaway on a common oval track found between turns two and three on the opposite side from the start/finish line.

BALL JOINT: A front suspension ball mounted in a socket that allows steering control in a stock car.

BANKING: The sloped turns located on a racetrack, measured in degrees from the horizontal.

BEHIND THE WALL: During a race, NASCAR requires major repairs to take place not on the pit road but on the other side of the pit road wall or in the garage area.

BIAS-PLY TIRES: A tire constructed through the use of overlapping layers or cords.

BLACK FLAG: The flag used by the flagman to signal a stock car driver that he must take his car off the track and report to his pit stall. Reasons for the black flag being displayed to a driver can range from a rules violation to the appearance of a mechanical problem that looks to be too unsafe to allow the car to continue in competition without repairs being made.

BODY TEMPLATES: Templates that outline different parts of the approved models that race in the Winston Cup Series. The NASCAR technical inspectors use the templates to ensure that the cars of the competitors are legal in the body dimensions.

BRAIN FADE: A momentary lapse in concentration that, in the case of any race car driver, can lead to disaster.

BREAK LOOSE: When a stock car's racing tires lose traction.

BUSCH GRAND NATIONAL SERIES: The second level of NASCAR competition, one division below Winston Cup. Most Winston Cup stars raced in the BGN series on their way up, and many continue to race in the series to gain additional experience.

CAMBER ANGLE: Positive camber is when a stock car's wheel is angled slightly out at the top; negative camber is when the wheel top angles in slightly. Measured in degrees.

CASTER ANGLE: Measurement in degrees of the steering axis from vertical, with positive caster showing the axis inclined to the rear, and negative caster showing the axis inclined forward.

CATCH CAN: A small device used to catch fuel overflow during a pit stop. The catch can helps prevent spillage of fuel on pit road.

CAUTION PERIOD: After an accident or after a car has had a mechanical failure requiring a racetrack cleanup, the cars pass under the yellow flag waved by the flagman and drive at reduced speed until the track is deemed safe for competition.

CHASSIS: The frame or core of a stock car, forming the heart of the vehicle construction. The chassis provides a place for mounting the motor, suspension and steering, drive train components, and the roll cage that protects the driver.

CHECKERED FLAG: For the leader of a race, the most cherished sight at the end of the last lap—the flag carrying the black-and-white block pattern.

COOLDOWN LAP: After taking the checkered flag, cars circle the track once more to slow down before leaving the racetrack surface.

CORNERING FORCE: The sideways pressure exerted on a tire as a car passes through a corner.

CREW CHIEF: The racing team member who oversees the race car's preparation and directs pit road activities during a race.

DIALED IN: The ideal state for a stock car to be in, set up to pick up the greatest speed on the straightaway and negotiate the racetrack turns as quickly as possible. A stock car that is "dialed in" has been worked on extensively to find the right combination of springs, shock absorbers, weight displacement, etc.

DOUGHNUTS: When stock cars running side by side make contact with each other, evidence of the impact is often left behind in the form of a black, circular outline made by one car's tire rubbing against the door panel of the other car.

DOWNFORCE: Aerodynamic forces that push down on a stock car as it circles the racetrack. Desirable to help the car maintain stability through turns, downforce can also create drag that slows the car.

DRAFTING: A valuable superspeedway technique, developed in the very first races at the huge Daytona International Speedway, in which one car will pull right up to another car's lead bumper. Together, the two cars slicing through the wind can run faster than a car running by itself.

DRAG: The resistance from friction that a car encounters as it moves through the air.

DRIVESHAFT: The shaft mounted between the transmission and the rear end. The driveshaft transmits the engine's power in order to turn the rear wheels.

DUCT TAPE: An invaluable mechanic tool used for everything from taping off the grille vents of a car to reduce air intake to impromptu repairs on a stock car's body. Nicknamed "200-mph tape."

DYNAMOMETER: A machine that measures engine performance, allowing the powerplants to be operated outside the car to study what is needed to obtain maximum performance.

ELAPSED TIME: Used to measure how long a stock car takes to complete a lap. In the pits and the garage area, it is rare to hear stock car performance judged in miles per hour. Instead, lap times are the standard.

FIRE: A race driver's worst enemy. Fire-retarding suits are worn by both drivers and the crew members who fuel the car during pit stops.

FIREWALL: The metallic plate that separates the driver and the car interior from the engine compartment.

FLAGMAN: The race official in the starter stand on the frontstretch who waves the flags that control the action on the racetrack.

FRONTSTRETCH: On a classic oval-shaped track, the straightaway area between the exit of turn four and the entrance to turn one. At tracks like Daytona International Speedway, the frontstretch is curved, giving the track a tri-oval shape. The frontstretch is where the start/finish line can be found.

FUEL CELL: A specially designed fuel tank used in stock cars. A bladder contains the fuel itself with baffles made of foam or other material that prevents the tank from rupturing in the event of a crash.

GARAGE AREA: The stall-like area used to prepare stock cars for competition and inspection before the race. In the NASCAR Winston Cup Series, the garage area is only accessible to crew members, NASCAR personnel, media members, and special guests.

GRAND NATIONAL: The NASCAR division that became the Winston Cup Series when R.J. Reynolds began its sponsorship. The name "Grand National" was revived later in the Busch Grand National Series.

GREEN: Reference to a fresh surface on the racetrack, either before any cars have taken to the track surface or after a heavy rain. A green racetrack can play havoc with a stock car's setup.

GREEN FLAG: The flag used to signal competitors that the race is under way at the start of the first lap or at the end of a caution period.

GROOVE: The preferred line around a racetrack that results in the quickest lap times.

GROUND EFFECTS: Aerodynamic term for the creation of negative pressure beneath a race car, used to help stabilize the vehicle.

HAULER: Nickname for the portable race shops that are the racetrack headquarters for each team. Parked in the garage area, the haulers are large trailers that not only carry the stock cars to the track but also have machine-working facilities, tool storage compartments, lounges, and many other features to maximize their use to team personnel.

HEEL AND TOE: A driving technique mastered by drivers such as Ricky Rudd, which can be particularly advantageous on tracks that require a great deal of shifting such as road courses. The driver uses the heel and toe of his right foot to simultaneously control the brake and accelerator.

HIGH GROOVE: Some drivers feel more comfortable with their cars' performance during a race when the cars run a "high groove" up closer to the track's outer retaining wall. Harry Gant was well known as a Winston Cup driver who often ran the high groove.

HOOKED UP: Similar to "dialed in" as a description of a stock car that is performing to its maximum potential.

HORSEPOWER: One horsepower is the force needed to raise 33,000 pounds (14,982kg) of weight 1 foot (30.4cm) in one minute. Also equivalent to 746 watts of power.

INFIELD: The center section of a racetrack, surrounded by the actual racing surface. Most larger NASCAR Winston Cup Series speedways and superspeedways sell infield tickets that allow spectating and camping in the infield on race weekends.

INTERMEDIATE TRACK: In the NASCAR Winston Cup Series, a speedway equal to or greater than 1 mile (1.6km) and less than 1.5 miles (2.4km) in length. Along with short tracks, superspeedways, and road courses, intermediate tracks are one of the four types of speedways the Winston Cup Series races on.

"JUST RACIN": An expression usually uttered by a driver who has fallen out of a race for one reason or another, used to explain the event that led to his downfall. In reality, "Just racin'" can mean anything from "That's the way it goes" to "Some idiot ran into me and knocked my car into the wall."

KINETIC ENERGY: Kinetic energy can be measured to determine the energy of a body—or stock car—in motion. It is equal to one-half of the mass multiplied by the velocity squared.

LAPPED CAR: A stock car goes down a lap when the leader of a race circles the track and passes that car. The car that has been passed by the leader is now a lapped car.

LEAD LAP: The number of the last lap completed by the leader of the race. In many instances, if a driver is on the same lap as the leader of the race—"on the lead lap"—that driver is still in contention to finish the race in one of the higher positions.

LIFT: An aerodynamic term that refers to air passing over a stock car that tends to make the vehicle want to rise up into the air. Lift is a particular concern at superspeedways, where the stock cars run at nearly 200 mph (321.8kph).

LOOSE: When an ill-handling stock car is said to be loose, the rear end of the car feels to the driver as though it wants to break loose and slide up toward the outer wall of a turn.

LOOSE STUFF: During long stock car races, small pieces of worn tire and other debris can accumulate at the top of the racetrack by the outer wall. If a car gets this high on the racetrack, it can lose control from running through the "loose stuff."

LOW GROOVE: Most stock car drivers prefer to run the "low groove," with their cars down at the bottom of the banking as low as possible without getting their left wheels on the flat track apron. A car that is set up perfectly will run right at the bottom of the track; a car that needs adjusting will drift high in the corners—unless the driver is purposely running a "high groove."

MARBLES: Another name for "loose stuff," the debris buildup near the outside wall of a racetrack turn.

MOMENTUM: Another calculation used for moving objects—including stock cars—is the formula for momentum: mass multiplied by velocity.

MOVE-OVER FLAG: If the flagman notices that a slower, lapped stock car is holding up one of the race leaders, he will wave this flag—identifiable by its blue color with diagonal orange stripe—at the slow car.

NACA DUCT: A duct shape designed according to standards of the National Advisory Council of Aeronautics. NACA ducts are often seen in stock cars mounted flush with side windows to direct airflow in the car.

NASCAR: Stock car racing's most important sanctioning body, the National Association for Stock Car Auto Racing. The Winston Cup Series is NASCAR's premier division and is the top stock car racing series in the world of motorsports.

NOMEX: A brand name for the fireproof material that most driver and crewman protective fire suits are made of.

OVERSTEER: The proper terminology for the condition that most stock car drivers would refer to as "loose," when the car's tail end feels like it wants to break loose and swing around toward the outside wall.

PACE CAR: The vehicle used to control the speed and formation of the stock cars at the beginning of a race and during any caution periods that may crop up during a race. In the Winston Cup Series, the pace car has flashing lights on the roof. When the stock cars are one lap away from taking the green flag to begin racing, the pace car driver turns off the flashing lights to inform the drivers that the competition is about to begin.

PANHARD BAR: Also known as a sway bar, the panhard bar is used in a stock car to control the amount of sideways movement of the body or chassis in relation to the rear axle. The panhard bar usually attaches to the chassis at one end and the axle or its housing at the other.

PIT BOARD: A sign on a pole held by one member of the pit crew used to guide the team's car to the proper location for a pit stop. The sign generally is designed to feature a shape or a graphic image that the team driver will immediately recognize, informing him he is nearing his pit location.

PIT ROAD: The area usually found by turning off a racetrack's frontstretch, where each team is given one pit stall. Here is where tire changes, fueling, window cleaning, and other in-race service requirements are completed. Some racetracks have pits on both the frontstretch and backstretch, with the slower race qualifiers relegated to the back pits.

PLOW: Another word used to describe a car that is hard to turn, as in, "The car is plowing through the turns." The same condition is described as "understeer," a "tight" race car, or a car that "pushes."

POLE POSITION: The position reserved at the start of the race for the fastest qualifier. In most stock car races, the cars line up in rows by twos, with the pole position being the inside (infield side) of the front row. The fastest qualifier is often said to be "sitting on the pole."

PROVISIONAL START: In the NASCAR Winston Cup Series, a handful of positions at the back of the starting lineup are reserved for drivers who are regular competitors but may have had trouble in qualifying for a particular event. Provisionals are offered first to the current Winston Cup champion, past Winston Cup champions, and so on according to a formula of descending merit.

PUSH: A car is said to have "developed a push" when it becomes hard to turn in the corners, with the front end feeling to the driver as though it wants to continue toward the outer wall of the track. Also referred to as a "tight" race car, one that "plows" through a turn, or one that has an "understeer" condition.

QUALIFYING: In Winston Cup racing, most qualifying sessions take place on the Friday of a race weekend to determine the top half of the starting grid, with second-round qualifying taking place the next day. The cars are generally timed in one- or two-lap runs to determine the race starting order.

RACING BACK TO THE FLAG: In the Winston Cup Series, if the leaders go by the start/finish line and a caution period starts due to an accident or other problem, the leaders are not officially under caution until the next time they reach the start/finish line. They can still pass each other for position until they drive under the yellow flag. Generally the leaders follow a gentleman's agreement to back off under these circumstances, but often a lapped car can get back on the lead lap by passing the leader before he takes the yellow flag.

RADIAL TIRES: Tires that differ in construction from bias-ply tires in that radial tires are constructed with a steel belt feature. Although bias-ply tires are used in many racing series, the NASCAR Winston Cup Series races exclusively on radial tires.

RAIN: The most disappointing weather in stock car racing, since the cars, with their slick tires, can not race in the rain. One of the most common racing expressions: "There's nothing sadder than a racetrack in the rain."

RED FLAG: A race is "red flagged" when the flagman waves a completely red flag from the flagstand. This occurs after a severe accident or if serious weather conditions arise.

RESTRICTOR PLATE: A square plate, distributed to the Winston Cup race teams by NASCAR, that mounts under the carburetor and restricts flow. The effect on the engine is reduced power. This has been NASCAR's preferred method to slow down the cars on superspeedways throughout the 1980s and 1990s.

RETAINING WALLS: The walls around a racetrack that are used to keep debris and crashing cars on the racetrack and out of the infield or grandstands.

RIDE: Drivers looking for a team to compete for are said to be "looking for a ride."

RIDE HEIGHT: A measurement taken from the ground to a specific point on the race car.

ROAD COURSE: A track that requires drivers familiar with the phrase "Go fast, turn left" to cope with right turns as well.

ROLL CAGE: A structure formed out of metal tubing that surrounds and protects a driver in the event of a stock car getting upsidedown or taking a violent side impact.

ROOF FLAPS: When instances of Winston Cup and other stock cars getting airborne became an alarming regularity on superspeedways, NASCAR developed a roof flap system to prevent such aerial excursions. When a stock car begins to turn around at high speeds, the roof flaps deploy and disturb the air flowing over the car, thus preventing it from taking off.

ROOKIE: A driver competing in his first season of a racing series. In the NASCAR Winston Cup Series, a rookie can be identified on the racetrack by the large yellow stripe attached to his stock car's rear bumper.

SANDBAGGING: A term that applies to a driver who may not be driving his car to its full potential during practice sessions or in the early stages of a race.

SCUFF TIRES: Often stock car teams in the Winston Cup Series will take the opportunity to wear in these sets of new tires by running several laps on them in practice sessions.

SEAT TIME: Time spent on the racetrack behind the wheel of a stock car.

SHORT TRACK: One of the four major types of tracks the Winston Cup Series races on, short tracks are ovals with a total length of less than 1 mile (1.6km).

SLINGSHOT PASS: On the very fastest speedways, one car will draft behind another and take advantage of the easier path through the air provided by the first car. The second driver can wait for the right moment, then suddenly pull out from behind the lead car and "slingshot" past the first car. Restrictor plates have hampered the success ratio of slingshot passes, as stock cars operating with the reduced power caused by the plates often need a second car to line up behind them in an attempt to get by another car in front.

SPOILER: An aerodynamic device, most commonly mounted at the top of a stock car's trunk area, designed to create downforce.

SQUIRRELLY: Word applied to a stock car that is not handling properly, usually when the car is too "loose."

START/FINISH LINE: The line across the front straightaway that marks the point where the race begins and ends. The flagstand is mounted at the outside of the start/finish line.

STICKER TIRES: Racing tires that, when brand-new, can be identified by the small manufacturer stickers that are affixed to the tire surface.

STRICTLY STOCK: NASCAR's first true stock car division, the Strictly Stock division's first race took place in June 1949. The division was soon renamed the Grand National division before becoming today's Winston Cup Series.

STROKER: A derogatory comment usually directed at a driver who is not competing as hard as he or she can.

SUPERSPEEDWAY: The fastest of the four types of racetracks the Winston Cup Series competes on. Superspeedways are 1.5 (2.4km) miles or greater in length, and on the largest superspeedways NASCAR requires the use of restrictor plates to keep the cars at speeds under 200 mph (321.8kph).

SWAY BAR: Another name for the panhard bar used to control the tendency of a stock car body or chassis to roll away when cornering.

TIGHT: A term used to describe a stock car that is difficult to turn in the corners. Although the driver turns the wheel, the front end of the car feels as though it wants to continue moving straight.

TIRE STAGGER: The difference in circumference between racing tires, with oval track rac-

ers preferring to use the larger-circumference tires on the right side to help the car turn left. Stagger plays a big role when cars are competing on bias-ply tires, and less so when radial tires are in use (radials are adjusted using air pressure).

TIRE TEMPERATURE: One of the most valuable tools used to set up a stock car for maximum performance at a racetrack is the study of tire temperatures recorded after several laps around the track. By analyzing the individual temperatures, crews can determine if the car's weight distribution requires alteration.

TRACK LENGTH: Official NASCAR track lengths are determined by measuring a racetrack's length 15 feet (4.5m) in from the track's outer wall.

"TRADIN' PAINT": Slang for stock cars making contact with each other during side-by-side speedway battles.

TRIOVAL: Used to describe tracks like Daytona International Speedway or Talladega Superspeedway, where the cars exit turn four and run through a curved frontstretch rather than a straightaway leading into turn one.

200-MPH TAPE: A colorful name for duct tape.

UNDERSTEER: The proper terminology to define what stock car drivers mean when they say their car "has picked up a push," "is tight," or "is plowing through the turns." In other words, it's difficult to get the car to turn.

WEDGE: A term that refers to the percentage of weight distributed on the wheels of a stock car. By adjusting wedge bolts at the rear of stock cars, crew members can alter the weight distribution of the car during a brief pit stop, thus drastically altering the handling of the car through the raising or lowering of a corner of the car. The ratchet wrenches that are used to adjust the bolts are turned, and it's common to hear the phrases "put a round in" or "took a round out" to describe these adjustments.

WHITE FLAG: When the flagman waves the white flag as the leader passes the flagstand, it informs the drivers that the final lap has begun.

WINNER'S CIRCLE: The goal of every Winston Cup stock car driver in every race is to complete the last lap and go directly to the winner's circle to be presented with the trophy, to be photographed by the media—and to be handed a large check.

WINSTON CUP: NASCAR's top stock car racing division, formed in 1970 when R.J. Reynolds and its Winston brand began sponsoring the series. The Winston Cup point fund began in 1971 at $100,000, but by 1997 it had grown to $4 million. The top twenty-five drivers in the championship points standings share in the fund, with the champion taking home $1.5 million. Between 1987 and 1997, the point fund doubled. This potential financial compensation, combined with the tremendous media coverage of the series, has made the Winston Cup Series the elite form of motorsports competition in the United States.

WINSTON CUP POINTS DISTRIBUTION:
The distribution of points in the NASCAR Winston Cup Series is handled on a per-race basis with each driver's finishing order responsible for his points allocation. At the end of the season in November, the driver with the most points wins the championship.

The points system was devised by racing journalist/historian Bob Latford. Many people have criticized the system in recent years for being a program that rewards consistency over winning performances. As proof they point to the fact that there is only a five-point difference between first and second places in each race. This is why Rusty Wallace could win ten races in 1993 and still lose the championship to Dale Earnhardt, winner of four fewer races that season. The points are distributed as follows:

1st place	175 points
2nd	170
3rd	165
4th	160
5th	155
6th	150
7th	146
8th	142
9th	138
10th	134
11th	130
12th	127
13th	124
14th	121
15th	118
16th	115
17th	112
18th	109
19th	106
20th	103
21st	100
22nd	97
23rd	94
24th	91
25th	88
26th	85
27th	82
28th	79
29th	76
30th	73
31st	70
32nd	67
33rd	64
34th	61
35th	58
36th	55
37th	52
38th	49
39th	46
40th	43
41st	40
42nd	37
43rd	34
44th	31
45th	28

Each driver who officially leads at least one lap of a race is awarded a five-point bonus. Also, the driver who leads the most laps of a race receives another five-point bonus.

YELLOW FLAG: The yellow flag, waved by the flagman at the start/finish line, warns drivers that there is an unsafe condition on the racetrack and that they must reduce their speed and fall in behind the pace car as the race goes "under caution."

APPENDIX*

NASCAR WINSTON CUP CHAMPIONS
including Grand National champions, 1949–1970

YEAR	DRIVER	CAR MAKE	WINS	POLES
1949	Red Byron	Oldsmobile	2	1
1950	Bill Rexford	Oldsmobile	1	0
1951	Herb Thomas	Hudson	7	4
1952	Tim Flock	Hudson	8	4
1953	Herb Thomas	Hudson	11	10
1954	Lee Petty	Chrysler	7	3
1955	Tim Flock	Chrysler	18	19
1956	Buck Baker	Chrysler	14	12
1957	Buck Baker	Chevrolet	10	5
1958	Lee Petty	Oldsmobile	7	4
1959	Lee Petty	Plymouth	10	2
1960	Rex White	Chevrolet	6	3
1961	Ned Jarrett	Chevrolet	1	4
1962	Joe Weatherly	Pontiac	9	6
1963	Joe Weatherly	Mercury	3	6
1964	Richard Petty	Plymouth	9	8
1965	Ned Jarrett	Ford	13	9
1966	David Pearson	Dodge	14	7
1967	Richard Petty	Plymouth	27	18
1968	David Pearson	Ford	16	12
1969	David Pearson	Ford	11	14
1970	Bobby Isaac	Dodge	11	13
1971	Richard Petty	Plymouth	21	9
1972	Richard Petty	Plymouth	8	3
1973	Benny Parsons	Chevrolet	1	0
1974	Richard Petty	Dodge	9	7
1975	Richard Petty	Dodge	13	3
1976	Cale Yarborough	Chevrolet	9	2
1977	Cale Yarborough	Chevrolet	9	3
1978	Cale Yarborough	Oldsmobile	10	8
1979	Richard Petty	Chevrolet	5	1
1980	Dale Earnhardt	Chevrolet	5	0
1981	Darrell Waltrip	Buick	12	11
1982	Darrell Waltrip	Buick	12	7
1983	Bobby Allison	Buick	6	0
1984	Terry Labonte	Chevrolet	2	2
1985	Darrell Waltrip	Chevrolet	3	4
1986	Dale Earnhardt	Chevrolet	5	1
1987	Dale Earnhardt	Chevrolet	11	1
1988	Bill Elliott	Ford	6	6
1989	Rusty Wallace	Pontiac	6	4
1990	Dale Earnhardt	Chevrolet	9	4
1991	Dale Earnhardt	Chevrolet	4	0
1992	Alan Kulwicki	Ford	2	6
1993	Dale Earnhardt	Chevrolet	6	2
1994	Dale Earnhardt	Chevrolet	4	2
1995	Jeff Gordon	Chevrolet	7	8
1996	Terry Labonte	Chevrolet	2	4

CLOSEST WINSTON CUP CHAMPION POINT MARGINS

POINT MARGIN	YEAR	CHAMPION	RUNNER-UP
10	1992	Alan Kulwicki	Bill Elliott
11	1979	Richard Petty	Darrell Waltrip
12	1989	Rusty Wallace	Dale Earnhardt
19	1980	Dale Earnhardt	Cale Yarborough
24	1988	Bill Elliott	Rusty Wallace
26	1990	Dale Earnhardt	Mark Martin
34	1995	Jeff Gordon	Dale Earnhardt
37	1996	Terry Labonte	Jeff Gordon
47	1983	Bobby Allison	Darrell Waltrip

*All records and data current through beginning of 1997 season

NASCAR WINSTON CUP SERIES POINT FUNDS

YEAR	TOTAL FUND VALUE	CHAMPION'S AWARD
1971	$100,000	$40,000
1972	100,000	39,000
1973	120,000	34,000
1974	140,000	46,000
1975	150,000	51,000
1976	150,000	44,000
1977	150,000	46,000
1978	175,000	49,000
1979	175,000	49,000
1980	210,000	49,500
1981	250,000	60,000
1982	300,000	75,000
1983	500,000	150,000
1984	500,000	150,000
1985	750,000	250,000
1986	2,000,000	400,000
1987	2,000,000	400,000
1988	2,000,000	400,000
1989	2,500,000	1,000,000
1990	2,500,000	1,000,000
1991	2,500,000	1,000,000
1992	2,500,000	1,000,000
1993	3,000,000	1,250,000
1994	3,000,000	1,250,000
1995	3,500,000	1,300,000
1996	4,000,000	1,500,000
1997	4,000,000	1,500,000

WINSTON CUP SERIES ROOKIE OF THE YEAR, 1971–1996

YEAR	DRIVER	RACES	WINS	TOP 5	POLES
1971	Walter Ballard	41	0	3	0
1972	Larry Smith	23	0	0	0
1973	Lennie Pond	23	0	1	0
1974	Earl Ross	21	1	5	0
1975	Bruce Hill	26	0	3	0
1976	Skip Manning	27	0	0	0
1977	Ricky Rudd	25	0	1	0
1978	Ronnie Thomas	27	0	0	0
1979	Dale Earnhardt	27	1	11	4
1980	Jody Ridley	31	0	2	0
1981	Ron Bouchard	22	1	5	1
1982	Geoff Bodine	25	0	4	2
1983	Sterling Marlin	30	0	0	0
1984	Rusty Wallace	30	0	2	0
1985	Ken Schrader	28	0	0	0
1986	Alan Kulwicki	23	0	1	0
1987	Davey Allison	22	2	9	5
1988	Ken Bouchard	24	0	0	0
1989	Dick Trickle	28	0	6	0
1990	Rob Moroso	25	0	0	0
1991	Bobby Hamilton	28	0	0	0
1992	Jimmy Hensley	22	0	0	0
1993	Jeff Gordon	30	0	7	1
1994	Jeff Burton	30	0	2	0
1995	Ricky Craven	31	0	0	0
1996	Johnny Benson	30	0	1	1

DAYTONA 500 WINNERS

YEAR	DRIVER	CAR MAKE
1959	Lee Petty	Oldsmobile
1960	Junior Johnson	Chevrolet
1961	Marvin Panch	Pontiac
1962	Fireball Roberts	Pontiac
1963	Tiny Lund	Ford
1964	Richard Petty	Plymouth
1965	Fred Lorenzen	Ford
1966	Richard Petty	Plymouth
1967	Mario Andretti	Ford
1968	Cale Yarborough	Mercury
1969	LeeRoy Yarbrough	Ford
1970	Pete Hamilton	Plymouth
1971	Richard Petty	Plymouth
1972	A.J. Foyt	Mercury
1973	Richard Petty	Dodge
1974	Richard Petty	Dodge
1975	Benny Parsons	Chevrolet
1976	David Pearson	Mercury
1977	Cale Yarborough	Chevrolet
1978	Bobby Allison	Ford
1979	Richard Petty	Oldsmobile
1980	Buddy Baker	Oldsmobile
1981	Richard Petty	Buick
1982	Bobby Allison	Buick
1983	Cale Yarborough	Pontiac
1984	Cale Yarborough	Chevrolet
1985	Bill Elliott	Ford
1986	Geoff Bodine	Chevrolet
1987	Bill Elliott	Ford
1988	Bobby Allison	Buick
1989	Darrell Waltrip	Chevrolet
1990	Derrike Cope	Chevrolet
1991	Ernie Irvan	Chevrolet
1992	Davey Allison	Ford
1993	Dale Jarrett	Chevrolet
1994	Sterling Marlin	Chevrolet
1995	Sterling Marlin	Chevrolet
1996	Dale Jarrett	Ford
1997	Jeff Gordon	Chevrolet

WINNERS OF THE WINSTON

YEAR	DRIVER	CAR MAKE
1985	Darrell Waltrip	Chevrolet
1986	Bill Elliott	Ford
1987	Dale Earnhardt	Chevrolet
1988	Terry Labonte	Chevrolet
1989	Rusty Wallace	Pontiac
1990	Dale Earnhardt	Chevrolet
1991	Davey Allison	Ford
1992	Davey Allison	Ford
1993	Dale Earnhardt	Chevrolet
1994	Geoff Bodine	Ford
1995	Jeff Gordon	Chevrolet
1996	Michael Waltrip	Ford
1997	Jeff Gordon	Chevrolet

ALL-TIME NASCAR GRAND NATIONAL/WINSTON CUP RACE WINNERS, 1949–1996

RANK	DRIVER	STATUS	VICTORIES
1	Richard Petty	Retired	200
2	David Pearson	Retired	105
3	Darrell Waltrip	Active	84
	David Pearson	Retired	84
5	Cale Yarborough	Retired	83
6	Dale Earnhardt	Active	70
7	Lee Petty	Retired	54
8	Ned Jarrett	Retired	50
	Junior Johnson	Retired	50
10	Herb Thomas	Retired	48
11	Buck Baker	Retired	46
	Rusty Wallace	Active	46
13	Bill Elliott	Active	40
	Tim Flock	Retired	40
15	Bobby Isaac	Deceased	37
16	Fireball Roberts	Deceased	34
17	Rex White	Retired	28
18	Fred Lorenzen	Retired	26
19	Jim Paschal	Retired	25
20	Joe Weatherly	Deceased	24
21	Benny Parsons	Retired	21
	Jack Smith	Retired	21
23	Speedy Thompson	Deceased	20
24	Buddy Baker	Retired	19
	Fonty Flock	Deceased	19
	Davey Allison	Deceased	19
	Jeff Gordon	Active	19

ALL-TIME NASCAR GRAND NATIONAL/WINSTON CUP POLE WINNERS, 1949–1996

RANK	DRIVER	STATUS	POLES
1	Richard Petty	Retired	127
2	David Pearson	Retired	113
3	Cale Yarborough	Retired	70
4	Darrell Waltrip	Active	59
5	Bobby Allison	Retired	57
6	Bobby Isaac	Deceased	51
7	Bill Elliott	Active	48
8	Junior Johnson	Retired	47
9	Buck Baker	Retired	44
10	Buddy Baker	Retired	40
11	Herb Thomas	Retired	38
12	Tim Flock	Retired	37
	Fireball Roberts	Deceased	37
14	Ned Jarrett	Retired	36
	Rex White	Retired	36
16	Geoff Bodine	Active	35
17	Fred Lorenzen	Retired	33
18	Mark Martin	Active	32
19	Fonty Flock	Deceased	30
20	Marvin Panch	Retired	25
	Terry Labonte	Active	25

ALL-TIME NASCAR GRAND NATIONAL/WINSTON CUP DRIVERS WITH MORE THAN 500 RACE STARTS, 1949–1996

RANK	DRIVER	STATUS	STARTS
1	Richard Petty	Retired	1,177
2	Dave Marcis	Active	815
3	Bobby Allison	Retired	717
4	Buddy Baker	Retired	698
5	Darrell Waltrip	Active	689
6	J.D. McDuffie	Deceased	653
7	Buck Baker	Retired	631
8	James Hylton	Retired	602
9	David Pearson	Retired	574
10	Ricky Rudd	Active	562
11	Buddy Arrington	Retired	560
12	Cale Yarborough	Retired	559
13	Dale Earnhardt	Active	542
	Terry Labonte	Active	542
15	Elmo Langley	Deceased	533
16	Benny Parsons	Retired	526

WINSTON CUP SERIES MOST POPULAR DRIVER, 1971–1996

YEAR	DRIVER
1971	Bobby Allison
1972	Bobby Allison
1973	Bobby Allison
1974	Richard Petty
1975	Richard Petty
1976	Richard Petty
1977	Richard Petty
1978	Richard Petty
1979	David Pearson
1980	David Pearson
1981	Bobby Allison
1982	Bobby Allison
1983	Bobby Allison
1984	Bill Elliott
1985	Bill Elliott
1986	Bill Elliott
1987	Bill Elliott
1988	Bill Elliott
1989	Darrell Waltrip
1990	Darrell Waltrip
1991	Bill Elliott
1992	Bill Elliott
1993	Bill Elliott
1994	Bill Elliott
1995	Bill Elliott
1996	Bill Elliott

ALL-TIME NASCAR GRAND NATIONAL/WINSTON CUP SERIES RECORDS, 1949–1996

Most wins in a career:	Richard Petty, 200
Most races in a career:	Richard Petty, 1,177
Most wins in a season:	Richard Petty, 27
Most consecutive wins:	Richard Petty, 10
Most wins from pole in a career:	Richard Petty, 61
Most wins from pole in a season:	Richard Petty, 15
Most wins at one racetrack:	Richard Petty, 15 (Martinsville and North Wilkesboro)
Most poles in a career:	Richard Petty, 127
Most poles in a season:	Bobby Isaac, 20
Most poles at one racetrack:	David Pearson, 14 (Charlotte Motor Speedway)
Best winning percentage in a career:	Tim Flock, 21.2
Best winning percentage in a season:	David Pearson, 61.1

ALL-TIME NASCAR GRAND NATIONAL/WINSTON CUP SUPERSPEEDWAY RACE WINNERS, 1949–1996

RANK	DRIVER	STATUS	VICTORIES
1	Richard Petty	Retired	55
2	Bobby Allison	Retired	52
3	David Pearson	Retired	51
4	Cale Yarborough	Retired	50
5	Dale Earnhardt	Active	44
6	Bill Elliott	Active	38
7	Darrell Waltrip	Active	37
8	Rusty Wallace	Active	26
9	Buddy Baker	Retired	17
10	Neil Bonnett	Deceased	15
	Davey Allison	Deceased	15

ALL-TIME NASCAR GRAND NATIONAL/WINSTON CUP RACES WON FROM THE POLE, 1949–1996

RANK	DRIVER	STATUS	VICTORIES
1	Richard Petty	Retired	61
2	David Pearson	Retired	37
3	Darrell Waltrip	Active	24
4	Bobby Isaac	Deceased	21
5	Bobby Allison	Retired	20
6	Herb Thomas	Retired	19
7	Cale Yarborough	Retired	16
	Tim Flock	Retired	16
9	Bill Elliott	Active	13
10	Junior Johnson	Retired	12
	Buck Baker	Retired	12

MOST MULTIPLE WINSTON CUP CHAMPIONSHIPS

NUMBER	DRIVER	YEARS
7	Richard Petty	'64, '67, '71, '72, '74, '75, '79
	Dale Earnhardt	'80, '86, '87, '90, '91, '93, '94
3	Darrell Waltrip	'81, '82, '85
	Cale Yarborough	'76, '77, '78
	David Pearson	'66, '68, '69
	Lee Petty	'54, '58, '59

"MODERN ERA" WINSTON CUP RACE WINNERS, 1971–1996

RANK	DRIVER	STATUS	VICTORIES
1	Darrell Waltrip	Active	84
2	Richard Petty	Retired	81
3	Dale Earnhardt	Active	70
4	Cale Yarborough	Retired	69
5	Bobby Allison	Retired	65
6	David Pearson	Retired	47
7	Rusty Wallace	Active	46
8	Bill Elliott	Active	40
9	Benny Parsons	Retired	21
10	Davey Allison	Deceased	19
	Jeff Gordon	Active	19

"MODERN ERA" NASCAR WINSTON CUP SERIES RECORDS, 1971–1996

Most wins:	Darrell Waltrip, 84
Most wins in a season:	Richard Petty, 13
Most consecutive wins:	Cale Yarborough, 4
	Darrell Waltrip, 4
	Dale Earnhardt, 4
	Harry Gant, 4
	Bill Elliott, 4
	Mark Martin, 4
Most wins from pole in a career:	Darrell Waltrip, 24
Most wins from pole in a season:	Darrell Waltrip, 8
Most wins at one racetrack:	Richard Petty, 15 (Martinsville and North Wilkesboro)
Most poles in a career:	Darrell Waltrip, 59
Most poles in a season:	Cale Yarborough, 14

Photo Credits

©Allsport:
Bill Hall: pp. 42; 105; 127; Craig Jones: pp. 104; 150; Ralph Merlino: p. 161
bottom; Jamie Squire: pp. 9; 21; 49; David Taylor: pp. 32; 57; 81; 113

©AP/Wide World Photos:
pp. 22 top; 27 top; 47; 56; 65; 68 top; 95; 109; 120 bottom; 124; 125 top;
131 top; 139 bottom; 147; 148 bottom; 156 top

©Archive Photos:
p. 131 bottom; Sporting News: p. 110; Reuters/Winston Luzier: p. 26

©Karen Barr:
Racing flag detail throughout

©Ken Brown/Competition Photographers:
pp. 24; 28 bottom; 38 both; 59 bottom; 60; 61 both; 82 top; 90; 94; 96;
103 bottom; 112 top; 114; 127 top; 130; 132; 133 both; 162 top

©Nigel Kinrade Photography:
Back endpapers; pp. 2; 5; 6-7; 30-31; 35 bottom; 37; 40; 41 both; 43; 44; 45; 48;
50 bottom; 64; 68 bottom; 70 top; 71; 72 bottom; 75; 76 both; 78 top; 80 bottom;
84; 85; 99 top; 101 bottom right; 106; 107 bottom; 108; 112 bottom; 115 both;
116-117; 119 bottom; 120 top; 123; 134; 136; 138; 139 top; 140 top; 146 top;
148 top; 151 top; 152; 153; 158; 160 top; 162 bottom

©Dozier Mobley Photography:
pp. 23; 28 top; 35 top; 46; 54 bottom; 58 bottom; 69 top; 72 top; 82 bottom; 83
bottom; 86; 97 both; 102; 103 top; 111; 121 bottom; 137; 140 bottom; 154; 160
bottom; DMP Archives: pp. 12; 14; 25 top; 33 both; 50 top; 54 top; 66; 73 top;
79; 83 top; 87 bottom; 88; 91 top; 101 bottom left; 118; 119 top; 121 top; 125
bottom; 126; 142; 149; 151 bottom; 156 bottom; 157; 161 top; 163

©Frank Moriarty:
pp. 55; 70 bottom; 98; From the Collection of Frank Moriarty: pp. 34; 100 all

©Steve Swope Photography:
pp. 36; 39; 53; 62; 63; 67; 73 bottom; 74; 78 bottom; 80 top; 92; 99 bottom;
128 bottom; 144; 146 bottom

©Tyler Photo Illustrators:
pp. 128 top; 141

©UPI/Corbis-Bettmann:
pp. 11; 13; 15; 16; 17; 22 bottom; 25 bottom; 29 all; 51; 52; 58-59; 69 bottom;
77; 89; 91 bottom; 93 both; 101 top; 107 top; 122; 135; 143; 145; 155

©Jeffrey S. Vogt/DBA Racing Photos:
Front endpapers; pp. 18; 19; 20; 27 bottom; 87 top; 129

INDEX